Puppet Play Therapy

Puppet Play Therapy is a comprehensive guidebook that describes the basic skills, techniques, and applications for selecting and working with puppets in specific types of settings and populations. Written by preeminent voices in the field, chapters offer invaluable guidance on selecting, using, and assessing puppet-based therapeutic interventions. Both beginning and experienced clinicians will also appreciate the inclusion of practical, step-by-step approaches and reproducible handouts that will aid them in their puppet play therapy sessions.

Athena A. Drewes, PsyD, RPT-S, is a licensed child psychologist, founder, and president emeritus of the New York Association of Play Therapy, as well as a national and international presenter and editor/coeditor on play therapy. Dr. Drewes is also director of clinical training and the APA-accredited doctoral internship at Astor Services for Children and Families, a large multi-service nonprofit mental health agency in New York.

Charles E. Schaefer, PhD, RPT-S, is cofounder and director emeritus of the Association of Play Therapy as well as professor emeritus of psychology at Fairleigh Dickinson University in New Jersey. He is also a renowned author, editor, and coeditor of over 100 research articles and 60 professional books.

Puppet Play Therapy

A Practical Guidebook

Edited by Athena A. Drewes and Charles E. Schaefer

Routledge
Taylor & Francis Group
NEW YORK AND LONDON

First edition published 2018
by Routledge
711 Third Avenue, New York, NY 10017

and by Routledge
2 Park Square, Milton Park, Abingdon, Oxon, OX14 4RN

Routledge is an imprint of the Taylor & Francis Group, an informa business

Library of Congress Cataloging-in-Publication Data
Names: Drewes, Athena A., 1948- editor. | Schaefer, Charles E., editor.
Title: Puppet play therapy : a practical guidebook/edited by Athena A. Drewes and Charles E. Schaefer.
Description: New York : Routledge, 2017. | Includes bibliographical references and index.
Identifiers: LCCN 2017030243| ISBN 9781138707214 (hbk : alk. paper) | ISBN 9781138707221 (pbk : alk. paper) | ISBN 9781315181349 (ebk)
Subjects: LCSH: Puppets—Therapeutic use. | Play therapy. | Child psychotherapy.
Classification: LCC RJ53.P85 P87 2017 | DDC 618.92/891653—dc23
LC record available at https://lccn.loc.gov/2017030243

ISBN: 978-1-138-70721-4 (hbk)
ISBN: 978-1-138-70722-1 (pbk)
ISBN: 978-1-315-18134-9 (ebk)

Typeset in Bembo
by Apex CoVantage, LLC

Dedicated to the magical world of puppet play therapy

Contents

Preface

The widespread popularity of puppets is evident by the fact that puppets are found in almost every play therapy room throughout the world. They have proven to be wonderful engagement tools and a safe way for children to act out conflicts, express feelings, reenact and gain mastery over stressful events, and learn and practice more adaptive behaviors. Unfortunately, most therapists, including play therapists, have received little or no training in the use of puppets in therapy.

The purpose of this book is to provide a practical guide in the use of puppets for therapeutic purposes. The aim is to present the basic skills, techniques, and applications underlying the effective practice of puppet play therapy, including both pioneering insights and new directions. Eclectic in scope, the volume also describes the major theoretical approaches underlying puppet play therapy so that the reader can select the principles and practices most compatible with his or her personal beliefs and values. The book is intended to be an essential guide for enhancing the clinical skills of both beginning and experienced professionals from mental health and allied fields.

Athena A. Drewes
Charles E. Schaefer

Editors

Athena A. Drewes, PsyD, RPT-S, is a licensed child psychologist, certified school psychologist, and registered play therapist and supervisor. She is director of clinical training and APA-accredited doctoral internship at Astor Services for Children and Families. She has over 40 years of clinical experience in supervising clinicians, specializing in working with children and teens experiencing sexual abuse, complex trauma, and attachment issues in school, outpatient, and inpatient settings utilizing an integrative play therapy approach.

She is a former member of the board of directors of the Association for Play Therapy and founder and president emeritus of the New York Association for Play Therapy. She has written extensively on play therapy and is a frequently invited guest lecturer throughout the United States and around the world.

Dr. Drewes has 11 edited/coedited books, including *School-Based Play Therapy, Second Edition*; *Cultural Issues in Play Therapy*; *Supervision Can Be Playful: Techniques for Child and Play Therapy Supervisors*; *Blending Play Therapy with Cognitive Behavioral Therapy: Evidence-Based and Other Effective Treatments and Techniques*; *Integrative Play Therapy*; and *The Therapeutic Powers of Play: 20 Core Agents of Change.* Her most recently published book, by the American Psychological Association, *Play Therapy in Middle Childhood*, includes a companion clinical video of Dr. Drewes' integrative prescriptive play therapy work.

Charles E. Schaefer, PhD, RPT-S, is professor emeritus of psychology at Fairleigh Dickinson University in Teaneck, New Jersey. He is cofounder and director emeritus of the Association for Play Therapy. Dr. Schaefer is the author/coauthor of more than 100 research articles and author/editor of over 60 professional books, including *Handbook of Play Therapy, Second Edition*; *Foundations of Play Therapy, Second Edition*; *The Therapeutic Powers of Play, Second Edition*; *Essential Play Therapy Techniques: Time-Tested Approaches*; *Short-Term Play Therapy, Third Edition*; and *Play Therapy for Preschoolers.*

Contributors

Jennifer C. Ablow, MA, PhD, associate professor, Department of Psychology, University of Oregon, Oregon

Susan M. Carter, PhD, RPT-S, licensed psychologist in private practice, Center for Change & Growth, PLC, Kalamazoo, Michigan

Jo Ann L. Cook, EdD, NCSP, ABSNP, RPT-S, private practice, Winter Park, Florida

David A. Crenshaw, PhD, ABPP, RPT-S, clinical director, Children's Home of Poughkeepsie, New York

Athena A. Drewes, PsyD, RPT-S, director of clinical training and APA-accredited doctoral internship at Astor Services for Children and Families, Middletown, New York

Pam Dyson, MA, LPC-S, RPT-S, DFW Center for Play Therapy Training, Plano, Texas

Brandon Eddy, MSc, Professor, Department of Community, Family & Addiction Services, Texas Tech University, Lubbock, Texas

Eliana Gil, PhD, RPT-S, ATR, LMFT, Gil Institute for Trauma Recovery and Education, Fairfax, Virginia; director, Starbright Training Institute, adjunct faculty member, Family Therapy Department, Virginia Tech, Virginia

Elizabeth Kjellstrand Hartwig, PhD, LPC-S, LMFT, RPT-S, Professional Counseling Program, Texas State University; president-elect, Texas Association for Play Therapy, Texas

Eleanor C. Irwin, PhD, clinical psychologist, drama therapist (RDT), certified child and adult psychoanalyst, clinical assistant professor of psychiatry, Department of Psychiatry, School of Medicine, University of Pittsburgh; faculty, Pittsburgh Psychoanalytic Center, Pennsylvania

Jillian E. Kelly, LCSW, RPT, private practice, Asheville, North Carolina

Susan M. Knell, PhD, LLC, clinical psychologist, Highland Heights, Ohio

Elsa Soto Leggett, PhD, LPC-S, RPT-S, CSC, program coordinator and associate professor in counselor education, University of Houston Victoria at Katy, Texas

Kristin K. Meany-Walen, PhD, LMHC, RPT, NCC, assistant professor of counseling, School of Applied Human Sciences, Cedar Falls, Iowa

Jeffrey Measelle, PhD, associate professor, Department of Psychology, University of Oregon, Oregon

Judi Parson, PhD, MA Play Therapy, MHthSc, Grad Dip Pediatrics, BN, RN, lecturer in Mental Health, Deakin University, Geelong, Victoria, Australia

Siobhán Prendiville, ME, MA, child and adolescent psychotherapist and play therapist, core trainer at Children's Therapy Centre, Westmeath, Ireland; Irish Association of Play Therapists and Psychotherapists (IAPTP)

M. Jamila Reid, PhD, Child & Teacher Professor, Incredible Years Program, Seattle, Washington

Charles E. Schaefer, PhD, RPT-S, professor emeritus of psychology at Fairleigh Dickinson University in Teaneck, New Jersey; cofounder and director emeritus of the Association for Play Therapy

Quinn K. Smelser, MA, LPC, RPT, NCC, The George Washington University, The Gil Institute for Trauma Recovery and Education, Fairfax, Virginia

Catherine Ford Sori, PhD, LMFT, full professor, MFC Track Leader, Division of Psychology and Counseling, Governors State University, University Park, Illinois

Brie Turns, MS, LMFTA, Department of Community, Family & Addiction Services, Marriage and Family Therapy Program, Texas Tech University, Texas

Joanne F. Vizzini, PhD, LCPC, NCC, licensed clinical professional counselor, Freedom Through Psychotherapy, LLC, Columbia, Maryland; former adjunct professor and clinical supervisor, Loyola University in Maryland; Puppet Therapy Institute; Puppeteers of America, UNIMA (International Puppetry Association)

Carolyn Webster-Stratton, PhD, professor emeritus, University of Washington; Incredible Years, Inc., Seattle, Washington

Section I

Introduction

1 Fundamental Concepts and Practices of Puppet Play Therapy

Charles E. Schaefer and Athena A. Drewes

Brief History

For over three thousand years, puppets have had a universal appeal to adults across the world, who have used them to entertain, inform, relate myth and legend, and enhance tribal rituals and religious ceremonies. There is something magical and wonderful about watching inanimate objects come to life. Because puppets display the human qualities of speech and movement, people identify with them and see their self or parts of their self in the puppets. Puppets transform internal mental states of the operator into a physical form, which enlivens communication and transports people of all ages to a world of fantasy and delight. Puppets are the quintessential childhood toy whose power to stimulate the imagination cannot be replicated by modern electronic toys that flash and beep.

Puppet Play Therapy

It was not until the 1930s that mental health professionals began to explore the value of puppets with children—both for diagnostic and therapeutic purposes. The earliest pioneers were Adolf Woltmann and Loretta Bender, who used puppet shows to help children in psychiatric hospitals freely express and find solutions to their problems through the processes of identification with and projection onto the puppets (Bender & Woltmann, 1936; Woltmann, 1940). The puppet shows contained plots based on themes or conflicts commonly experienced by children, such as sibling rivalry or the expression of aggression. The children were asked to provide solutions to the conflicts and problems expressed by the puppet characters, and these solutions were used as a basis for therapy.

Puppet play therapy is a form of play therapy that involves the use of puppets by mental health professionals for diagnostic and therapeutic purposes. Puppet play therapy has become a mainstream practice in contemporary child psychotherapy. Moreover, the use of puppets to promote healing and development has expanded widely in recent years. Puppets are now being applied effectively across the human life cycle—from infancy to old age. In addition, parents and professionals are finding puppet play to be beneficial for children in medical, educational, and home settings. Section Four of the book describes the application of puppet play across diverse environments.

Fundamental Concepts of Puppet Play Therapy

Therapeutic Powers of Puppet Play

The main ways that puppet play can foster therapeutic change in clients are by the following healing processes:

1. Self-Expression

Talking through puppets can provide the necessary psychological distance for clients to disclose troublesome thoughts and feelings that are not easily expressed in their own voice. People feel safe having the puppets describe their inner world because they could always deny that the puppet talk refers to them. The children can project onto the puppet feelings and thoughts, without taking responsibility for the action and words projected, since they view them as the words and actions of someone else.

2. Access the Unconscious

Puppets provide a window to a client's unconscious processes through such defense mechanisms as *projection*, that is, unconscious attribution of one's own feelings or desires onto a puppet; *symbolization*, where one object stands for another, for example, a witch puppet can represent a mean mother figure; and *displacement*, that is, directing negative feelings toward a family member to whom they were originally intended onto a puppet.

3. Catharsis

Instead of acting out feelings of violence or frustration themselves, clients can imbue puppets with those feelings. If they have an angry feeling, for example, and it is safely expressed through a puppet, it can be followed by great relief and joy.

4. Direct Teaching

Puppets have been found to capture children's interest, attention span, and involvement in learning (Remer & Tzuriel, 2015), thus facilitating the acquisition of more adaptive thoughts, feelings, and behaviors, such as rational thinking, emotion regulation, and social skills.

Also, puppets can be used by teachers and clinicians to teach conceptually through visual symbols—for example, an angry puppet face is the symbol for angry feelings—and integrate oral expression, comprehension, and retention of knowledge (Peyton, 2001). Puppets can help children readily remember what they have processed, associating what they hear the puppet say with what they see. The visual element combines with the conceptual element to form a potent blend of visual education (Peyton, 2001).

5. Abreaction

By puppet reenactment of stressful or traumatic events, clients can gain: (1) emotional release of blocked affects related to feeling powerless and anxious during the event, and (2) the opportunity to repeatedly practice corrective actions so as to obtain a sense of mastery over the traumatic experience.

6. Awareness of Feelings

Puppets can model for a client how to label and express their feelings, as well as empathize with the feelings of others. This expands the child's "feeling" vocabulary. Children will confide in puppets and will often do something to please a puppet that they would not do for another child or adult, thus developing empathy.

7. Rapport

The fun of playing with puppets can help a therapist establish rapport with children, who are by nature playful. Even "hard to reach" children tend to respond positively to puppet play. Puppets can quickly break down resistances and help to enhance trust and motivation that might otherwise take weeks to develop.

8. Problem-Solving

A therapist's "helper" puppet can be the voice of reason and suggest ways for a child to solve his or her presenting problem. Conversely, a child can act as a "helper" for a puppet who has a problem similar to the child's, such as troublesome worrying. Also, by playing different roles in puppet play, clients may find their own solution to real-life problems.

9. Behavioral Rehearsal

Therapists can use puppets to model coping strategies for a stressful event that a child will soon experience, such as a medical procedure or starting school. The goals are to reduce the unknown aspects of the stressor and demonstrate coping strategies, such as deep breathing and self-talk (Shapiro, 1995).

10. Assess Family Dynamics

Puppet play assessments provide therapists with the opportunity to directly observe family interactions, that is, patterns of communication, roles, and coalitions, rather than rely on assumptions about family relations based on background material.

Theoretical Approaches

These and additional therapeutic powers of puppet play have been applied in distinctive ways by all the major play therapy approaches. Section Three of this book contains an overview of how puppet play therapy is practiced by therapists following different play therapy models—both directive and nondirective. It describes the specific application of the healing powers of puppet play by the following theoretical orientations: child-centered, psychodynamic, Adlerian, and solution-focused.

Types of Puppets

A puppet is an inanimate object that is manipulated by human agency so that it moves and appears to be alive. There are six general types of puppets: (1) hand puppets, (2) marionettes, (3) shadow puppets, (4) Muppets, (5) dummies, and (6) finger puppets.

1. Hand Puppets

They can be used from ages 3 to 103! These comprise a broad array of puppets that are worn on the hand and operated by the puppeteer. They include mouth puppets, which have a movable mouth that is manipulated by the puppeteer's hand to facilitate self-expression. Hand puppets are more convincing in their movement and capable of more aggressiveness and expression than string marionettes (Bender & Woltmann, 1936). They should be lightweight, comfortable, portable, and inexpensive. Glove puppets are slightly more complex, with an internal division for fingers allowing independent manipulation of the puppet's arms as well as the head.

2. Marionettes

A small figure of a person or animal having jointed parts operated from above by pulling strings and rods. Typically, a puppet stage is used to conceal the puppeteer's hands.

3. Shadow Puppets

These are mostly rod puppets that are flat, opaque, or colored figures that cast a silhouette when manipulated behind a light source and a screen.

4. Muppets

A Muppet is a cross between a hand puppet and a marionette. One or two Muppeteers operate the mouth in a manner similar to a hand puppet, while the extremities are operated by strings and rods like a marionette.

5. Dummies

The most realistic type of puppet is the ventriloquist's dummy. The operator places his or her hand inside the dummy and manipulates the dummy's jaws, arms, and legs by strings and rods. Quite a bit of skill is needed by the ventriloquist.

6. Finger Puppets

These are tiny puppets that fit over a finger. They are the easiest type of puppet for a young child to operate. They can be easily stored, and a child can support a whole family of characters on the fingers of just one hand.

Each type of puppet has its own particular advantage, but hand puppets are the "must-have" play therapy puppet. They are lightweight, comfortable, highly portable, relatively inexpensive, and easy to operate by people from early childhood to old age. Since they are the simplest, most versatile, and most popular type of puppet, they will be the specific focus of this guidebook.

Selection of Puppets for the Playroom

As a general practice it is best to display a diversified collection of 15–20 puppets (Carter & Mason, 1998). Too few puppets will not allow for enough range of expression; too many offer too many choices, which is likely to overwhelm the client. A basic collection should include:

Realistic Family Figures (e.g., Mom, Dad, two children)
Wild and Tame Animals (e.g., wolf, dog, mouse)
Human Characters (e.g., police officer, doctor)
Fantasy Figures (e.g., witch, good fairy, devil, superhero)

The puppets in one's standard collection should include symbols for people a child may meet in his or her life, such as a good fairy for a helpful woman, or should symbolize internal personality characteristics, such as a mouse for timidity.

Every play therapist, of course, will have his or her personal favorite puppets. A recent survey of American play therapists (Schaefer, 2017), about the puppets that have proven most useful in their practice, found they reported the following puppets most often. The reason they believe these specific puppets have been so therapeutic for children is also summarized below.

1. *Dragon.* (Express and master scary and traumatic experiences.)
2. *Turtle.* (Many shy children wish to draw in their heads and hide in social situations.)
3. *Family.* (Portray family interactions.)
4. *Shark.* (Express aggression and feeling protected.)
5. *Bird.* (Flies and easily escapes danger.)
6. *Dog.* (Comforting and nurturing.)
7. *Dinosaur.* (Express themes of power and protection.)
8. *Alligator*—With mouth that zips to open and close. (Express oral aggression by angrily eating up anything in its path.)
9. *Snake.* (Express power and aggression.)
10. *Wizard.* (Has magical powers to make things better in one's life.)

Additional guidelines for the selection of puppets for your collection:

Choose puppets that

- are easy for children to manipulate.
- are soft and "cuddly" as opposed to firm and rigid.
- are washable or can be cleaned.
- have a "personality." This is an intangible quality that is easier to recognize than to define. But when you look at the puppet you intuitively know how that puppet should talk and act.
- are visually and texturally appealing.
- have a movable mouth (for children over age 5).
- are culturally diverse, including skin color.
- are likeable.

Basic Puppetry Skills

> *On sensitive hands, puppets can live, but they demand more than your hands, you must give them your heart.*
>
> —Tom Tichenor

The following basic puppetry skills will enhance an adult's ability to make hand puppets come alive. Like any other skill, they need to be practiced frequently so as to develop proficiency. Practicing in front of a mirror is particularly recommended.

1. Movement

Movement is the essence of bringing a puppet to life (Astell-Burt, 2001). As much as possible, make your puppet's movements mimic the real-life movements of the animal or human character the puppet represents. Thus, a puppy would likely move quickly with lots of energy, while the movement of an "old man" puppet would tend to be slow and deliberate. A puppet that is sad might express it by dropping its head. Manipulation, that is, making your puppet move, is not as easy as it might seem. Initially, you are likely to move your puppets too much, so they appear hyperactive, or too little, so they seem dull or lifeless.

Vary the movement and keep the action both continuous and lively enough so as to maintain the interest of the child. As long at the puppet's head, mouth, or body is moving during the dialogue, the child will not be concerned about where the actual origin of the voice is.

2. Focus

It is essential that a puppet should look at and establish eye contact with the person or puppet to whom it is speaking. Also, when your puppet is speaking, look at the puppet to draw attention to it, rather than looking at the person(s) to whom the puppet is speaking.

3. Mouth Action

When people speak, their lower jaw moves up and down, while their upper jaw remains stationary. So try to move the lower jaw of the puppet more than the upper jaw. Since your thumb in the head of a hand puppet controls the lower jaw, move it downward when the puppet speaks while keeping the other four fingers stationary on top of the head.

4. Lip Synchronization

Synchronize opening your puppet's mouth an inch or two with each important syllable or word spoken. Reserve a wide-open mouth for exaggeration or loud expressions. Keep in mind that the beginning and ending syllables of a sentence are the most noticeable to an audience for mouth synchronization. What happens in between is not so noticeable. The most common mistake in lip synchronization is closing the mouth on each syllable, which will seem like the puppet is "eating its words."

5. Appropriate Voice

Alter your voice to match the character of the puppet. A weak voice for a dinosaur or a loud voice for a mouse will seem inappropriate for the puppet and be difficult to believe. Exaggerate your voice; make it fun, dramatic, magical! A unique voice makes the puppet easy to identify with and interesting to listen to. Discover a voice contrasting to your own; it can be shocking, surprising, dramatic, fun. Look at the puppet and see what characteristics its features suggest (sleepy eyes may connote a slow, tired voice; many teeth, a chattering voice; a large mouth, a commanding deep voice).

Create a new voice by changing pitch to achieve higher or lower tone, inflection to emphasize certain words, loudness, word speed, and breath quality.

Use extremes: very high or low whisper; protracted yawn; slow or fast; growling, choppy, deep, or squeaky; grumpy or happy. Eloooongate wooords to make a slow voice; to make it assertive, use a strong, upbeat, and clear voice.

6. *Posture*

Keep your arm holding the puppet at a right angle to the floor and avoid tilting it side to side or front to back for no reason. This will create an illusion of the puppet having feet and thus make it seem more natural.

7. *Personality*

Create an engaging personality for the puppet that fits the physical and psychological characteristics of the puppet. This will make the puppet more interesting and appealing.

What does the puppet look like or represent? Give it a name, things it likes, a job, humor, friends, pet phrases, favorite foods, personal history, special interests.

Is it attractive, exotic, neat, adorable, homely, messy, funny-looking? How does your puppet feel? Is it happy, afraid, grouchy, nervous, sad, excitable, angry, surprised?

Give it an idiosyncrasy that sets it apart: has an allergy, is always sneezing, falls asleep periodically, forever confused. Personality quirks make the puppet seem more human and more endearing. How will it behave? Will it be regal, friendly, shy, sophisticated, dignified, weak, pompous, strong, forgetful, silly, or serious?

8. *Larger Than Life*

The characteristics of a puppet should be portrayed larger than its live counterpart in order to captivate and enthrall the viewer. A timid mouse puppet should be more timid; a wicked witch puppet more wicked; a silly character puppet, extra silly.

9. *Facial Expressions*

Whenever appropriate, use your fingers to wrinkle the puppet's face to emphasize certain types of emotions, for example, fear, joy.

10. Name

Give each of your puppets a name so they will seem more real, for example, Tucker, Dino, Buddy.

11. Duration

The duration of a puppet performance by a young child should be kept short to keep the child's interest and attention—generally no more than 10–15 minutes.

12. Warm-up

Once a child selects a puppet and is ready to play with it, ask the puppet a few simple questions about itself, for example, "What is your name?" "What kind of puppet are you?" "Are you a good or bad puppet?" This warm-up activity will help the child get used to animating the puppet before engaging in a subsequent puppet play therapy activity.

Practical Issues

Pitfalls of Puppet Play

Many children will try to make aggressive-looking puppets, such as crocodiles and lions, bite or hit others, including the therapist. To forestall this, you might quickly ask the child to talk about, rather than act out, this type of puppet; for example, ask the puppet's name, how old it is, where it lives.

Puppetry and other types of fantasy-based therapy should be used with caution with children who are exhibiting symptoms of psychosis or severe emotional disturbance. Their fragile grasp of reality may be weakened by fantasy play, and it is likely to be frightening to them (Woltmann, 1964).

Storing Puppets

You should treat puppets as real, and not throw them in a box, but rather have them out on display, on top of and on the shelves of bookcases. Using a shoe bag or rack, which has separate "pockets" to store items, that hangs on the back of a door is a very easy way to store puppets, placing them separately in each pocket. You can also make a puppet rack, with a post, dowels to hold the puppets, and "legs" that make it stand up in a corner of a room (see Figure 1.1).

Figure 1.1 Puppet Stand
Photo by Athena A. Drewes

Puppet Theaters

Puppet theaters vary from the more traditional ones that sit on the floor and the children can go behind (see Figure 1.2) to tabletop size, along with using the top of a table or bookcase. You can make a quick puppet stage by turning a table on its side, or use a stick covered with fabric and stretched between the backs of two chairs, or putting a blanket over a table or chair and crouching down behind and putting the puppet hand up. But it is not necessary to have a puppet theater. Dramatic puppet play can be conducted without one, and having the puppet visible to the viewer.

Figure 1.2 Puppet Theater

Photo by Athena A. Drewes

Sources for Obtaining Hand Puppets

A wide selection of high-quality animal, people, and fantasy puppets can be ordered online from the following sites:

- Folkmanis: www.folkmanis.com
- The Puppet Store: www.thepuppetstore.com
- PuppetU: www.puppetu.com

You can also use paper plates or tongue depressors to make puppets (see Figures 1.3 and 1.4).

Figure 1.3 Tongue Depressor Puppets
Photo by Athena A. Drewes

Figure 1.4 Paper Plate Puppet
Photo by Athena A. Drewes

Alternatively, instructions for making a variety of puppets yourself, including paper bag, sock, finger, and Muppet-like puppets, can be found at: www.wikihow.com/Make-Puppets. Solid-color fabric hand puppets can be made; or muslin puppets, ready to add buttons, paint, feathers, yarn, or colored fabric for personalizing a puppet, are available at Lakeshore: www.lakeshore-learning.com. There are 15 muslin fabric hand puppets, called Collage Puppets, in each package.

References

Association for Play Therapy. (1997). A definition of play therapy. *The Association for Play Therapy Newsletter, 16*(1), 7.

Astell-Burt, C. (2001). *I am the story: The art of puppetry in education and therapy*. London, UK: Souvenir Press (E&A) Ltd.

Bender, L., & Woltmann, A. (1936). The use of puppet shows as a psychotherapeutic method for behavior problems in children. *The American Journal of Orthopsychiatry, 6*(3), 341–354.

Carter, R., & Mason, P. (1998). Selection and use of puppets in counseling. *Professional School Counseling, 1*(5), 50–53.

Peyton, J. (2001). *An analysis of the qualities in puppets*. Retrieved April 2, 2017, from www.puppetool.com/!getpublicfile.php?fid=155

Remer, R., & Tzuriel, D. (2015). I teach better with the puppet. *American Journal of Educational Research, 3*(3), 356–365.

Schaefer, C. E. (2017). Play therapists report their most useful puppets. *Play Therapy Magazine, 12*(3), 25–27.

Shapiro, D. (1995). Puppet modeling techniques for children undergoing stressful medical procedures. *International Journal of Play Therapy, 4*(2), 31–39.

Woltmann, A. (1940). The use of puppets in understanding children. *Mental Hygiene*, 24, 445–458.

Woltmann, A. (1964). Psychological rationale for puppetry. In M. R. Hamout (Ed.), *Child psychotherapy: Practice and theory* (pp. 395–399). New York: Basic Books.

A Glossary of Relevant Terms

Hand Puppet. A type of puppet that is controlled by the hand or hands that occupy the interior of the puppet.

Play Therapy. "The systematic use of a theoretical model to establish an interpersonal process wherein trained play therapists use the therapeutic powers of play to help clients prevent or resolve psychosocial difficulties and achieve optimal growth and development" (Association for Play Therapy, 1997).

Puppet. An inanimate object, often resembling a human or an animal figure, that can be manipulated by a human so that it appears to be alive.

Puppet Play. The term refers to playing with children as opposed to playing for children, i.e., puppet theater.

Puppet Play Therapy. An approach wherein a mental health professional uses puppet play for the purpose of psychotherapy. A form of play therapy that utilizes puppets to implement the therapy.

Puppet Theater. A type of theatrical presentation using two- or three-dimensional puppets that are operated by actors called puppeteers who are generally hidden from view behind a screen.

Puppeteer. A person who animates puppets.

Puppetry. The art of manipulating an inanimate object in the form of a living character. Puppetry is basically a form of artistic expression that is a variation of storytelling or dramatic expression.

Therapeutic Puppet Play. The use of puppets to improve the mental health of self or others. Therapeutic puppet play is not limited to psychotherapy. Rather, the term "therapeutic" is meant in a more general sense of fostering psychological well-being.

2 Puppet Play Therapy With Children of All Ages

Eleanor C. Irwin

Marionettes and puppets, used for centuries as entertainment all over the world, have retained wide popularity even in our digitally obsessed day. Variations of Punch and Judy shows that originated in Italy in the 18th century spread rapidly to England, France, Germany, and Russia, and some are still shown on YouTube today. Popular hand puppets for children are King Friday and Lady Elaine from *Mister Rogers' Neighborhood*, as well as Kermit the Frog and the Cookie Monster from *Sesame Street.* Meanwhile, adults have been equally taken with live actors and puppets on Broadway shows like *Avenue Q* and *The Hand of God*.

The appeal of puppets across ages and cultures lives on, with increasing use in many domains and, not surprisingly, psychotherapy. These funny bits of play featuring people, animals, and symbolic character types usually entertain, but they can also be shockingly violent and raw. Real yet not real, puppetry can portray penetrating insights about the human condition, yet may also be easily dismissed as "make-believe." And in this paradox lies the core of its value to psychotherapy.

Factors Leading to Success in Puppet Play

Because they provide ready access to children's imagination, puppets are helpful additions to playrooms, aiding in diagnosis (understanding) and treatment (helping) of those who hope to find relief from painful "bad feelings" (Schafer, 2003). To enhance the deeper value of puppet play, one needs an empathic therapist (Schore, 1994) who understands nonverbal communication, along with a broad assortment of aesthetically pleasing hand puppets. A skilled therapist who is comfortable with play can help little ones able to engage in representational play (Sandler & Rosenblatt, 1962); latency-age children who have interiorized their fantasy lives (Piaget, 1962); and adolescents who struggle with identity, role confusion, relationships, school issues, and "second separation-individuation" issues. The goal of puppet play is to help all children reveal what has been concealed through symptom formation, and, with the help of a treatment alliance, bring about positive changes in their lives.

The announcement, "This is play—not real, but pretend," offers the psychological safety of disguise, a promise of not revealing (or being punished for) hidden secrets. What the therapist knows but the player does not (yet) realize, of course, is that the *feelings* are real, while the *story* is make-believe. By "buying off" the harsh and often condemning superego via disguise, puppets promote dramatic play, promising relief from hidden shame, guilt, and humiliation.

What Can the Therapist Learn From Puppet Play?

Both the form and the content give valuable, but different, kinds of information. *Content* gives clues about the underlying conflict in the story, that is, what the story is about, the characters, plot, and conflict, while the *form* tells us how the story is played, the child's strengths and weaknesses, and his or her defenses.

While the puppet characters are projections of the self and/or significant others, they are often disguised by the child's defenses, constituting a different kind of "language." Key defenses used in play are symbolism, projection, and displacement, which can be roughly defined in the following ways: Symbolism is the capacity of the human mind to have one thing (unconsciously) stand for another; projection refers to the tendency to attribute to another (to "cast out") unacceptable ideas or impulses; and displacement alludes to the tendency to redirect onto someone else (or to something else), one's dangerous or unacceptable ideas. Since everyone, to some extent, utilizes these defenses, one can see clearly how puppet play can happily "rid" one of seemingly dangerous, frightening feelings, as the following example illustrates.

Five-Year-Old Joey: An Example of How Puppet Play Can Help

After being hit by a drunk driver, Joey experienced grand mal seizures, waking to find a doctor giving him shots. Confused and frightened, he recovered, but was tormented with bad dreams and panic attacks, especially before clinic visits. Exhausted by their son's "tantrums" and worn out by his sleep problems, the parents pleaded for help for themselves and relief for their previously calm and loving child.

In the first session, asked to tell a story using the 20 or so puppets spilled out on the floor, Joey immediately chose a bright red devil and a realistic-looking boy puppet. Ignoring the puppet stage, he settled into my office chair, put the puppets on the desk, and started to play. To give some structure, I interrupted, asking him to introduce the puppets and say where the story takes place (i.e., the story line of who, what, and where, with the motivational "why" at the end).

Impatiently, Joey began: "Well . . . it's 'bout the devil doctor n' a boy, at the hos'pittal." Quickly taking a pencil from my desk, the devil doctor gleefully and repetitively "stabbed" the boy, saying, "You need this one, and this one, 'n wait—(with a red pencil) . . . here's a BIG one!"

So there we had it: a straightforward plot, unelaborated, titled "The Devil Doctor and His Big Needles." "Interviewing" the child at the end, I usually ask who he would like to be and not like to be in the story (assuming that both polarities are part of the self). Joey emphatically said he wanted to be the devil even though he was *bad!* Taking the role of the nurse, I interviewed the devil doctor, asking why the boy needed so many big shots. "AH! He's BAD—'n he's 'posed to get 'em!" the doctor said. "Bad?" I inquired. "In what way?" "Well," the devil said, "bad for ridin' his bike on the street!" (i.e., the accident was Joey's fault—his punishment for not listening!).

Still to come was the working through of his confused understanding, but Joey eventually came to see that he was not responsible for the accident, the drunk driver was. Puppet therapy provided, first, pleasure; second, abreaction; and third, a strong treatment alliance (akin to a positive transference) that helped Joey to enjoy his sessions and feel more hopeful. Less confused, anxious, and burdened by past issues, Joey went to first grade with the inner structure of a latency child (Sarnoff, 1976).

The Healing Power of Puppet Play

Joey's play spoke to what is potentially healing in this modality. Telling the story from his point of view, Joey *projected* his rage and hatred for the doctor (*symbolized* as the devil), while also *displacing* his aggression (and self-hatred) onto the devil doctor, whom he blamed for causing his problems. To this array of psychological mechanisms, we have to add *turning passive to active* (Freud, 1920; Waelder, 1933), which links such play to the *repetition compulsion* and *attempts at mastery* through role reversal. As Waelder has so succinctly written, play is the child's way of "assimilating piecemeal" experiences that are too much to be "assimilated instantly in at one swoop" (Waelder, 1933, p. 218). With decreasing anxiety, Joey moved from being a passive victim to an active aggressor, poignantly illustrating Erikson's comment that "to 'play it out' is the most natural self-healing measure childhood affords" (1950, p. 222).

Puppet Play Procedure

Range of Puppet Choices

Choice and variety are important in helping to make puppet play psychologically safe and rewarding. In addition to having a trained play therapist, it helps to have (1) a variety of puppets; (2) a stage or something to hide behind, if the child wishes; and (3) a semi-structured interview that can help mine the diagnostic data from the session(s).

To add variety, choices can include the following categories: (1) realistic family characters (mother, father, children) and fantasy puppets (e.g., royal family of king, queen, prince, princess, guard, and so forth); (2) domestic and wild animals (dog, cat, and bird, but also a monkey, wolf, gorilla, snake, alligator, or other animal with aggressive-looking teeth); (3) symbolic character types (witch, monster or bad guy, giant, devil, skeleton); (4) "occupation" puppets (doctor, nurse, and especially a policeman, who frequently serves as the voice of the punitive superego, or sometimes the father figure); and (5) amorphous-looking "characters" that can symbolically represent anything (e.g., a wooden spoon with big felt eyes or a big mouth, a flower, a fragment of fuzzy or gauzy material, a star on a stick that can represent lightning or have magic wish-fulfilling properties).

The therapist is not limited by available puppets, however, because playroom toys can easily be incorporated into puppet plays. Sometimes miniature life people and animals are included, as children "break boundaries" from the stage to the playroom, finding just what they need to elaborate their fantasies (as illustrated in the case examples).

While purchasing such a broad assortment of puppets can be expensive, experience suggests that initial costs are worth the investment. Unlike art materials that are "consumed" and need to be replaced, puppets can even outlast the therapist (!), with the possible exception of the symbolic bad mother (witch) and bad father (devil), whose rough treatment usually means a shorter shelf life. It is also important to look for unusual, well-made puppets, not just the furry, poorly delineated kind, each looking more or less like the other. Children, like adults, are intrigued by novelty and quality.

Self-Made Puppets

Fortunately, therapists need not depend solely on ready-made puppets or toys, because puppets can easily be made to suit an immediate purpose. Art materials like paper plates, Popsicle sticks, Styrofoam balls or cups, papier-mâché, yarn, beads, or whatever is handy can be decorated to fit the child's fantasy (like "teardrop germs" in Tammy's story, which is told later).

Use of a Stage

A small stage can be helpful, not just for puppet play but for many other dramatic play activities. For example, a popular stage, like the versatile one from Community Playthings (Ulster Park, New York), can be used as a classroom, store, cave, hideout, jail, or torture cellar with spooky things that "go bump in the night." But if a stage is not available, one can make a collapsible cardboard "theater," or something that gives the illusion of space, fostering the separation between actor and audience. If the story is compelling, the child will find a comfortable way to enact it. Although in full view, psychic distance allows the child to pretend that he or she cannot be seen—a wonderful example of the "willing suspension of disbelief." A brother and sister, for example, involved in filial therapy, played out their story while behind the sofa; another child used a chair; while still others crouched behind the sandbox or table, illustrating improvisational theater at its best. The therapist helps by being the "audience," maintaining the illusion, looking steadily, and later talking.

Use of a Semi-Structured Interview

One of the first steps in working with children is to help them feel comfortable, because anxious children cannot play. The universal "play signal" (Piers, 1972) usually helps: "Let's make a puppet story. Pick out some puppets you'd like to play with." Then, spilling out puppets on the floor, one can watch the selection process, sometimes sitting on the floor beside the child (Irwin, 1983). When the child is finished, the remaining puppets are put away and the child is helped to find a comfortable play space. It is important to remember that since this is improvisational play, there are no hard and fast rules. The main idea is to help the child tell a "made-up story—not one from a book or movie, TV show or video game."

Richard Gardner (1971) wrote about an interesting storytelling technique that I have often adapted for puppet play. Gardner uses the format of a television show and announces the child's name (e.g., "Master Steven") as the storyteller on a TV program. This helpful "warm-up" technique is especially useful with anxious children who find it hard to be imaginative.

Using the format of "who, what, where, and when," one can suggest that the child find a comfortable space and introduce the characters, one by one. If the child seems a bit shy or nervous, one can talk briefly *to* the puppet, asking for pretend bits of information about the puppet to help the child get into the spirit of play.

After the characters are introduced, one can ask where the story might take place, and then announce that the story is about to begin. If the child is hesitant, one can help by alluding to the show: "And now Mrs. Witch will be coming out to meet you. Good morning, Mrs. Witch! What kind of a day are you having?"—titrating the amount of help given, according to the child's need. Most children are familiar with puppets, however, and rarely need additional help.

Puppet plays, in some ways, are like waking daydreams. Just as there is the manifest part of a dream, followed by the "dream work" that elaborates underlying meaning, similarly, there is an initial puppet story (manifest material) and "puppet work" that helps enlarge the child's fantasy. And as with a dream, the therapist takes notes to capture significant pieces of information, although the need for an exact record diminishes as intuitive understanding grows.

Most important in understanding the meaning of the story are the names of the characters, the gist of the plot, crucial parts of dialogue (the "who, what, where, and when"), and the name of the show. Once the story is over, the therapist can ask various characters to "come out" and be "interviewed"; this helps one to understand the "why" of the story. Pretending a pencil is a microphone, one talks directly to the puppet (not to the child), asking questions to clarify ambiguity and/or provide elaboration to enhance meaning. One might say, for example, "Tommy, could the policeman come out? I'd like to talk to him. 'Good day, Mr. Policeman! My, you sure worked hard! Can you tell me more about how you knew the tall man was guilty?' " and so forth.

Once core players are interviewed, the therapist can inquire about (deeper) issues regarding self and other identifications: for example, "Tommy, if you could be anybody in the story, who would you most like to be? . . . AND, is there anyone you wouldn't like to be?" One can also ask about a title for the story, and "the moral" or lesson to be learned: for example, "If other kids were watching this show, what would they learn . . . What would they say is the story's main idea?"

Most kids can tell a story with this kind of safe structure and playful beginning. Some authors (Hawkey, 1951) have said that occasionally an anxious youngster asks the therapist to tell a story. If this happens, one could ask the child to select the characters and suggest an opening scene, and then make up a story based on what is known about the child. Gardner's mutual storytelling technique (1971) is also instructive in this regard because he asks the child to tell a story and then tells the story back (more or less), but with a healthier resolution to the conflict.

Puppet Stories With Preschoolers

Young children (4–6) are easily engaged in puppet stories, although sometimes their stories may be repetitive and lack coherence, reflecting their transitional phase between their own inner reality and external reality. Gould (1972) writes about this phase, calling it "fluctuating uncertainty," suggesting the child is unsure about real/not real. Happy to express fantasies about their inner life, young children are not bound by reality, but play out their thoughts and fears. Their themes often center on body integrity, babies, playing/being dead, getting injured, having an operation, battling fires, and bad guys. Trying to manage their aggressive drives, their stories circle around violent, dangerous themes—biting and clawing, pooping and peeing, attacks and counterattacks, devouring animals, and powerful guns that can kill. And, of course, if the play gets too scary, play disruption may occur, indicating that anxiety about the real/unreal has been trespassed, as in the following example.

Billy: Fearing His Littleness in Comparison to the Superhero's Bigness

Play can serve as a defense against underlying anxiety, but that was not the case with 4-year-old Billy, who was often in a perpetually anxious state. Playing out a show about superheroes killing bad guys, he suddenly left the play area, zipped open his pants, pulled out his penis, and said, "Want to see my wee-wee? It's BIG!" Having not yet developed the defense of repression, Billy was unable to stay with the symbolization in the story. Playing out a theme of powerful superheroes seemed to stimulate scary feelings of littleness and impotence. Experiencing play anxiety, he seemed to ask for reassurance and confirmation about his maleness and power.

I told Billy that he had a very fine penis, just right for his age. And, over time, as he got older, it would get bigger, until one day it would be very big, just like daddy's. But for now, it was better to go back to the story, and then we could talk some more about superheroes and little guys.

Because children like Billy have not yet developed the defense of repression, they are not able to keep unconscious thoughts and feelings out of conscious awareness, and need help.

Evidence of Abuse in Puppet Play With Vulnerable Children, Revealing Secrets

Because the action of puppet play evokes powerful active memories that are not yet repressed or suppressed, children sometimes play out episodes of traumatic experiences. Barbie's puppet play depicted a "Witch mommy" who left the house while her little girl was in bed. Then Alvin (the paramour) came into the little girl's room and "knifed her." At this point in her story, Barbie jumped up, stopped playing, and said she had to go to the bathroom. Leaving the bathroom stall door open, she urinated and then stared into the toilet. When I asked what she expected to see, she said she thought she saw blood, because that's what happened when Alvin "knifed" her.

While the majority of puppet stories do not open such a frightening Pandora's box, one is reminded of Terr's (1994) investigations of trauma in which memory is suddenly stimulated by a connection to a past experience that allows the "hidden" trauma to be recalled. Barbie seemed to make such a connection, albeit in the therapeutic safety of the playroom with a trusted person.

Puppet Play With Latency Children

In the middle years (ages 6–12), kids are full of fantasies, often with complicated plots elaborated in dramatic play. More likely to use the stage, their stories are often structured with complex plots with a beginning, middle, and end and a "moral." Perhaps the invitation to "let go" with puppets is felt as a relief from the usual school orientation, with the playroom offering an opportunity for controlled regression. With greater impulse control, capacity to delay gratification, a rich fantasy life, improved language skills, and an appreciation of humor (albeit often of the pregenital, regressive bathroom type), they are ideal players.

Eight-Year-Old Tammy, Referred for Anorexia

Blonde, excessively thin Tammy had a pinched, withdrawn, and sad look. Her parents referred her, they said, because she stopped eating after their divorce. Tammy's first puppet story was about Princess Isobel, the king, and the queen. The royal couple fought—a lot!—but kissed and made up, and then had a big feast for everyone. But alas, Princess Isobel couldn't eat because of scary germs everywhere that could kill everybody. Angry, the parents punished Isobel by putting her in the castle jail.

Tammy interrupted the play at this point (anxious?) and asked what she could use as germs. As I wondered what *she* thought, she decided to draw colorful "teardrop germs" hand puppets on a paper plate, with a Popsicle stick on the back. Returning to the story, she waved the germs around the still-feasting king and queen, but from her jail cell she was the only one who could see the dangerous germs. Everyone enjoyed the feast but the jailed princess, who whispered, "You are going to *die*—the germs will make you sick!" Since it was the end of her session, we carefully wrapped the "germ puppets" in tissue paper, put them into a shoebox, and safely "hid" them on a high shelf until her next session. Returning, she played "Chapter 2." The queen visited Isobel in jail, offering her "good food" (i.e., sand on a plate). Hungry, Isobel ate the food, but then the germs flew out, making her sick—and suddenly, the "teardrop germs" killed her! The queen was sad, but then said, "Oh well, now the germs are gone!"

Since Tammy insisted that the princess be buried, we made a "casket" (a tissue box) for her, and buried her in the sandbox. When the royal family visited the (sandbox) grave, Tammy waved the germs and in a haunted voice, whispered, "Eat the good food!" (i.e., sand). Hungry, the king and queen ate the sand "food," and then they, too, died.

Variations of this story alternated with artwork, and, in time, Tammy became less depressed and talked about her anger at her mother, whom she blamed for the divorce ("Mom always starts it!"). She surprised her dad by making (and eating!) spaghetti, a recipe she said she learned from a TV show.

This example illustrates the creativity of much latency play but also stresses the importance of following the child's lead and facilitating the play, whether in puppetry, sand play, or artwork.

Adolescence: Turn to Reality

Adolescents often tell stories that deal with their immediate concerns—school, sexual activity, drinking, or quarrels with parents or friends. Responding to the invitation to use puppets, they improvise as they play the story out, then and there. Puppet stories are often stimulated by discussions about interpersonal conflicts, which, after all, are the core of dramatic enactments. When an adolescent begins to describe an argument or battle with another, one can say, "Show me what happened—don't tell me. Pick some puppets and let's see what happened."

Jimmy: School Problems and His Escape With Pot

Personable and popular, Jimmy seemed to be liked by everyone but often fought with his parents, who pushed their only son to do well academically. In his first session, Jimmy talked of being lucky, getting out of predicaments easily, and said he didn't care about school or his "crappy" teachers, except for shop. And it was no big deal that he liked to smoke pot before his first class with his friends. "HEY! It helps me get through the day!"

However, in his second session, his attitude was somber. He said there was trouble, a big fight with his parents. The school called and told his parents that he'd been late eight times in six weeks. Furious, he said, they "threw the book" at him.

Hearing this, I said, "Okay, let's hear the argument. Pick someone to be your parents and someone to be you." Smiling broadly, Jimmy chose an old man (a "bum" puppet), a witch, and a prince figure for himself. The story began with the "bum" father's phone call with the school. Turning to the prince, the father, angry, demanded to know why the prince was always late. With a cavalier attitude, the prince said the school was always wrong, always making mistakes; they must have gotten him mixed up with someone else.

When the witch joined in, the battle really heated up. The argument got louder and the bum got angrier, insisting that the prince was lying. The punishment, the father said, was: no cell phone, no allowance, no seeing Janie (his girlfriend) on Saturdays . . . and then, suddenly, the yelling and the story stopped. Jimmy's face lost its look of bravado. Throwing the bum and witch puppets on the floor, he said, "Can you believe it? They really said I couldn't see Janie! Those jerks!"

The drama was over. The discussion turned serious, to the punishments, hatred for school, need for pot because school was hard, his sense that he couldn't do the work; maybe he should just be an auto mechanic.

This was a new turn in our session. Jimmy seemed to be a smart kid—verbal, quick thinking, with good native intelligence. However, when I said as much, he pulled some papers from his backpack and shoved them at me. Taken aback by the crumpled, messy English exam with poor spelling and even worse handwriting, it suddenly occurred to me that this charming and funny kid might have a heretofore undiagnosed learning problem. By virtue of his good native intelligence he had gotten by before, but by tenth grade he could no longer fake his way.

After some discussion, we had a family meeting and then a school conference, making a plan for him to be tested for ADD (of the inattentive type), because he did indeed seem to have a clear pattern of learning problems. Testing was the beginning of Jimmy's turnaround.

Summary

Puppets offer a safe way for children of all ages to communicate fantasies, ideas, and feelings. They can be helpful in aiding diagnosis and treatment, as well as in forging a treatment alliance. A creative and trained therapist who can facilitate play using an array of aesthetic and interesting puppets can further the goal of aiding children to find their voices, thereby effecting meaningful therapeutic change.

References

Erikson, E. H. (1950). *Childhood and society.* New York: Norton.

Freud, S. (1955). Beyond the pleasure principle. In J. Strachey (Ed. and Trans.), *The standard edition of the complete works of Freud* (Vol. 18, pp. 1–68). London: Hogarth. (Original work published in 1920).

Gardner, R. (1971). *Therapeutic communication with children: The mutual storytelling technique.* New York: Science House, Inc.

Gould, R. (1972). *Child studies through fantasy: Cognitive-affective patterns in development.* New York: Quadrangle Press, 77–84.

Hawkey, L. (1951). The use of puppets in child psychotherapy. *British Journal of Medical Psychology*, 24, 206–214. In C. Schaefer (Ed.), *Therapeutic use of child's play* (pp. 359–372). New York: Jason Aronson.

Irwin, E. (1983). The diagnostic and therapeutic use of pretend play. In C. Schaefer & K. O'Connor (Eds.), *Handbook of play therapy* (pp. 148–173). New York: John Wiley & Sons.

Piaget, J. (1962). *Play, dreams and imitation in childhood.* New York: Norton.

Piers, M. (Ed.). (1972). *Play and development.* New York: Norton.

Sandler, J., & Rosenblatt, B. (1962). The concept of the representational world. *Psychoanalytic Study of the Child, 17*, 128–145.

Sarnoff, C. (1976). *Latency.* New York: Jason Aronson.

Schafer, R. (2003). *Bad feelings: Selected psychoanalytic essays.* New York: Other Press.

Schore, A. (1994). *Affect regulation and the origin of the self: The Neurobiology of emotional development.* Hillsdale, NJ: Erlbaum.

Terr, L. (1994). *Unchained memories: True stories of traumatic memories, lost and found.* New York: Basic Books.

Waelder, R. (1933). The psychoanalytic theory of play. *Psychoanalytic Quarterly*, *2*, 208–224.

Section II

Puppet Assessment Techniques

3 The Berkeley Puppet Interview for Child Assessment

Jeffrey Measelle and Jennifer C. Ablow

Federal and state policies mandate that health and educational agencies detect, treat, and monitor young children with mental health problems and/or socioemotional needs. For example, Part C of the IDEA (Oser & Cohen, 2003), Head Start requirements (Currie & Neidell, 2007), and Healthy People 2020 (Kindig, Asada, & Booske, 2008) each specify that at-risk children be identified to receive evidence-based services as early as possible. Although it is estimated that 25% of young children have a mental or behavioral disorder, and that 60% of all children start school in need of intervention, 80% will not receive services that could prevent or reduce costly long-term problems (Costello & Angold, 2016). The sources of such problems are numerous. For example, precise detection of symptoms and impairment in young children has been impeded by gaps in our understanding of the antecedents of psychopathology, particularly forms of impairment that, because they are low in frequency or complex in character, are not detected until the emergence of more pronounced difficulties in mental health (Kazdin, 2017).

It is agreed that a lack of psychometrically sound tools with which to screen, diagnose, and monitor young children's health, mental health, and socioemotional status is a serious public health concern. Reviews of this problem cite the absence of self-report tools for young children as a critical issue in need of redress (Luby, 2006; Paynter, 2015; Ialongo, Edelsohn, & Kellan, 2001). With young children, parents are typically tapped as the "knowledgeable informants" despite evidence of reporting biases and poor agreement with other adults (Hinshaw, Han, Erhart, & Huber, 1992; Luby et al., 2002). Most problematically, parents and teachers frequently fail to detect young children's more internalized socioemotional distress (Ablow et al., 1999; Whalen, Sylvester, & Luby, 2017). The lack of age-appropriate instrumentation has meant that young children's subjective evaluations of their own needs have not been assessed routinely in scientific, health, or educational settings. In our own work, we have argued that this is a root cause of under-detection (Ablow & Measelle, 1993; Measelle, Ablow, Cowan, & Cowan, 1998).

Eliciting reliable self-reports from young children is complicated by a variety of developmental factors, such as shorter attention spans and less mature expressive skills (for review, see Measelle et al., 1998). Methods that are not interesting and engaging for young children or that rely *exclusively* on children's verbal abilities are less likely to work for young children, especially those who are inhibited or language-delayed. Moreover, conscious or unconscious anxieties about divulging information to a stranger (i.e., an adult interviewer) may prevent some children from disclosing pertinent information. Research demonstrates, however, that young children benefit from the use of age-appropriate props such as puppets, drawings, and other visual aids to help children talk about themselves and their experiences (Greenspan & Greenspan, 1991; Irwin, 1985; Valla, Bergeron, & Smolla, 2000). Early studies have shown that puppets in particular are able to keep 4- to 8-year-old children of varied clinical and socioeconomic backgrounds engaged, even when discussing sensitive topics such as death (Bernhart & Prager, 1985), sadness (Irwin, 1985; O'Conner, Schaefer, & Braverman 2015), or aggressive behavior (Bender & Woltman, 1937). In short, when children are involved in more age-appropriate activities, they are more likely to talk openly about their experiences (Ceci & Bruck, 1993).

The Berkeley Puppet Interview (BPI)

The Berkeley Puppet Interview (BPI), building on a rich tradition of using puppets in clinical settings, was developed to address the absence of standardized methodologies appropriate for measuring young children's perceptions of themselves and their interpersonal environments (Ablow & Measelle, 1993). Using an interactive technique for interviewing children, the BPI blends structured and semi-structured interviewing methods with motivational interviewing techniques for children (see Fig. 3.1). During the actual

Figure 3.1 Typical BPI Interview Arrangement With 6-Year-Old Boy
Photo by Jennifer Ablow

BPI interview, two identical hand puppets (puppy dogs named "Iggy" and "Ziggy") make opposing statements about themselves and then ask children to describe themselves. For example:

Iggy: I have lots of friends.
Ziggy: I don't have lots of friends.
Iggy: How about you?

OR

Ziggy: My parents fight a lot.
Iggy: My parents don't fight a lot.
Ziggy: What about your parents?

Rather than using a forced-choice or recognition-task response format, the BPI allows children to respond in ways that are most natural and comfortable to them, with the goal of promoting a fluid and unselfconscious dialogue between a child and the puppets (see Fig. 3.2). The majority of young children interviewed with the BPI respond verbally, either by describing themselves or by indicating which puppet is most like them. Other children use limited verbal responses, such as naming one of the two puppets, or by responding in nonverbal ways, such as pointing to a puppet. To capture the range of individual differences in young children's responses, the BPI uses an extensive, rule-based coding system. Regardless of whether children's responses are verbal, nonverbal, elaborated, or limited, the BPI's coding system provides coders with the parameters needed to make sense of the varied ways that 4- to 8-year-old children respond to interview items. Specifically, guidelines have been developed to help coders decipher figures of speech, reasoning

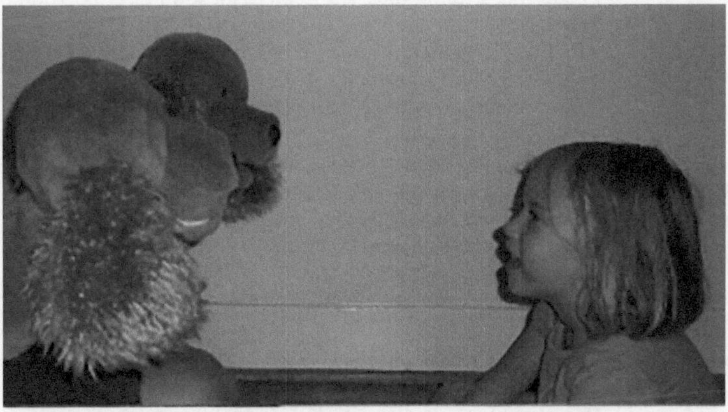

Figure 3.2 Typical BPI Interview Arrangement With 4-Year-Old Girl
Photo by Jennifer Ablow

processes, and conditional responses that reflect ambivalent self-perceptions or uncertainty due to a lack of experience with a particular issue. In short, by allowing children to respond in their own idiosyncratic ways, one of the BPI's central achievements is its ability to promote a fluid and unselfconscious dialogue between children and the puppets about a variety of topics.

Table 3.1 provides a summary of what we view to be the BPI's core interactive, age-appropriate features. More specifically, Table 3.1 considers the necessary and recommended materials needed to conduct the BPI as developed for standardized applications as well as the interactive features of how the puppets work with children to get comprehensible and scorable responses.

Table 3.1 Age-Appropriate Features of In-Person BPI

Domain	*Feature*
Materials	• Two identical, non-gendered hand puppets (dogs) named Iggy and Ziggy (I&Z) • Movable mouths • Nondescript but cuddly/appealing features (e.g., floppy ears) increase child's engagement and motivation • No other props needed (e.g., stage, table, chairs)
Task structure, demands, item wording	• Clear, simple task introduction ensures procedural accuracy • Non-challenging, factual practice items ensure comprehension and establish veridical self-reporting as expectation • Puppets offer pairs of opposing statements about themselves; lower socially desirable responding • Behaviorally or contextually anchored items provide retrieval cues that increase accuracy (Depression: "I cry/don't cry a lot at school.") • Symptom/problem and strength/competence items • Not forced-choice or Likert-based responding; child responds to "How about you?" and puppets establish degree ("Do you do that a lot or not a lot?") • Open-ended follow-ups can seek clarification or elaboration or can be interspersed to maintain engagement • Modular, customizable content: researcher selects relevant question domains from psychometrically established item pools • Recommended length of interview protocols: 10–25 minutes
Child response modalities	• Verbal responses • Nonverbal responses (pointing/touching corresponding puppet) • Variable (e.g., start nonverbal but shift to verbal) • Puppets can offer restatements that help child's comprehension • Puppets' acknowledgements ensure accurate scoring ("Oh, yeah, that's like me too, I'm a sad kid.")
Social/ interactive features	• Puppets are presented as interested age-mates ("We want to get to know you!") • Contingent verbal and nonverbal behaviors convey puppets' interest, engagement, and capacity to respond to child • Puppets able to detect and adjust to child's attention levels • Puppets able to detect and adjust to child's affect • Puppets able to detect and adjust to child's verbal capacities

Originally, the BPI was developed as a two-part interview (Ablow & Measelle, 1993), with one part targeting children's perceptions of their academic and social competence and their emotional well-being, including feelings of depression, anxiety, and aggression (described in Measelle et al., 1998). Part two of the original BPI targeted children's perceptions of their family environment, in particular, children's appraisals of their parents' relationship dynamics (e.g., conflict, affection) as well as children's perceptions of their relationships with parents and siblings (partially described in Ablow, Measelle, Cowan, & Cowan, 2009).

The BPI, however, has intentionally been designed as a method rather than as a single interview or limited set of content domains. Indeed, since its development, our objective has been to collaborate with scientists and clinicians to develop and validate a variety of content domains. As such, we view the BPI as an age-appropriate method that takes a modular approach to the assessment of children. As of today, items and scales have been developed and refined in a variety of domains, which are summarized in Figures 3.3 and 3.4. Specifically,

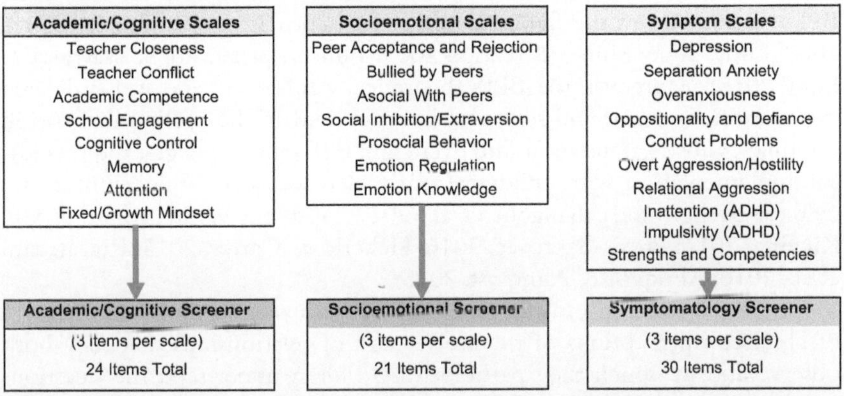

Note**:** The **BPI Family Domain** and attendant subscales are not presented here. This domain includes children's multiscale assessment of their relationships with parents and siblings as well as perceptions of parents' marital relationships.

Figure 3.3 BPI Self Domains, Subscales, and Related Screeners

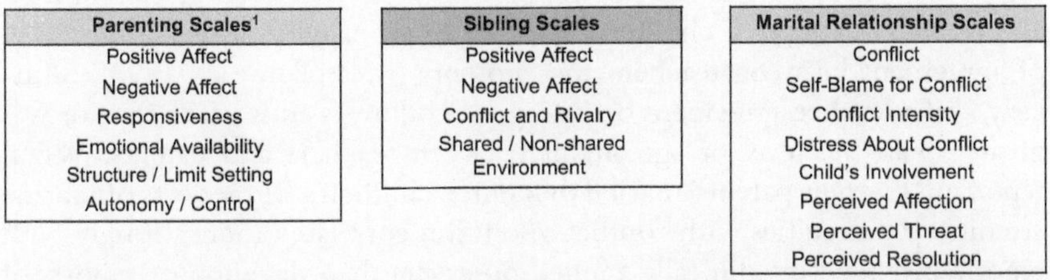

[1]Parenting scales have been developed for both mothers and fathers as well as items for "parents" if the distinction is not important.

Figure 3.4 BPI Family Environment Domains and Subscales

Figure 3.3 presents the "self" domains and Figure 3.4 presents domains to assess children's appraisals of relationships within the family.

Evidence of the BPI's Scientific and Clinical Utility as an Assessment Tool

The BPI has provided a strong challenge to the suggestion that 4- to 8-year-old children cannot provide valuable information about themselves. Since publication of initial scientific reports (Ablow & Measelle, 1993; Measelle et al., 1998; Measelle, John, Ablow, Cowan, & Cowan, 2005), investigations with the BPI have produced replicated evidence that young children may be the best informants about their internal states of distress (Luby, 2006; Ringoot et al., 2013), that early interventions can produce changes in children's self-appraisals that help drive behavioral change (Cowan, Cowan, Ablow, Johnson, & Measelle, 2005), and that young children's reports of their traits predict real-world outcomes five and ten years later (John, Measelle, Ablow, Cowan, & Cowan, In press). Scientific reviews have identified the BPI as a standard in the field of child assessment (Briggs-Gowan & Carter, 2008; Luby, 2006; Shiner & Caspi, 2003; Nilsson et al., 2015; Navsaria & Luby, 2015). Moreover, the BPI's theoretically informed and well-validated items/scales/domains and screeners have resulted in the tool's utilization in multiple contexts, translation into over eight different languages, and successful implementation with children from varied socioeconomic, clinical, and cultural backgrounds (Ringoot et al., 2017; Göttken, White, Klein, & von Klitzing, 2014; Prosic-Santovac, 2016; Heberle & Carter, 2015; Rijlaarsdam et al., 2016; Almqvist & Almqvist, 2015).

Substantial research indicates that the BPI is a reliable and valid measure of children's perceptions of themselves and of relationships that they both observe and in which they participate. Children understand the questions and become unselfconsciously engaged in dialogue with the puppets, giving differentiated and coherent responses in the process. One of the key findings in these studies has been that agreement between 4- to 8-year-old children and adult informants tends to be as strong as if not stronger than the level of agreement between pairs of adult informants. For example, agreement between young children's reports of their depressed-anxious mood and teachers' ratings of children's internalizing behavior exceeded the level of agreement between teachers and mothers (Measelle et al., 1998). Similarly, child-teacher agreement on ratings of children's antisocial behavior was greater than the level of agreement between teachers and parents. When reporting on their parents' marital dynamics, children's BPI reports of marital conflict or difficulties with conflict resolution correlated more strongly with reports provided by clinically trained observers than did spouses' reports of these same behaviors with each other (Ablow et al., 2009). These data are important in light of the field's tendency to view young children's perceptions/reports as less valid and to rely on adult informants when attempting to identify children's emotional and behavioral problems or when describing which aspects of young children's familial environments may or may not be distressing to them.

Clinically, the BPI has also served as a useful assessment tool as well as a resource to support therapeutic processes with young children. As a method, the BPI supports delivering specific sets of questions. However, skilled interviewers can also utilize open-ended follow-ups to explore children's responses. In research contexts, a premium is typically placed on administering predetermined sets of interview items within a reasonable amount of time (that reflects both children's attentional capacity as well as the time allotted to the BPI in what are typically dense data collection protocols). However, clinical work affords interviewers with greater latitude to follow up with children on particular statements they might make. To illustrate the BPI's utility as a clinical assessment and therapeutic tool, the following case examples highlight the method's semi-structured and open-ended features.

Case Illustration 1: During an interview with a 7-year-old male, the child was asked:

Iggy: When my parents fight, I don't think something bad will happen.
Ziggy: When my parents fight, I do think something bad will happen.
Iggy: How about you?
Child: When my parents fight, I do think that something bad will happen. Because when my parents fight, my dad gets mad and he always does something physical.
Ziggy: Oh I see. Like what? What does your dad do?
Child: When he gets mad he twists our arms or he grabs my mother's mouth like this (*demonstrates*) and makes her stop talking about what he doesn't want her to talk about.
Iggy: That sounds kind of hard.
Child: Yeah.

In the context of a larger interview with additional items assessing marital dynamics, the interviewer astutely first acknowledged the child ("Oh I see"), but then took the opportunity to probe a bit further with the puppets. The interviewer did not need to probe beyond the initial follow-up, recognizing that the interview was still in progress and that there would likely be other opportunities during or after the interview to explore possible concerns of physical abuse or domestic violence in the family.

Case Illustration 2: In the context of a large intervention study with a sample of middle-class families, an entire BPI interview was completed with a 4.5-year-old girl who had stopped talking when she turned 3 years of age because, according to her parents, she did not like the sound of her voice. After administering the standardized introduction and asking a handful of practice items designed to get the child speaking and to demonstrate comprehension for the task demand, the interviewer established a nonverbal way for the child to respond.

Ziggy: So, it's okay if you don't want to use your words to tell us about you.
Iggy: Yeah, that's okay. Instead, you can point at me if you're like me or point at Ziggy if you're like Ziggy.
Ziggy: Or, you can pat our heads if you'd like. You decide! Okay?
Child: (*Nods head in agreement.*)

The child then preceded to complete a 20-minute interview nonverbally by pointing, patting the corresponding puppet, or nodding or shaking her head. If the interviewer was not sure she comprehended the child's nonverbal response, she easily sought and obtained clarification through the puppets.

Ziggy: We're sorry. Can you say that again? Are you a sad kid most of the time?
Iggy: Or, not a sad kid most of the time?
Child: (*Pats Ziggy's head.*)
Ziggy: Oh, I see, most of the time, you're a sad kid like me.
Child: (*Nods head in agreement.*)

Case Illustration 3: One of the best indicators that a child is both engaged with the puppets and comprehending what is being asked is when a child offers comforting statements to the puppet who just made a negative statement about themselves. Often, these instances give the interviewer an opening to probe the child's ideas and thoughts beyond the immediate question. In the next example, a 5-year-old boy responded to the puppets' statements as follows:

Iggy: When kids at school are playing, I ask them if I can play too.
Ziggy: When kids at school are playing, I don't ask them if I can play.
Iggy: How about you?
Child: Ziggy, you should ask them to play so you're not so lonely.
Ziggy: Hmm, I see. But what do you do? Do you ask them or not ask them to play?
Child: I ask if I can play with kids.
Iggy: How do you do that?
Child: I just go up to someone I know and ask if it is okay to play too. They always say "yes." If I don't know them, I'll ask a kid who looks friendly if I can play.
Ziggy: Okay, we understand now. Thanks!

The Range of Children

Most children will complete the BPI interview with little difficulty, including children referred for socioemotional or behavioral assessments. Children almost universally enjoy the experience of talking with Iggy and Ziggy, and often show disappointment when the interview session is over. However, some children do get tired, bored, anxious, excited, or uncooperative during an interview. In these situations, interviewers are encouraged to use a variety of strategies to support and encourage the child. Occasionally, short breaks can be helpful, though the risk that a child will not resume after a break is a possibility. For children presenting with different behavioral and socioemotional needs, we offer a variety of suggestions based on extensive experience using the BPI with at-risk populations of children.

Building Rapport With the Child

Establishing rapport with the child is an important objective before commencing the interview process. We also find it useful to talk generally about the idea that we have two puppet friends who are interested in meeting the child, and that they are excited to tell the child all about themselves. We recommend that the interviewer *not* actually introduce (show) the puppets until they themselves have established rapport with the child. In our experience, rapport building does not take long at all when the prospect of meeting the puppets is introduced.

Tone of Interview

It is essential that the interviewer adopt a neutral but warm tone when interviewing all children. The same neutral tone should be used for each puppet so that the child knows that either statement is acceptable. In other words, it is important that the positive statement not sound more upbeat or the negative statement sound more downbeat. Also, avoid adopting voices that are either overly animated or unnatural to the interviewer; these are both difficult to sustain across the interview and often seem inauthentic to the child. In addition, the interviewer should adopt a comfortable and measured pace that ensures clarity of delivery and a child's comprehension. For example, a slight pause should occur between question stems to avoid merging the two statements into one long utterance, and to represent clearly to the child that each puppet is offering a distinct perspective. After the question stems are presented, a slight pause allows the child to respond fully. It is important for the interviewer to be sure that the child has completed his or her thought and is ready to go on to the next item. At all costs, avoid creating an atmosphere of haste by moving rapidly from one item to the next.

Children With Language Difficulties

It is not sufficient to simply re-ask an item if a child is having comprehension difficulties. Rather, re-asking the item in a truncated form will typically improve a child's comprehension. With children who are having a difficult time expressing or articulating themselves verbally, truncation of the item before asking the child "How about you?" will also help. As a general principle, presenting the truncation of the item as part of the query will enable a child who is struggling to articulate the crux of the item more easily. For example:

Ziggy: It's hard for me to work on something for a long time.
Iggy: It's not hard for me to work on something for a long time.
Ziggy: So how about you? Is it hard . . .
Iggy: . . . Or not hard to work on things for a long time?

In general, once it becomes clear that a child has comprehension issues or an expressive language problem, the interviewer should identify the child's most comfortable form of expression, and then integrate this style into the administration of the items. The goal is to help the child by adapting the interview's delivery to fit the mode of expression that is most comfortable for the child. This will almost always involve the use of item truncation.

As well, there are times when the latency of a child's response suggests that the child has become distracted or has not fully comprehended an item. At these times, the child will benefit from the interviewer facilitating his or her response with a truncated redelivery of the item.

General Considerations That Help Most Children

To avoid contributing to a child's self-consciousness, interviewers should avoid making value judgments in response to the child (i.e., "that's good" or "that's bad"). Furthermore, interviewers should try to always acknowledge a child's response (positive or negative), because not doing so can inadvertently increase some children's self-consciousness. To validate children's responses and to convey interest and attentiveness, one or both puppets should always acknowledge a child's response with neutral statements such as, "Oh, that's like me," "That's how I feel too," or even, simply, "Oh, I see." To avoid sounding redundant, use different yet appropriate follow-up statements throughout the interview. Keep the item just presented in mind and use an appropriate response that is matched to the item. For example, if the item presented had to do with a parent (e.g., "My mom likes to play with me."/"My mom doesn't like to play with me."), follow the child's response with "That's like my mom too." Concordance between the actual question stem and follow-up helps to promote a natural dialogue.

Externalizing Behavior

Children who express their distress with or dislike of the situation through restless, distracted, or even aggressive behavior during the BPI interview can be helped to stay on task through a combination of strategies. To help less attentive children, interviewers should use the child's name frequently and encourage the child through preemptive and regular praise (e.g., "You know what!? You are doing such a good job talking with us. You are working so hard. We are really enjoying getting to know you!") Occasionally, it may be helpful or necessary to negotiate a process with the child whereby a set number of questions is asked in exchange for incentives (like stickers, short breaks, etc.) to reward on-task behavior.

If a child's behavior becomes truly problematic during the interview (e.g., acting aggressively toward the puppets), the interviewer is encouraged to lower the puppets and talk with the child about expectations. In the BPI method, puppets can do a lot of effective encouraging and structuring of on-task behaviors. However, to ensure that a child will continue to see the puppets as enjoyable age-mates, we suggest that interviewers assume responsibility for more directive or corrective interventions with more difficult children.

Internalizing Behavior

Although rare, if the interview questions seem to upset a child, it is helpful to offer support and encouragement to the child by acknowledging the difficulty of the child's feelings and empathizing through the puppets (e.g., Ziggy: "I feel that way too; that can be hard"). It also can be useful to ask the child open-ended questions to let the child express more of what might be on his/her mind, should this appear helpful or indicated. As with more distractible or disruptive children, praise and encouragement both normalizes a child's statements and encourages the child to continue. We believe that the BPI is highly effective for children dealing with internalizing problems, precisely because one of the puppets is always sharing a similar sentiment, and because the puppets convey neutrality and their matter-of-fact interest in the child ("Oh, I see. I get scared a lot too").

Some children will be anxious or overly stimulated at the outset. In most cases, shy/anxious/fearful children simply need to see that the puppets are friendly and to gain an understanding of the task's demands. Typically, after one or two practice items are delivered (e.g., "I like pizza."/"I don't like pizza. How about you?"), these children find a way to communicate and settle into the interview.

Children With Neurodevelopmental Symptoms

Children with known or suspected neurodevelopmental disorders, such as autism, are unlikely to be able to complete the BPI when symptoms are moderate to severe, or where communication is markedly impaired. Researchers and clinicians should consider carefully the possibility that some children will even experience puppets as socially aversive.

The BPI's manual provides an extensive set of procedural guidelines and suggestions. Some of the more central suggestions are as follows.

Summary of BPI Interviewing Guidelines

1. Establish rapport with children before turning to the actual puppet interview. Introduce each puppet to the child. Explain what is going to happen in the interview. Use one or two practice questions to engage the child and to demonstrate how the interview works. Do not begin the actual interview until you are certain the child is engaged and understands the process.
2. Interview with a neutral, nonjudgmental tone. The interviewer should adopt a clear, comfortable, gentle pace. Avoid creating an atmosphere of haste by moving rapidly from one item to the next. As well, interviewers are strongly encouraged not to see the BPI as a source of entertainment or to adopt animated personas when interviewing a child. Indeed, we have found that individuals with either extensive child play therapy or child theater experience often struggle to adopt a more neutral, matter-of-fact tone when interviewing children.
3. To convey interest in the child's response, follow his/her endorsement with a simple statement of acknowledgement, such as "That's like me too." However, do not follow up children's responses with an evaluative statement (e.g., "Oh that's good," or "That's too bad," etc.).
4. When encountering more difficult/challenging children, it will be important to use encouragement and positive feedback as a way to help children stay on task. As a rule, we strongly encourage interviewers to offer praise and encouragement preventatively, before behavior problems begin to emerge. By encouragement and positive feedback, we mean statements such as:

   "You are working so hard!"
   "We are really enjoying talking with you."
   "We really like getting to know you."
   "We like telling you things about ourselves."
   "We really like hearing about you."
   "We're having a lot of fun talking with you."
   "We only have a few more things to talk about before we take a break. But you're doing such a good job."

5. Say the child's name frequently to make sure he or she is alert and paying attention, as well as to personalize the interviewing process, but not so often as to diminish its effect.
6. If a question needs to be repeated, be certain to restate both options. Do not restate a question by repeating only one of the statements.
7. At times, it is not clear whether a child has understood an item. With children who appear to have difficulty tracking and/or responding to the intent of an item, interviewers should use a *truncating tactic* as part of the interview process. For example, after delivering each item half in the standard way, the interviewer would then redeliver the item in an abbreviated

manner, providing the child with two verbally succinct alternatives from which to choose. This is an especially useful tactic when children seem to have comprehension difficulties with longer, more complicated items:

Iggy: If a kid doesn't do what I say, I tell him I won't be his friend anymore.
Ziggy: If a kid doesn't do what I say, I don't tell him that.
Iggy: How about you, Betsy? When a kid doesn't do what you say, do you tell her you won't be her friend anymore . . .
Ziggy: . . . Or not tell her that?

8. If a child is having trouble comprehending items, avoid statements that give the child a choice, such as "Should we try that again?" Second, if the interviewer is going to ask a child with an expressive language problem to "try again," the interviewer needs to make it possible for the child to succeed in expressing his or her thoughts/feelings by using item truncations. We have seen children's affect change as a result of having their difficulties repeatedly acknowledged and the interview process not modified to reflect their language abilities.
9. The objective of the BPI is not to encourage extraneous conversation between the interviewer and child during the interview. However, clinical issues may arise that warrant a break in the interview's flow where the interviewer might wish to ask unscripted follow-up question(s). For example, when a child is revealing difficult feelings and thoughts, we have found it useful and important to acknowledge that "these are hard questions but you're doing really well and we like talking to you." Again, conversation should be used judiciously and with a purpose.
10. After the last question has been asked, the puppets should inform the child that the interview is complete. More importantly, the puppets should thank the child for talking with them (e.g., "Thanks for talking with us") and let the child know that they had fun talking with and learning about him or her. In addition, we like to have the puppets ask the child if he or she would like to ask the puppets anything before they leave.

Summary

The BPI was designed to collect young children's perceptions of self and others in an age-appropriate manner. Extensive research and clinical work with the BPI has provided extensive evidence of its reliability as a method with which to obtain a wide range of information from children 4 to 8 years old. For individuals or groups interested in implementing the BPI, we strongly suggest formal training when standardized delivery is an objective (i.e., across multiple interviewers or when repeat administrations are planned). In more ideographic contexts, the BPI method is quite flexible and can be adapted to a variety of delivery circumstances.

References

Ablow, J. C., & Measelle, J. R. (1993). *The Berkeley puppet interview manuals*. Berkeley, CA: University of California.

Ablow, J. C., & Measelle, J. R. (2009). Capturing young children's perceptions of marital conflict. In M. S. Schulz, M. K. Pruett, P. Kerig, & R. Parke (Eds.), *Strengthening couple relationships and interventions for optimal child development: Lessons from research and intervention* (pp. 41–57). Washington, DC: APA.

Ablow, J. C., Measelle, J. R., Cowan, P. A., & Cowan, C. P. (2009). Linking marital conflict and children's adjustment: The role of young children's perceptions. *Journal of Family Psychology, 23*, 485–499.

Ablow, J. C., Measelle, J. R., Kraemer, H. C., Harrington, R., Luby, J., Smider, N., Dierker, L., Clark, V., Dubick, B., Heffelfinger, A., Essex, M. J., & Kupfer, D. J. (1999). The Macarthur three-city outcome study: Evaluating multi-informant measures of young children's symptomatology. *Journal of the American Academy of Child and Adolescent Psychiatry, 38*, 1580–1590.

Almqvist, A. L., & Almqvist, L. (2015). Making oneself heard: Children's experiences of empowerment in Swedish preschools. *Early Child Development and Care, 185*(4), 578–593.

Bender, L., & Woltman, A. G. (1937). Puppetry as a psychotherapeutic measure with problem children. *New York State Association of Occupational Therapists*, 7, 1–7.

Bernhardt, B. R., & Prager, S. B. (1985). Preventing child suicide: The elementary school death education puppet show. *Journal of Counseling and Development, 63*, 311–312.

Briggs, -Gowan, M.J., & Carter, A. S. (2008). Social-emotional screening status in early childhood predicts elementary school outcomes, *Pediatrics, 121*(5), 957–962.

Ceci, S. J., & Bruck, M. (1993). Suggestibility of the child witness: A historical review and synthesis. *Psychological Bulletin, 113*(3), 403.

Costello, E. J., & Angold, A. (2016). Developmental epidemiology. In D. Chichetti (Ed.), *Developmental Psychopathology: Volume I* (Third Edition, pp. 1–35). New York: Wiley.

Cowan, P. A., Cowan, C. P., Ablow, J. C., Johnson, V., & Measelle, J. R. (2005). The family context of parenting in children's adaptation to school: Support for early intervention. In *Monographs in parenting* (pp. 1–414). M. H. Bornstein (Series Editor). Mahwah, NJ: Erlbaum Publishers.

Currie, J., & Neidell, M. (2007). Getting inside the "black box" of Head Start quality: What matters and what doesn't. *Economics of Education Review, 26*(1), 83–99.

Göttken, T., White, L. O., Klein, A. M., & von Klitzing, K. (2014). Short-term psychoanalytic child therapy for anxious children: A pilot study. *Psychotherapy, 51*(1), 148.

Greenspan, S. I., & Greenspan, N. T. (1991). *The clinical interview of the child* (2nd ed.). Washington, DC: American Psychological Association.

Heberle, A. E., & Carter, A. S. (2015). Cognitive aspects of young children's experience of economic disadvantage. *Psychological Bulletin, 141*(4), 723.

Hinshaw, S. P., Han, S. S., Erhart, D., & Huber, A. (1992). Internalizing and externalizing behavior problems in preschool children: Correspondence among parent and teacher ratings and behavior observations. *Journal of Clinical Child Psychology, 21*, 143–150.

Ialongo, N. S., Edelsohn, G., & Kellan, S. G. (2001). A further look at the prognostic power of young children's reports of depressed mood and feelings. *Child Development*, 72(3), 736–747.

Irwin, E. C. (1985). Puppets in therapy: An assessment procedure. *American Journal of Psychotherapy, 39*, 389–399.

John, O. P., Measelle, J. R., Ablow, J. C., Cowan, C. P., & Cowan, P. A. (In press). Young children's self-reported personality traits predict academic and social outcomes 5 and 10 years later. *Psychological Assessment.*

Kazdin, A. E. (2017). Addressing the treatment gap: A key challenge for extending evidence-based psychosocial interventions. *Behavior Research and Therapy, 88*, 7–18.

Kindig, D. A., Asada, Y., & Booske, B. (2008). A population health framework for setting national and state health goals. *Jama, 299*(17), 2081–2083.

Luby, J. L. (2006). *Handbook of preschool mental health: Development, disorders, and treatment.* New York, NY: Guilford Press.

Luby, J. L., Heffelfinger, A., Measelle, J. R., Ablow, J. C., Essex, M. J., Dierker, L., Harrington, R., Kraemer, H. C., & Kupfer, D. J. (2002). The MacArthur health and behavior questionnaire compared to the DISC-IV: Greater sensitivity in identification of DSM-IV internalizing disorders in young children. *Journal of the American Academy of Child and Adolescent Psychiatry, 41*, 458–466.

Measelle, J. R. (2005). Children's self-perceptions as a link between family relationship quality and social adaptation to school. In P. A. Cowan, C. P. Cowan, J. C. Ablow, V. Kahen-Johnson, & J. R. Measelle (Eds.), *The family context of parenting in children's adaptation to school* (pp. 163–188). *Monographs in parenting.* M. H. Bornstein (Series Editor). Mahwah, NJ: Erlbaum Publishers.

Measelle, J. R., Ablow, J. C., Cowan, P. A., & Cowan, C. P. (1998). Assessing young children's self-perceptions of their academic, social and emotional lives: An evaluation of the Berkeley puppet interview. *Child Development, 69*, 1556–1576.

Measelle, J. R., John, O. P., Ablow, J. C., Cowan, P. A., & Cowan, C. (2005). Can young children provide coherent, stable, and valid self-reports on the big five dimension? A longitudinal study from ages 5 to 7. *Journal of Personality and Social Psychology, 89*, 90–106.

Navsaria, N., & Luby, J. (2016). Assessing the preschool-age child. In M.K. Dulcan (Ed.), *Dulcan's Textbook of Child and Adolescent Psychiatry* (pp. 37–56), , Arlington, VA: American Psychiatric Association Publishing.

Nilsson, S., Björkman, B., Almqvist, A. L., Almqvist, L., Björk-Willén, P., Donohue, D., & Hvit, S. (2015). Children's voices: Differentiating a child perspective from a child's perspective. *Developmental Neurorehabilitation, 18*(3), 162–168.

O'Connor, K. J., Schaefer, C. E., & Braverman, L. D. (2015). *Handbook of play therapy.* New York: John Wiley & Sons.

Oser, C., & Cohen, J. (2003). *Improving part C early intervention: Using what we know about infants and toddlers with disabilities to reauthorize part C of IDEA.* Washington, DC: Zero to Three Policy Center.

Paynter, J. M. (2015). Conducting Developmental and Cognitive Assessments with Young Children with Autism Spectrum Disorders, *Journal of Psychologists and Counsellors in Schools, 25*(1), 126–128.

Prosic-Santovac, D. (2016). Popular video cartoons and associated branded toys in teaching English to very young learners: A case study. *Language Teaching Research, 21*(5), 568–588.

Rijlaarsdam, J., Tiemeier, H., Ringoot, A. P., Ivanova, M. Y., Jaddoe, V. W., Verhulst, F. C., & Roza, S. J. (2016). Early family regularity protects against later disruptive behavior. *European Child & Adolescent Psychiatry, 25*(7), 781–789.

Ringoot, A. P., Jansen, P. W., Rijlaarsdam, J., So, P., Jaddoe, V. W. V., Verhulst, F. C., & Tiemeier, H. (2017). Self-reported problem behavior in young children with and without a DSM-disorder in the general population. *European Psychiatry, 40*, 110–115.

Ringoot, A. P., Jansen, P. W., Steenweg-de Graaff, J. C. J., Measelle, J. R., van der Ende, J., Jaddoe, V. W. V., Hofman, A., Verhulst, F. C., & Tiemeier, H. (2013). Young children's self-reported peer relations, emotional and behavioral problems: The psychometrics of the Berkeley puppet interview. *Psychological Assessment, 24*, 1273–1281.

Shiner, R., & Caspi, A. (2003, January). Personality differences in childhood and adolescence: Measurement, development, and consequences. *Journal of Child Psychology and Psychiatry, 44*(1), 2–32.

Valla, J. P., Bergeron, L., & Smolla, N. (2000). The Dominic-R: A pictorial interview for 6-to 11-year-old children. *Journal of the American Academy of Child & Adolescent Psychiatry, 39*(1), 85–93.

Whalen, D. J., Sylvester, C. M., & Luby, J. L. (2017). Depression and anxiety in preschoolers: A review of the past 7 years. *Child and Adolescent Psychiatric Clinics of North America, 26*(3), 503–522.

Appendix

Sample Berkeley Puppet Interview Items

The BPI is considered a method rather than a single or specific set of questions. The BPI method is designed to be flexible, enabling users to develop their own set of questions and content domains. Here we provide a few examples to convey the language and complexity that has proven effective in research.

Depression

I don't like myself.
I like myself.
I'm a lonely kid.
I'm not a lonely kid.

Anxiety

I don't worry a lot.
I worry a lot.
I don't get tummy aches a lot.
I do get tummy aches a lot.

Social Inhibition

When I meet new kids, I'm not shy.
When I meet new kids, I am shy.
It makes me nervous and shy to ask other kids to play.
It doesn't make me nervous and shy to ask other kids to play.

Hostility/Aggression

I hit kids a lot.
I don't hit kids.
I think it's fun to tease and pick on other kids.
I don't think it's fun to tease and pick on other kids.

Inattention

I have a hard time paying attention.
I don't have a hard time paying attention.
It's hard for me to remember what my teacher tells me to do.
It's not hard for me to remember what my teacher tells me to do.

Parental Warmth and Positive Affect

My mom says she loves me.
My mom doesn't say she loves me.
My dad is not nice to me.
My dad is nice to me.

Parental Anger and Hostility

When my mom is mad, she spanks me.
When my mom is mad, she doesn't spank me.
My dad yells at me when he is mad.
My dad doesn't yell at me when he is mad.

Marital Conflict

My parents fight in front of me.
My parents don't fight in front of me.
My parents fight a lot.
My parents don't fight a lot.

Marital Conflict Self-Blame

My parents' fights are not about me.
My parents' fights are about me.
When my parents have a fight, I don't think that they are mad at me.
When my parents have a fight, I think that they are mad at me.

Marital Conflict Resolution

After my parents have a fight, they say they are sorry to each other.
After my parents have a fight, they don't say they are sorry to each other.
After my parents have a fight, they don't make up.
After my parents have a fight, they make up.

Peer Acceptance and Rejection

I have lots of friends at school.
I don't have lots of friends at school.
Other kids don't ask me to play with them.
Other kids ask me to play with them.

Bullied by Peers

Kids do mean things to me, like push or trip me.
Kids don't do mean things like that to me.
Kids say mean things to me.
Kids don't say mean things to me.

4 The Family Puppet Interview

Catherine Ford Sori

Historically, the fields of play therapy and family therapy developed along parallel paths, with few recognizing the exponential gains that could be realized by integrating both fields (Sori & Gil, 2015). In 1975 Irwin and Malloy began to bridge this gulf when they introduced the "Family Puppet Interview" (FPI). This innovative "family play therapy" (FPT) technique was designed to uncover, through metaphoric story, a family's communication style, problems, and experiences. The FPI is an interactive, structured assessment and treatment activity that involves the entire family, and which generates a "wealth of interactive data" to reveal important "symbolic family fantasy material" (Irwin & Malloy, 1975, p. 179). It offers a format for families to communicate symbolically about difficult issues and emotions from a safer, less guarded position, and provides a novel method for families to experience one another within the context of play. Family members select puppets and create an original story, and then perform it for the therapist, speaking through the puppets. Irwin and Malloy (1975) provide follow-up questions, such as asking each for a title or moral of the story, inviting members to reflect on a puppet's actions or emotions, and finally asking if the story reminds family members of anything they are experiencing in their own lives.

Twenty years later, Gil (1994) published *Play in Family Therapy*, the first text to detail the extraordinary benefits and innovative methods of FPT, including the FPI. Here Gil first introduced the concept of spending additional time exploring clients' stories from within the metaphor before moving on to the questions outlined in Irwin and Malloy (1975). Gil designed ways to "amplify the metaphor," allowing deeper access to the rich symbolic material in clients' narratives. This expansion keeps families in the symbolic story longer, engaging the right hemisphere of the brain to draw deeper on clients' intuition, creativity, and emotions, allowing unconscious material to surface (see Crenshaw & Tillman, 2013; Gil, 1994, 2011, 2015; Gil & Sobol, 2005). To "stay in the metaphor," Gil might ask puppets to expand the story or explore the impact on each, or direct two distant puppets to interact. The value of this is that "the magic of the family's metaphor is not interrupted by the clinician's focus on distanced observation, retrospection, or interpretation" (Gil, 1994, p. 51). The potential benefits include reducing clients' defenses, increasing the family's pleasure and delight as they relate in a unique way, and hinting at novel solutions to problems that they had not considered. After this expansion, clinicians "come out of the metaphor" and utilize the more analytical, left-hemisphere questions presented by Irwin and Malloy (1975). Gil (2011) stated that "great potential is unleashed when the more analytical, insight-oriented left hemisphere of our brain can evaluate and feel enlightened by the more creative, symbolic workings of the right hemisphere of our brain" (p. 209). The focus of this chapter is the FPI, including Gil's amplification methods (1994, 2011, 2015), along with innovative ways to expand the benefits of this activity.

Materials and Preparation for the Family Puppet Interview

The FPI requires a collection of about 20 to 30 puppets. Too many choices may overwhelm clients, but enough are needed to suggest a variety of characteristics. Children relate well to representations of animals, including domestic, farm, zoo, and wild animals. Other categories are dinosaurs, sea creatures, flying creatures, insects, and fantasy animals (e.g., unicorn). Look for puppets of the same species (perhaps different sizes) that could represent animal families (e.g., lion and cub). More important than quantity, however, is that the puppets have symbolic potential. Select puppets that represent diverse characteristics, such as good and evil (angel and devil), aggression (alligator, dinosaur), and vulnerability (human baby, lamb, puppy). Other recommendations are those with special powers (angels, witch), fairy tale or fantasy figures (king, queen, alien), those seen as wise (owl, wizard), or those that have superior strength (lion, gorilla). Puppets with occupations (police officer, doctor, and firefighter) and that are ethnically diverse are particularly valuable. Many clients are drawn to puppets that can "hide" (turtles, clams), that illustrate transformation (caterpillar that turns into a butterfly), or that contain an element of surprise (genie in a bottle, jack-in-the-box). Professional puppets are durable, colorful, and captivating, but are costly. Puppets can be fashioned from socks and yarn, or stuffed animals found at retail shops or garage sales (see Foraker-Koons & Sori, 2015). An added benefit is that young clients may enjoy assisting in their transformation. The best hand puppets allow the lower jaw to be manipulated to indicate speech, and the head and arms to move to emulate natural movements (Carter & Mason, 1998). Puppets of various proportions allow therapists to speculate on how both size and characteristics may be metaphoric representations of the family's relationships, roles, and issues, including power and control. It is useful to video record FPI sessions if the equipment is available (see below).

Conducting a Family Puppet Interview

There are a few things to keep in mind when deciding which puppets to make available. Sometimes family members all select puppets with similar characteristics (e.g., a turtle and a clam are both land and water creatures with shells in which to hide), or someone might want two identical puppets (e.g., "twin monkeys"). Gil and Sobol (2005) caution against limiting the number of puppets that people wish to use, stating:

> A child who has to have more than anyone else communicates his or her needs: perhaps the child feels neglected in the family; perhaps the child needs to feel special or different. Enmeshed family members may need to pick the same puppet, or sometimes one individual's choice (a fish) may set the tone for everyone else (turtle, seahorse, whale, starfish), indicating that person's influence over the family.
>
> (p. 351)

Karakurt (2012) suggests that when someone chooses multiple puppets, each might represent different aspects of the self (e.g., an angry monkey along with a lost, helpless lamb).

Instructions

Begin the FPI by bringing the family into a room where approximately 30 puppets have been laid out. To introduce the activity, provide simple, clear instructions, such as:

> I'd like you to look through these puppets and select some that seem interesting to you. Then I'd like you to make up a story together that has a beginning, a middle, and an end. There are only two rules: First, the story must be original, not one you already know, like a fairy tale or a movie. The second rule is that after you create your story, you will act it out for me by speaking through the puppets, not just telling me the story. I'll leave now for about 30 minutes so you can pick your puppets and create your story. Just open the door when you are done and I'll come back to be your audience.

If adults express doubt or are reluctant to participate, Gil (2011) suggests asking them to trust you and try to be curious, and reassure them the emphasis is on playing together. Although most children are eager to use puppets, occasionally a child may be sullen and disinterested. To pique their interest, explain that you will be video recording their "performance" (assuming you have signed consent to record) so you can all enjoy watching it together the following week!

Observations of Both Process and Content

Throughout all phases of the FPI, it is essential to keenly observe both the family's process (how they relate and interact), as well as the content of their story (what the metaphors might represent). Observe families closely as they select the puppets (Gil & Sobol, 2005), either from behind a one-way mirror or by viewing a recording after the session. (Staying in the room, even sitting quietly in a corner, may make some clients self-conscious and inhibit their creativity.) Notice which puppets are considered, discarded, and kept; as well as the family dynamics around puppet selections. What is the degree of interest? Do siblings vie for a parent's attention or spar over a particular puppet? (If so, what happens?) Are puppets chosen or assigned? Does anyone attempt to limit, discourage, or suggest an alternate selection? How many puppets does each select? Is anyone unable to find a puppet that is interesting? Are family members engaged with one another or working quietly alone?

Observation of Story Creation

Once puppets are selected, the process of how the family creates their story "demonstrates and clarifies how the family organizes to undertake and complete a task" (Gil, 1994, p. 49). Notice the level of ease or difficulty in getting started, and each person's contribution to story development. How is the story line decided? Do distinct leaders and followers emerge? Whose ideas are privileged; whose are ignored or rejected? Are roles assigned or chosen? Does one person take over while another withdraws? Are parents encouraging, intrusive, or dismissive? What is the emotional climate as they explore possibilities and make decisions about their choices?

The content is often a metaphoric representation of concerns, struggles, family secrets, forbidden topics, stifled emotions, loss (including parental abandonment), and strained relationships the family is experiencing. As the story develops, what themes are suggested? What real-life threats or dangers may be alluded to? Is the family able to resolve the problem? Try also to identify individual and family strengths and signs of resiliency, which may be utilized later to engender hope and provide a positive foundation for change.

Family's Performance of the Story

After the family signals for you to return, one way to ease them into the activity is to ask the puppets' names and invite them to tell you a sentence or two about themselves (Gil, 1994). If they have difficulty getting started, a prompt such as, "I wonder where this story takes place and what is going to happen?" may be effective. If a client steps out of the role and addresses the therapist, try guiding them back into the metaphor by looking at the puppet (not the client), addressing the puppet by name, and encouraging the puppets to interact (e.g., "Red Robin, can you tell that to Busy Bee and ask how she felt?").

Observations of both process and content take on greater significance in the family's performance. Process observations include noticing the level of engagement and enjoyment for each family member. Does everyone participate? How do the puppets interact? What emotions are displayed by the puppets? Is the dialogue coherent or chaotic? Additional insight may be gained in a subsequent viewing of the video following the session. Process observations can be used to assess parenting styles (authoritarian, permissive, or authoritative), parent-child attachment, how well individuals and families function, and themes that may allude to the family's current experiences. These observations can be viewed through various theoretical lenses (e.g., structural, narrative, experiential, solution focused) that can inform family assessment, hypotheses, goals, a treatment plan, and subsequent interventions.

Content observations during the performance should be compared to those witnessed as the family created their original story. Are the same themes evident, altered, or are new themes introduced? What roles are suggested? Does the story include a healthy resolution to the problem? Sometimes the family's original story veers off in a new direction during the performance, which may expose more serious issues, suggest alternate interpretations of metaphors, reveal more hidden problems and deeper feelings, or expose topics that families had guarded against.

Processing and Amplifying the Metaphor

To keep the family "in the metaphor," look directly at the puppets (not the family members) when asking questions and processing the story (Bromfield, 1995). If clients do not respond through the puppet, a prompt directly addressing the puppet can help get them back in character. Amplified questions move beyond the content of the story, allowing clinicians to "stay in the metaphor" for a longer period to explore significant elements of the story (Franklin, 2015; Gil, 2011). These open-ended questions focus on the metaphor long enough to expand awareness and allow unconscious thoughts or repressed emotions to surface. Clinicians might wonder what happens to the puppets after the story ends; ask for more details; challenge family members to expand on new ways of interacting; invite two puppets to discuss something or plan an activity together; and so on (see Gil, 1994, 2011, 2015). The emphasis should be in expressing curiosity, while clinical interpretations should be minimal (Gil & Sobol, 2005) and *never* shared with clients. After this amplification process, clinicians can move "out of the metaphor" and pose the questions recommended by Irwin and Malloy (1975) (see above), including asking if any part of the story is similar to something they are experiencing in their own lives.

If there is insufficient time left to process the story, provide a brief summary of the plot, applaud the family's effort and creativity, and let them know how much you enjoyed it. Inform them you will look forward to viewing the recording together at the next session, and ask them to reflect on this experience during the coming week. Gil (2011) points out that developing process questions while "staying in the metaphor" can be difficult for those new to this technique, but becomes easier with practice. A week's delay allows time to review the recording and craft amplification questions to explore the characters, metaphors, themes, emotions, and meanings in more depth at the next session. This time can also be used to develop a treatment plan and decide how best to utilize the puppets and metaphors in future sessions.

Using the Puppets and Metaphors Throughout Treatment

The actions of the puppets, metaphoric content of the story, and new ways of interacting can be referenced, expanded, and built upon throughout treatment. Gil (2015, p. 174) sometimes uses costumes and asks the family to "reenact their puppet story, this time taking on the roles they had created and acting them out." Clients may ask to use their puppets to revisit an emotion, or to have a difficult conversation where the puppets provide a safe emotional distance (much as costumes would).

Second FPI

If a family is asked to participate in a subsequent FPI, they may request the same puppets or want to introduce new ones into the second story. Comparing recordings of both FPIs is useful to highlight change, encourage clients, and clarify areas requiring further treatment. This offers a unique tactic to measure clients' headway in resolving problems, improving family functioning, enhancing relationships, and other treatment goals.

Methods to Expand the Benefits of the FPI

The puppets chosen for the FPI can be applied creatively in several ways as a family nears termination. The family might review the FPI again, after which the therapist, as a TV "reporter," uses play microphones to interview each puppet, who are "experts" in noticing how puppets can work together to make things better. Sharing the puppets' expert knowledge may help "viewers" who might be in similar situations!

The puppets used in a family's FPI have been incorporated into "puppet reflecting teams" (Sori, 2011a), providing families with a fresh, surprising perspective of how others see them. This is an excellent mechanism to move stuck cases forward. Karakurt (2012) discusses the successful use of the FPI in various cultures, and a culturally relevant adaptation of the FPI is the

"Rappin' FPI" (Sori, 2010), which has special appeal to teens. As a homework assignment, family members are asked to work together to fashion a rap, and perform it in the next session using their puppets from the FPI. Questions can explore what this process was like, what surprised them, what was the most difficult part, and what each enjoyed most. (Presenting the family with a recording of their rap is a valuable reminder of their experiences in therapy.)

An alternative application is for the therapist to create a rap about the family, incorporating the puppets utilized in their FPI (Sori, 2011b). Roles are reversed, as the therapist is now the performer, and the family becomes the audience. This is an unexpected and playful way to celebrate and highlight progress, especially at termination. Clients are delighted to see it performed by a self-deprecating therapist willing to shed a bit of "professional" veneer. Be prepared for the family to jump to their feet and join in by clapping their hands and moving to the beat!

Case Illustration

This case (introduced in less detail in Sori, 2015) involved a family with a newly divorced mother, Scarlett, and three teens. John (17) enjoyed sports, and was a senior linebacker on his school's football team; Josiah (13), unlike his brother, preferred reading and chess over sports; and Justine (15) was quite popular but was the designated Identified Patient, having developed behavioral issues recently at school. The family presented as talkative and warm and seemed to enjoy being together. When asked about the recent divorce, all agreed that they were "fine" with it, and that everything was "fine" except for Justine's behavior at school. With little context to go on, the therapist decided to conduct a family puppet interview the following session.

In the second session, after showing the family a pile of about 30 puppets, the therapist asked them to select puppets that seemed interesting. Together they were to make up an original story (not one they knew already) with a beginning, middle, and end, which they would act out through the puppets. She would leave so they could begin, and would return when they signaled they were ready, to be the "audience" as they performed their story talking through the puppets.

From behind a one-way mirror, the therapist watched Mom select a large cow ("Elsie") that she described as "loving and nurturing"; John chose a large gorilla ("Bruzer") who was "King of the Jungle"; Justine dove immediately for a mother koala bear carrying a baby on her back ("Patty and Baby Mimi"), saying "Patty looks out for all the smaller animals"; while Josiah, modeling after his older brother, selected a smaller gorilla named "Cool Dude," who was "really cool, and almost as strong as Bruzer" (which irritated "Bruzer"). Everyone participated in creating a story about trying to find a friend named "Stanley" who was lost in the woods. When they signaled they were ready, the therapist returned.

After being introduced to each character, the performance began, but with little resemblance to the original story. "Elsie" (Mom) started the story but was loudly interrupted by "Patti" (Justine) yelling that "Elsie's" ideas were stupid and wouldn't work because she didn't know what she was doing. "Bruzer" (older brother) joined in, saying that he should be in charge of finding Stanley because he was the biggest animal in the forest and everyone was afraid of him. A new plot twist developed when "Elsie" (Mom) moaned how terrible it was that "Stanley" was lost because he was such a good friend, and "Bruzer" retorted, "He's no friend to me." "Elsie" reminded him that he should be grateful because of all the extra food he gets from "Stanley." Unlike their original story, everyone began shouting so loudly that no one could be understood. The cacophony stopped abruptly when Justine pulled out a large stingray puppet, "Stanley," who had a long, sinister looking stinger. "Elsie" greeted Stanley warmly, but the others seemed less excited to see him, and that ended the story.

Taking a moment to collect herself, the therapist offered a synopsis of the plot and the puppets' actions. Amplification questions directed to the puppets included: What was it like for them when "Stanley" was lost and no one could find him? Who was most and least pleased to see "Stanley" emerge from the forest? What did they think "Stanley" did in the forest, and how did he become lost? How was it to have a friend with such a large and threatening stinger in their midst? How might they determine if "Stanley" a posed a threat? If he did, how might they find protection from his giant stinger? To this last question, "Bruzer" immediately responded that he was the biggest and strongest in the forest—even bigger than "Stanley the Stingray"—and he could protect them. "Elsie" interjected that "Stanley" really was not dangerous, he just appeared to be. The children's sullen faces and silent voices seemed to shout their objection.

When asked if there might be anything in the story similar to something going on in their own lives, Mom admitted that this was the second time she had divorced the children's father because of domestic violence, which the children had sometimes witnessed. With little time remaining in the session, the therapist applauded this step Mom had taken to protect herself and her children from such disturbing violence. The therapist asked if "Elsie" and "Bruzer" could talk during the week about how to keep all the animals safe from the stingray.

The therapist recognized that safety seemed to be a major theme in this family that they had not been prepared to disclose, but the FPI cut through their restraints and allowed it to be revealed in their metaphoric story. The therapist's hypothesis was that "Stanley the Stingray" represented their father. In considering the puppets' roles, John's puppet ("Bruzer") seemed to be the main protector in the family. "Patty/Mimi" (Justine) was the "protector of small animals," and the most raucous and vociferous challenger to "Elsie" (Mom), proclaiming how ineffectual Mom's efforts to organize the family really were. Josiah's selection of puppets may have represented two opposing forces within him: "Cool Dude" (smaller gorilla) wanted to emulate his older brother, and "Stanley the Stingray" suggested anger or ambivalent feelings toward his father. "Elsie the Cow" (Mom) originally described herself as "loving and nurturing," but this was called into question when the other puppets declared her incompetent.

In the following session, after viewing the FPI video with the family and discussing how they had enjoyed it, the therapist asked if they might think of things they would like to work on in counseling. Individual, dyadic, and overall family goals were set by the family (and therapist) that reflected both the story's content and the family's process in creating and performing it.

A week after that the therapist decided to meet first with the sibling subsystem, where Justine exposed a terrible secret they had kept from Mom: Dad had physically abused her shortly before the separation. He had chased Justine through the house, beating her repeatedly with a belt until John intervened, snatching the belt from his father's hands. Afterward, there was a tacit agreement not to tell their mother, fearing for her safety if she confronted their father. After some discussion, all agreed it was time to share this secret with Mom. Scarlett was horrified to learn her daughter had also experienced her ex-husband's violence, and dismayed that the children kept it a secret to protect her from "Stanley the Stingray." They implored her to change the locks to stop "Stanley" from barging in unannounced, keeping them in a perpetual state of anxiety and fear that their mother would take him back again. The therapist retrieved the puppets they used in the FPI and asked each to tell "Elsie" how this affected them, and what she could do to help the animals of the forest feel safe.

"Elsie" took steps to protect the forest animals, and the family progressed quickly toward their goals. Mother became a capable parent who could provide nurturance and fun times, as well as safety and structure. The puppet's quarreling voices quieted; they learned to listen better, and to trust "Elsie" to keep them safe from any stingrays in the forest.

In the last session, the therapist performed a "therapeutic letter rap" for the family, incorporating puppets used in the FPI. The purpose was to highlight their growth, their progress toward goals, and their numerous strengths in a playful manner. The visual element of the puppets enhanced the dramatic impact of the rap and provided deeper levels of meaning. The therapist's execution of the rap using the puppets and toy microphones triggered gales of laughter. Their enthusiasm was apparent as they all leapt to their feet to clap, dance, and join in on the chorus, and this final session ended with "high fives" all around. Each was delighted to receive a written copy of the "rap"—a concrete record in a playful format documenting the many transformations the therapist had witnessed in the family. The metaphors in the FPI sidestepped the family's initial guardedness and provided an entrance "through the back door" to uncover and explore the family's issues. The FPI catapulted the family forward, and they made rapid progress. It is doubtful if they (or the therapist) will ever forget the richness of this experience.

The FPI (and other FPT techniques) can be viewed as "trans-theoretical" (Schaefer & Drewes, 2014; Gil, 2015), and incorporated with most play and family therapy theories (see Dermer, Olund, & Sori, 2006). Play is therapeutic for adults as well as children, and the benefits are multiplied when families play together. The FPI can breathe new life into hurting families who experience renewed joy in playing together. Any obstacles to integrating elements from both fields can be overcome by those who are curious, adventuresome, and eager to discover new possibilities for growth and healing (see Gil & Sori, 2015).

References

Bromfield, R. (1995). The use of puppets in play therapy. *Child and Adolescent Social Work Journal, 12*(6), 435–444.

Carter, R., & Mason, P. (1998). The selection and use of puppets in counseling. *Professional School Counseling, 1*(5), 50–53.

Crenshaw, D., & Tillman, K. (2013). Access to the unconscious. In C. E. Schaefer & A. A. Drewes (Eds.), *The therapeutic powers of play: 20 core agents of change* (2nd ed., pp. 25–38). Hoboken, NJ: Wiley.

Dermer, S., Olund, D., & Sori, C. F. (2006). Integrating play in family therapy theories. In C. F. Sori (Ed.), *Engaging children in family therapy: Creative approaches to integrating theory and research in clinical practice* (pp. 37–65). New York, NY: Routledge Press.

Foraker-Koons, K., & Sori, C. F. (2015). A guide to making puppets without breaking the bank. In C. F. Sori, L. Hecker, & M. Bachenberg (Eds.), *The therapist's notebook for children and adolescents* (2nd ed., pp. 327–330). New York, NY: Routledge.

Franklin, P. (2015). Tell me all about it: Using objects as metaphors. In C. F. Sori, L. Hecker, & M. Bachenberg (Eds.), *The therapist's notebook for children and adolescents* (2nd ed., pp. 9–12). New York, NY: Routledge.

Gil, E. (1994). *Play in family therapy*. New York, NY: Guilford Publications.

Gil, E. (2011). Family play therapy: Igniting creative energy, valuing metaphors, and making changes from the inside out. In C. E. Schaefer (Ed.), *Foundations of play therapy* (2nd ed., pp. 207–226), NY: John Wiley.

Gil, E. (2015). *Play in family therapy* (2nd ed.). New York, NY: Guilford Publications.

Gil, E., & Sobol, B. (2005). Engaging families in therapeutic play. In C. E. Bailey (Ed.), *Children in therapy: Using the family as a resource* (pp. 341–382). New York, NY: Guilford.

Gil, E., & Sori, C. F. (2015). Obstacles and opportunities in utilizing family play therapy. In E. Gil's (Ed.), *Play in family therapy* (2nd ed., pp. 33–56). New York, NY: Guilford.

Irwin, E. C., & Malloy, E. S. (1975). Family puppet interview. *Family Process, 14*, 170–191.

Karakurt, G. (2012). Puppet play with a Turkish family. *Journal of Family Psychotherapy, 23*, 69–78.

Schaefer, C. E., & Drewes, A. (Eds.). (2014). *The therapeutic powers of play: 20 core agents of change* (2nd ed.). Hoboken, NJ: Wiley.

Sori, C. F. (2010). Rappin' family puppet interview. In L. Lowenstein (Ed.), *Creative family therapy techniques* (pp. 63–66). Toronto, Canada: Champion Press Books.

Sori, C. F. (2011a). Puppet reflecting teams in family therapy. In H. G. Rosenthal (Ed.), *Favorite counseling and therapy techniques* (2nd ed., pp. 281–290). New York, NY: Routledge.

Sori, C. F. (2011b). Using hip-hop in family therapy to build "rap" port. In H. G. Rosenthal (Ed.), *Favorite counseling and therapy homework assignment* (2nd ed., pp. 299–308). New York, NY: Routledge.

Sori, C. F. (2015). Using the family puppet interview in assessment and goal setting. In C. F. Sori, L. Hecker, & M. Bachenberg (Eds.), *The therapist's notebook for children and adolescents* (2nd ed., pp. 21–26). New York, NY: Routledge.

Sori, C. F., & Gil, E. (2015). The rationale for integrating play and family therapy. In E. Gil's (Ed.), *Play in family therapy* (2nd ed., pp. 1–32). New York, NY: Guilford Press.

5 Puppet Sentence Completion Task (PSCT)

Susan M. Knell

Sentence completion (SC) tasks are a form of projective techniques, which were traditionally based on the psychoanalytic notion of projection. In projection, an individual "externalizes" needs, feelings, conflicts, and motivations onto ambiguous stimuli (Rabin, 1960). For adults and adolescents, sentence completion tasks (SCT) are one of the most frequently used projective techniques (Lubin, Larsen, & Matarazzo, 1984). Individuals complete a sentence stem, with the flexibility of stems used cited as one of the reasons for the popularity and wide use of SC (Goldberg, 1965).

The use of SC tasks is thought to date back to the end of the 1800s (Ebbinghaus, 1897; cited in Hart, 1986), with the use of incomplete sentences to assess mental abilities. The complexity of the response was thought to reflect greater intellectual potential. Subsequently, others continued to develop this technique for use as an intellectual assessment, with its introduction as a metric of emotional/personality development appearing in the mid-20th century. Clinicians such as Tendler (1930) introduced the use of sentence stems to pull for emotional responses. Over the next several decades, various forms were used, with the SC added to the psychological test battery for US soldiers in WWII (as described in Hart, 1986), and later for nonmilitary use.

Sentence Completion Tasks With Young Children

Most traditional SC tasks were initially developed for adolescents and adults, and their use with young children is problematic. Assessment and treatment of preschool-age children can be challenging, particularly due to a lack of assessment tools that are developmentally sensitive to their needs. Difficulties include issues with administration, understanding by the child, and interpretation of the results.

When administering projective techniques with children, their age, developmental level, willingness to participate, and ability to understand the task must be taken into consideration (Hart, 1986). In addition, the child's comfort with the examiner and mood are contributing factors that are important in understanding the assessment results. It is essential that the examiner have a clear working knowledge of developmental issues that may affect responses, in order for interpretation to be based in a normative perspective. Interpretations must also be made with collaborative information from various sources, which may include clinical interviews with parents, child, and significant others (e.g., teachers). Finally, since most children express themselves through play, and it is generally considered the most reliable modality for working with children, its use in therapy is well documented. Integrating play into the assessment process offers a more developmentally appropriate method of gathering assessment and diagnostic information.

Use of Puppets in Assessment of Children

The use of puppets in both assessment and therapy with young children is both developmentally appropriate and well documented (e.g., Irwin, 2000). Integrating puppets into assessment provides a more developmentally sensitive approach, which likely will lead to more reliable clinical information.

The examiner must engage the child in a way that increases his or her comfort and promotes the child's understanding of the task. Being playful when integrating puppets into the assessment can be useful. (Imagine an examiner using puppets in a monotone voice, with a completely straight face/expression, and think about the likelihood that the child would become engaged in the task under these circumstances!)

Like other objects of play, puppets provide a nonthreatening means of expressing conflicts and feelings. From the child's perspective, it might be the puppet expressing the conflict or feeling and not the child per se. Irwin (1985) described an assessment technique utilizing puppets to tell a pretend television story, which was followed by a clinical interview to provide clarity regarding the meaning of the story. Later, Irwin (2000) presented a review of puppet use in diagnosis and treatment with children and families. In addressing developmental considerations, Irwin stated, "Young children often present their conflicts with startling clarity and lack of disguise, thus helping to illuminate the diagnostic picture" (p. 685). She also noted that puppet play in the younger age group was less censored and thus more openly full of conflict.

Research on Sentence Completion Tasks

Sentence completion tasks have not been psychometrically validated, particularly because of the various forms and range of responses. Various researchers have documented empirical data supporting specific forms of the SCT (e.g., Weiss, Zilberg, & Genervo, 1989), but generalizability to other forms is not appropriate. Most often, the SCT is used in clinical settings, and qualitative analysis of responses is recommended. Obviously, interpretation is primarily a function of the examiner's skill, experience, and theoretical orientation. For children, the most studied SC is the Hart Sentence Completion Test for Children (HSCT; Hart, 1986). This measure was developed to provide a standardized scoring procedure focusing on four dimensions—family, social, and school environment, and self-perception—and is designed for use with 6- to 18-year-olds.

The Puppet Sentence Completion Task

The use of more traditional sentence completion tasks is typically not appropriate for children under the age of 6 to 7 years. Most children under this age have difficulty comprehending the expectation of the task, and therefore are unable to respond in a coherent manner. Because of the rich clinical material that can be gathered from a sentence completion task, Knell (1992, 1993) proposed the use of a puppet sentence completion task (PSCT). The rationale behind this measure was to present a more developmentally sensitive task to younger children, so that they could understand and respond in an age-appropriate way. The puppet sentence completion task (Knell, 1992; Knell & Beck, 2000) was developed to make the traditional child SCT more appropriate for preschool-age children, and it is presented in this chapter.

Age Range

The PSCT can be used with children from 3 to 7 years old. These ages are approximate boundaries given the individual differences of children in the preschool and early school-age years. Although there are certainly 2.5-year-old-children who would be able to complete the PSCT, the average child would not have verbal skills sufficient for the task before the age of 3 years. Typically, the younger the child, the less sophisticated the verbalizations. Despite its limitations for very young children, it still potentially provides important clinical information. Nonetheless, the task tends to elicit more clinical information from older preschool-age children (4- to 5-year-olds). At the upper age range, older children (6- to 8-year-olds) may have the verbal abilities to complete the task, but may find that they are uninterested in the puppets. Therefore, children in the 6- to 8-year-old range often are able to move quickly from the puppet task to a more traditional sentence completion task, but may be helped, at first, by the structure of the PSCT.

Population Considerations

With the exception of age considerations, there are no limitations on the use of the PSCT. Most children could potentially complete this task, although children with some developmental delays, autism, or significant speech impairments might not be able to complete the task without some modifications. A hearing-impaired child fluent in sign language could be given the task by a sign-fluent examiner or with the use of a sign interpreter. A child with a mental age below 3 years, regardless of chronological age, would probably be unable to complete the PSCT.

Materials

Puppets are the primary materials needed, although other play materials should be on hand if the child is not interested in the puppets.

Selection of Puppets

Many different kinds of puppets can be introduced for use in this task. The child should have some choices, but not be overwhelmed by large numbers of options. Puppets should represent different categories (e.g., people vs. animal puppets). The puppets should be either placed in front of the child, or in an accessible place (e.g., bottom shelf of an open toy cabinet). In either case, the puppets should be at the child's eye level. As part of the procedure, the child is told that he or she should choose a puppet. It is helpful to observe the manner of choice, as well as the category of puppet, the child picks. Does he or she quickly make a choice or take a great deal of time? Does the child seem interested in making this choice, and eager to continue with the task, or does the child exhibit and/or express disinterest? It is particularly helpful to note the child's verbalizations during the process. Does the child give any reasons why the particular puppet is chosen? Does the child turn to the examiner and request that he or she make the choice for the child? These types of observations can potentially add a great deal of understanding to the child's level of functioning, emotional issues, and needs.

Selection of Sentence Stems

The PSCT was first introduced as a way to utilize a more traditional sentence completion task in a developmentally appropriate way. The stems were derived from standard stems, reflecting areas that might elicit valuable clinical information (e.g., family, self-esteem, feelings, potential traumas). Since no standardized sentence completion test exists, sentence stems were added or deleted as clinical judgment demanded. The PSCT as first described (Knell, 1992, 1993) was designed for use with a general preschool-age population. The goal was to provide a set of common sentence stems that could be used with most children. A number of optional stems related to possible victimization or maltreatment issues were added at the end of the task. Even for children not known to have been maltreated, these stems were useful in order to assist in ruling out the possibility of abuse or trauma. However, they could be excluded if it was considered clinically inappropriate to include them. Special stems, unique to particular life situations or presenting problems, can be added by the examiner for specific populations (e.g., children of divorced parents). Some commonly used additional stems, related to presenting problems commonly seen in the preschool- and early school-age population, are provided in the optional section of the PSCT (see Appendix).

Ruma (1993) noted that in play therapy with sexually abused children, the therapist may at times introduce themes that are common among maltreated children. She describes efforts to encourage the child without leading. Sentence stems that pull for common sequelae of maltreatment offer such an opportunity. Sentence stems such as "The worst secret is . . ." or "When I am in bed I think about . . ." may provide structure for traumatized or abused children to convey information that would be difficult to reveal in an interview.

For some children, this structure may be too overwhelming. Such children may respond to these sentence stems by their silence or lack of intelligible response. One example was a 4.5-year-old child, Richard, who had been abused by his babysitter (Ruma, 1993). Although he had disclosed some information about the maltreatment, he had become very reluctant to elaborate on what he had disclosed or discuss any new information. He was able to respond to many sentence stems in the PSCT, but when presented with the stem, "A secret I am not supposed to tell is . . . ," Richard was unable to give a response. Although Richard did not reveal any new information, his difficulty in responding corroborated the abuse information he had already disclosed.

Administration of the PSCT

Establishing rapport is a critical first step in the administration of the PSCT. Once the child seems comfortable in the playroom with the examiner, the PSCT can be introduced. There is no hard-and-fast rule about when to administer the PSCT. Preferably, it should be given before too many sessions have taken place. For some children, the first session can include the PSCT. For others, it may be preferable to wait until the child is more comfortable and rapport has been established. Because the PSCT is a fairly structured activity, it is harder to introduce it if most of the time with the child has involved unstructured, spontaneous play. Therefore, it is recommended that the task be administered sometime within the first two to three sessions.

The procedure for administration of the PSCT (see Appendix) is relatively straightforward. The examiner lets the child choose a puppet, and then the examiner chooses two puppets. The child can be offered the option of picking the puppets for the examiner. The PSCT is broken down into two parts. In Part I, the examiner reads the sentence stems for the first puppet (Puppet A). After the sentence stem is read, the examiner's second puppet (Puppet B) responds. The examiner then turns to Puppet C (the one held by the child) and indicates that the child should respond for the puppet. The manner in which the examiner indicates that it is the child's turn may be through voice inflection, or through hand movements pointing to the child's puppet, or both. There are a total of five sentence stems in Part I. However, the examiner moves on to Part II of the PSCT as soon as it is clear that the child understands the tasks. Thus, all five sentence stems in Part I are not necessarily given to the child if it is clear that the child understands the task after a few stems are given. Many children catch on quickly and do not seem to like the repetition that is necessary in Part I. In this situation, it is appropriate to move to Part II as quickly as possible. This will be clear by the responses that the child gives for Puppet C.

If the child does not understand the task, the examiner can begin with the first sentence stem and have the puppets prompt the child. It is important not to continue to Part II until it is clear that the child understands Part I.

In Part II, the examiner's first puppet states the sentence stem directly to the child's puppet, and the child responds for his or her puppet. Most children will give only one response, but some will give a response for the puppet and one for themselves. Both responses should be noted. It is not always possible or necessary to give all the sentence stems in Part II. Some children, particularly younger preschoolers, cannot tolerate responding to all of the sentence stems. Others, particularly older children, may be able to do the whole task. When it becomes clear that the PSCT must be shortened, it is recommended that the examiner choose sentence stems that are clinically relevant, or stems that "pull" for certain themes. This often necessitates skipping over some items in order to get to more relevant sentence stems before the child's interest level drops. Any or all of the optional sentence stems can be used when they are clinically relevant for the child. The order of administration is not critical, and the examiner should be flexible in administering the task, in order to ensure that clinically relevant items are given before the child loses interest.

With the child and parents' permission, it is often helpful to tape the administration of the PSCT. This is particularly helpful with young children whose language articulation skills are not fully developed. This allows the examiner to focus on the child, rather than focusing on asking the child to repeat words that are not readily understood. It also allows the examiner to keep both hands free for puppets, rather than using one hand for recording the child's responses. Although it is not necessary to have two hands for puppets in Part II, the examiner will need to have puppets on both hands in Part I. For Part I, written recording of responses is awkward. Of course, using a tape recording necessitates that the examiner has the time to listen and transcribe the tape as soon as possible after the session is over.

It can be helpful to ask the child for further clarification or information about particular sentence stems. The examiner may want to ask the child to explain his or her response, or may ask a specific question about the response. Because the PSCT is not a standardized, normed measure, the examiner can use clinical judgment in deciding which responses to pursue further, and when to go on to the next sentence stem. Such decisions are based on the examiner's reflection on the child's response, and clinical sense of when it is best to capture material immediately and when waiting is more appropriate.

Case Illustrations

Case Example

Jack was a 7-year, 8-month-old boy, referred because of his anxiety and difficulties regulating his emotions. He became upset if reprimanded at school, and often felt that he was blamed for things that he didn't do. At home, he would get upset if his three older siblings criticized him.

Jack gravitated to the puppets during his first session with the therapist, and immediately began communicating through a puppet he had chosen. At the second session, the PSCT was introduced, though it was very clear that he did not need the introductory parts of the task, as he immediately understood and responded to the sentence stems. (The sentence stems are followed by Jack's responses, which are in **bold**; questions by the examiner are in parentheses with a question mark.)

I am afraid of **sometimes scary stuff** (like?) **monsters.**

I am happiest **when it's Saturday** (why?) **because I don't have school and I don't have turtle math** (He was speaking for the turtle puppet on his hand, and it was a Saturday session).

I am saddest when **my sisters are mean to me.**

I get scared when **my parents fight.**

My biggest problem is **stuff** (like?) **sometimes it's hard with my parents, sometimes they disagree with me and it hurts my feelings, like they think I am not helping, and I am.**

At school sometimes **the teacher blames me for things I didn't do** (like?) **accidentally I did something, but somebody else does something else and I get blamed.**

My teacher is **nice to me usually, but not always** (When not nice?) **when she yells at me** (when?) **when I'm not good.**

Further Considerations in the Administration of the PSCT

Adding Clinically Relevant Stems Prior to Administration of the PSCT

Because of the nature of the PSCT, it is possible to individualize the task for each administration. The optional stems do not always meet the needs of all children. Sentence stems can be added to the basic task before administration to make the task relevant to the child and his or her presenting problems. Stems can be added that may pull for information about particular issues unique to the child's environment, family constellation, or life stressors. The limits of sentence stems are endless. The following case example illustrates the use of additional sentence stems, added prior to administration of the PSCT, used to capture clinical information about toileting issues.

Case Example

Seth was a 3-year, 5-month-old boy with presenting problems related to toileting and behavioral concerns. His mother reported that he was often noncompliant and was having a difficult time managing his behavior in his preschool setting. He had been toilet trained for urination, but preferred to withhold his bowel movements rather than use the toilet. If he withheld his bowel movements for long periods of time, his stools were hard, and thus, his pediatrician had recommended stool softeners.

Due to those toileting concerns, several sentence stems were added prior to the administration of the PSCT. The first few sentence stems were part of the regular administration. The added ones were specifically used to elicit information from Seth about toileting concerns.

I love to **play outside.**
I am afraid of **monsters.**
I am happiest when **smile, happy, big potty.**
I go **poop, flush the toilet.**
When I go to the bathroom, **I can't.**
I wash my hands when **you go to potty.**
I go to the potty **go wee wee and flush toilet.**

It is important to know and use the child's own words for bodily functions (e.g., with this child, "wee wee" for urination, "poop" for bowel movements). These names can usually be gathered in the preliminary interview with parents.

Seth's responses suggest that he was able to talk about the toileting issues. His quick response of "I can't" to the stem, "When I go to the bathroom" suggests that he is aware of the concerns his parents had about his refusal to use the toilet for a bowel movement. Further, his response of "smile, happy, big potty" may suggest that he would be pleased if he could use the toilet for bowel movements or perhaps that his parents might smile and be happy when he does. Alternatively, they do not smile when he does not use the toilet, and it is his wish that they would! Similarly, when he stated he would "flush the toilet" after he had a bowel movement, this may be a reflection of his fantasy about being able to use and flush the toilet without difficulty, or of the pressures on him to do so.

Adding Clinically Relevant Stems During Administration of the PSCT

At times the examiner may seek further clarification of responses by asking the child to expand upon his or her response. For Jack, the examiner asked a few times for clarification (e.g., asking what some of the scary things were that he was afraid of, and why he was happiest on Saturdays). Other times, it can be helpful to get this clarification through additional sentence stems.

These may be added in advance, when the examiner has some knowledge about specific issues for the child, or can be added *spontaneously during the administration* of the task in response to the child's responses. An example of this latter form of clarification is provided by the following case example.

Case Example

Brian was a 5-year, 8-month-old boy who was referred because of behavioral problems in his babysitter's home. According to the parents, Brian was fairly well behaved at home and did well in structured settings. However, when at his babysitter's home, Brian had a number of instances of pushing, shoving, hitting, and kicking the babysitter's son. A sense of urgency existed on the parent's part because the babysitter had threatened to stop caring for Brian if he continued to be aggressive. Several sentence stems were added to the PSCT in order to gather information regarding Brian's perceptions of the situation at the babysitter's. These sentence stems specifically related to the babysitter and her son. In addition, during the administration of the PSCT, it was clear that further clarification of Brian's responses was needed. This was done by adding sentence stems spontaneously based on Brian's responses. (Sentence stems in regular type were added to the protocol prior to administration of the PSCT in order to gather specific information about Brian's perceptions of the babysitter's home. Sentence stems in capital letters are the ones that were added *spontaneously* by the examiner during the administration of the PSCT.)

Karen (babysitter) is **mean.**
KAREN IS MEAN BECAUSE **I do something wrong and she gets mad at me.**
WHEN SHE GETS MAD AT ME **I go. I make a picture.**
THE PICTURE IS **hearts.**
Steven (babysitter's son) is **nice.**
SOMETIMES STEVEN IS MEAN WHEN **he's mean I go tell Karen.**
AND KAREN, SHE **sometimes puts her kids in time-out. She does that to me, too.**
WHEN I'M IN TIMEOUT I FEEL **lonely.**
WHEN I'M LONELY I FEEL **sad.**

In the example, the examiner had planned to use the sentence stems related to the babysitter and her son in order to elicit Brian's feelings about the situation. However, the additional sentence stems were added in to elicit even more information based on Brian's responses. This example shows how the spontaneous addition of sentence stems can generate much information about the child's feelings. Obviously, these sentence stems could not have been designed in advance.

Using Toys Other Than Puppets in the PSCT

Despite the designation of this task as a puppet sentence completion, flexibility is still the mainstay of the assessment process. There are some children, even at the preschool age, who are uninterested in puppets, or who refuse to play with them. Even with such children, it is still possible to proceed with the PSCT. The example that follows illustrates the use of the PSCT with a child who did not want to use puppets.

Case Example

Mark was a 3-year, 9-month-old child who refused to use the toilet for bowel movements. Mark was toilet trained for urination at approximately 2.5 years old, and would eagerly use the toilet for urination, but refused to sit on the toilet for a bowel movement. Instead, Mark would ask for a diaper (which he no longer wore), and then would use the diaper for his bowel movements. Although the parents continued to comply with this request, his preschool refused to allow him to stay in school unless he was "completely toilet trained." They would not permit him to put on a diaper for bowel movements, and therefore he was only allowed to stay in school for a half day. Mark was motivated to stay in school, because he expressed to his parents that he felt that he was missing out on fun activities in the second half of the day. When the parents refused to give Mark a diaper, he would withhold his bowel movements. This option was not appropriate, because of the concerns regarding fecal impaction that might result from withholding of his stools.

Other presenting problems included Mark's aggressive behavior and noncompliance. At the time of referral he was dealing with feelings regarding the birth of a younger sibling, as well as fears of monsters and witches. Mark's parents also reported that he showed much interest in toy cars, to the point of knowing names and much identifying information about cars. In preparation for the assessment, many sentence stems were added to the standard list in order to gather information regarding Mark's feelings about his toileting issues. Mark, however, refused to use the puppets presented to him. In order to proceed with the task, a set of toy cars was substituted for the puppets. In the following examples, the examiner spoke as if the cars were stating the sentence stems and Mark replied to the stems as if he were speaking for the cars.

> My diaper is **My diapers are all gone, so I poop in the toilet.**
> They're all gone? **I leave them and throw all in my diaper pail, so I can go poop in the toilet and squeeze my poop out.**
> Mr. Car (addressing the toy car in Mark's hand), I am afraid of witches. **Know what I'm afraid of? I'm scared of a creature like a tree. I'm afraid it will come out of my bed.**
> I'm sad when **my mommy and daddy leave and I just cry.**

Adding Therapeutic Sentence Stems to the PSCT

With some children, the sentence stems can be designed to be "therapeutically leading." That is, the stems can be created to fit the child's situation, but in a more psycho-educational manner that also helps the child therapeutically. This is typically more appropriate after the examiner feels that there is sufficient assessment information and such therapeutic stems will not contaminate the information obtained. It could also be used later in therapy if the sentence stems are part of the play therapy, rather than used exclusively for diagnostic purposes. Examples for a later part of Mark's PSCT follow:

> My problem is **I don't know.**
> Some kids have potty problems. Do you have a potty problem? **Yes, I have. NO. I go poop. I squeeze it out and wipe. I put my poop in the toilet and I flush it down.**

Mark's responses suggest that he is well aware of the concerns that his parents have regarding his lack of toilet use for making bowel movements. However, he insists that he does not have a "potty problem," and he just "squeezes it out, wipes, and flushes it." Interestingly, Mark first responded that he did have a potty problem, but quickly changed his response to "no."

Summary

The PSCT is a developmentally appropriate measure designed to be used with preschool and young school-age children. It is based on the SCT used with older children and adults but is designed to facilitate participation from young children. Several aspects of the PSCT make it more conducive to gathering information from young children. The task itself is not begun until it is clear that the child understands the directions. Flexibility is offered by giving the child the opportunity to complete the sentence stem either through the "voice" of a puppet or without the puppet as a prompt. For some children, the puppet provides a tool so they do not have to tell the examiner directly how they are feeling. For other children, once the puppets help structure the task, they are comfortable responding freely without the puppets. In either case, the use of puppets (or another appropriate play material) provides a safe, familiar structure for the administration of this task.

It is important that the data gathered from this task are used in conjunction with all information gathered, and not in isolation. Interview information (e.g., parent interview, including developmental history; child play interviews) as well as more objective methods (e.g., Child Behavior Checklist; Achenbach & Rescorla, 2000; Manual for the ASEBA—Preschool Edition; LaFrenier & Dumas, 1995) is useful. Information from other significant adults, such as teachers and caregivers, can often be important. The ultimate goal is to conceptualize a sense of the child's perceptions of his or her situation from all of the information gathered.

References

Achenbach, T. M., & Rescorla, L. A. (2000). *Manual for the ASEBA preschool forms and profiles.* Burlington: University of Vermont, Department of Psychiatry.

Ebbinghaus, H. (1897). Uber eine neue Methode zu Prufung geistiger Fahigkuten und ihre Anwendung bei Schulkindern [Concerning a new method of testing intellectual abilities and their use in school children], *Zeitschrift fur Psychologie, 13*, 401–459.

Goldberg. P.A. (1965). A review of sentence completion methods in personality assessment. In B. I. Murstein (Ed.), *Handbook of projective techniques* (pp. 777–822). New York: Basic Books.

Hart, D. H. (1986). Sentence completion techniques. In H. M. Knoff (Ed.), *The assessment of child and adolescent personality* (pp. 245–272). New York: Guilford.

Irwin, E. C. (1985). Puppets in therapy: An assessment procedure. *American Journal of Psychotherapy, 39*(3), 389–400.

Irwin, E. C. (2000). The use of a puppet interview to understand children. In C. Schaefer, K. Gitlin, & S. A. Sandgrund (Eds.), *Play diagnosis and assessment* (pp. 682–703). New York: Wiley.

Knell, S. M. (1992). *The puppet sentence completion task.* Unpublished manuscript.

Knell, S. M. (1993). *Cognitive behavioral play therapy.* Hillsdale, NJ: Aronson.

Knell, S. M., & Beck, K. W. (2000). Puppet sentence completion test. In K. Gitlin-Weiner, K. Sandgrund, & C. Schaefer (Eds.), *Play diagnosis and assessment* (pp. 704–721). New York: Wiley.

LaFrenier, P. J., & Dumas, J. E. (1995). *Social competence and behavior evaluation: Preschool edition.* Los Angeles: Western Psychological Services.

Lubin, B., Larsen, R. M., & Matarazzo, J. D. (1984). Patterns of psychological test usage in the United States: 1935–1982. *American Psychologist, 39*, 451–453.

Rabin, A. L. (1960). Projective methods and projection in children. In A. I. Rabin & M. R. Haworth (Eds.), *Projective techniques with children* (pp. 2–11). New York: Grune & Stratton.

Ruma, C. D. (1993). Cognitive—behavioral play therapy with sexually abused children. In S. M. Knell (Ed.), *Cognitive behavioral play therapy* (pp. 193–230). Hillsdale, NJ: Aronson.

Tendler, A. D. (1930). A preliminary report on a test for emotional insight. *Journal of Applied Psychology, 14*, 123–136.

Weiss, D. S., Zilberg, N. J., & Genervo, J. L. (1989). Psychometric properties of Loevinger's sentence completion test in an adult psychiatric outpatient sample. *Journal of Personality Assessment, 53*, 478–486.

Appendix

Puppet Sentence Completion Task Revised—1998

Directions: The examiner should let the child choose a puppet. After the child has chosen a puppet, the examiner chooses two puppets. If the child so wishes, the examiner can let the child pick the puppets for the examiner. The following code is used in the directions:

Puppet A—Examiner's
Puppet B—Examiner's
Puppet C—Child's

Part I

Directions: Puppet A states the sentence stem. Puppet B quickly responds. The examiner then turns to Puppet C (held by the child) for a response. The examiner supplies answers for Puppet B. Move to Part II as soon as it is clear that the child understands the task by providing a response for Puppet C.

Puppet A:	My name is ________________
[Turn to Puppet B:]	My name is ________________
[Turn to Puppet C:]	My name is ________________
Puppet A:	My favorite ice cream is ________________
[Puppet B:]	*chocolate ice cream*
[Puppet C:]	________________
Puppet A:	I am ________________
[Puppet B:]	*4 years old*
[Puppet C:]	________________
Puppet A:	My favorite toy is ________________
[Puppet B:]	*my teddy bear*
[Puppet C:]	________________
Puppet A:	My favorite color is ________________
[Puppet B:]	*blue*
[Puppet C:]	________________

If the child does not understand the task, go back through and have Puppet B prompt the child to help Puppet C give a response. Continue until the task is clearly understood by the child. Do not go on to Part II until it is clear that the child understands the task. If the child does not seem to understand what is expected in Part I, Part II will probably not be understood.

Note: Some children catch on quite quickly and do not seem to like the repetition necessary in Part I. For these children, it is permissible to go directly to Part II. Although it is preferable to write down the child's responses immediately, because the therapist has a puppet on each hand it may be necessary to record responses immediately following administration of Part I.

Supplemental note: The responses listed in Part I are examples. If the examiner feels that other responses make more sense, or would elicit more cooperation from the child, these can be used.

Part II

Directions: In Part II, Puppet A states the sentence stem. The sentence is stated directly to Puppet C. The response made by the child (Puppet C) should be written in the blank space immediately. Some children will give two responses, one for the puppet and one for themselves. Both responses should be noted.

1. My favorite food is
2. I love to
3. Outside I play with
4. Mommy is
5. Daddy is
6. My favorite TV show is
7. (If applicable) My brother's name is
8. (If applicable) My sister's name is
9. I like to pretend to be
10. If I were bigger I would
11. At night when I sleep I
12. I am afraid of
13. I hate
14. The best secret is
15. The worst secret is
16. Mommy is nice when
17. Daddy is nice when
18. Daddy is mean when
19. Mommy is mean when
20. I am happiest when
21. I am saddest when
22. I get scared when

23. My biggest problem is
24. The worst thing about me is

Optional Sentence Stems

25. With my hands I like to touch
26. With my hands I don't like to touch
27. Someone I don't like to touch me is
28. Someone I like to touch me is
29. My body is
30. I don't like to be touched on my
31. A secret I am not supposed to tell is
32. I am maddest when
33. When I heard about my parents' divorce, I felt
34. Divorce is
35. Visiting my mom/dad is
36. When I visit my mom/dad, I
37. My stepmom/stepdad is
38. My potty (toilet) is
39. When I go potty (to the bathroom), I
40. Diapers are
41. When mommy leaves I feel
42. Being alone is
43. My tummy (stomach) is
44. My biggest wish is
45. I cry when
46. ____________________
47. ____________________
48. ______________________

Section III

Theoretical Approaches

6 The Child-Centered Approach to Puppet Play With Children

Elizabeth Kjellstrand Hartwig

The use of puppets in child-centered play therapy provides children with opportunities to express their inner world. Children are naturally drawn to puppets for a variety of reasons: They're colorful and soft, easy to use, and can be used in a variety of ways. In a study on the use of toys in child-centered play therapy, Ray et al. (2013) explored the frequency of toy use in the playroom. In this study the puppet theater was used at a frequency of 32%, meaning that nearly one-third of the interactions in the playroom involved the puppet theater, and specific puppets were used for a total frequency of 25%. This finding demonstrates that puppets are useful tools for children in the playroom.

Overview of Child-Centered Theory

Child-centered play therapy (CCPT) is a nondirective approach to working with children. CCPT is based on the core conditions of person-centered therapy: empathy, genuineness, and unconditional positive regard (Rogers, 1980). Axline, a student and colleague of Rogers, contributed to the field of play therapy with the development of nondirective play therapy. Axline (1947, pp. 73–74) offered eight guidelines that defined the nature of CCPT and promoted Rogers' core conditions:

1. The therapist must develop a warm, friendly relationship with the child, in which good rapport is established as soon as possible.
2. The therapist accepts the child exactly as he or she is.
3. The therapist establishes a feeling of permissiveness in the relationship so that the child feels free to express his or her feelings completely.
4. The therapist is alert to recognize the feelings the child is expressing and reflects those feelings back to him or her in such a manner that the therapist gains insight into the child's behavior.
5. The therapist maintains a deep respect for the child's ability to solve his or her own problems if given an opportunity to do so. The responsibility to make choices and to institute change is the child's.

6. The therapist does not attempt to direct the child's actions or conversation in any manner. The child leads the way; the therapist follows.
7. The therapist does not attempt to hurry the therapy along. It is a gradual process and is recognized as such by the therapist.
8. The therapist establishes only those limitations that are necessary to anchor the therapy to the world of reality and to make the child aware of his or her responsibilities in the relationship.

These guidelines provide a foundation for the child-centered play therapy approach.

In his book *Play Therapy: The Art of the Relationship*, Landreth (2012) formalized the process of CCPT by providing guidelines for playroom materials, facilitative responses, therapeutic limit setting, and working with parents. Landreth emphasized the importance of building a relationship with a child in play therapy and trusting the child to lead his or her own healing process. Ray (2011) later expanded the CCPT approach in her book *Advanced Play Therapy* by introducing the concept of play themes, exploring the role of aggression in children, and describing play therapy in various settings.

The concept of symbolic play is a crucial element of a child's cognitive and social development (Piaget, 1951; Vygotsky, 1976). Symbolic play is a child's ability to use objects, actions, or ideas to represent people, objects, and actions as representations of their world. In child-centered play therapy, children use the toys in the playroom as part of the symbolic play process. Ginott (1994) affirms, "Through the manipulation of toys, the child can show more adequately than through words how he feels about himself and the significant persons and events in his life" (p. 51). Puppets are valuable tools in this process because they can represent people (e.g., family members, police officer, cheerleader), feelings (e.g., butterfly—happiness, turtle—fear), and concepts (e.g., dragon—power, dog—friendliness or loyalty). Landreth (2012) notes that symbolic play "allows children to freely assimilate their experiences without environmental constraints" (p. 17). Children can also use puppets as a self-metaphor. They may choose a puppet that represents personal qualities they already have (e.g., an owl for intelligence) or a puppet that represents qualities they would like to have (e.g., an alligator for power). Through symbolic play, children can explore their thoughts about themselves, others, and their world using puppets.

Description of Implementing Key Items With Puppets

Selection and Display of Puppets

Similar to the rationale for selecting toys for the playroom, the selection of puppets is a thoughtful process that is based on sound rationale. Landreth (2012) recommended that practitioners select toys and materials that facilitate a wide range of creative and emotional expression, engage children's interests, facilitate exploratory play, allow nonverbal expression, allow success without a prearranged structure, allow for noncommittal play, and are durable for active play (p. 156). Given these guidelines, practitioners should choose puppets that allow children to express a range of emotions and represent images or symbols to which children could relate. Landreth suggested three broad categories of toys: real-life, acting-out aggressive-release, and creative expression and emotional release. Real-life puppets allow for children to express themselves using concrete representations of family members, pets, and community members. Aggressive-release puppets are used to express frustration, anger, or hostility. Creative expression and emotional release puppets offer children a range of emotions to express. This author recommends a sample set of 15 to 20 hand puppets with puppets from each of these categories:

Real-Life

- Family members that represent diverse families and family structures: puppets from two multicultural families that include two fathers, two mothers, two sons, and two daughters;
- Puppets for special populations: military puppet, kangaroo joey (adoption or parent-child issues);
- Pets: dog, cat, horse, bird;
- Community members: police officer, doctor, firefighter, nurse.

Aggressive-Release

- Puppets that can appear aggressive: dragon, snake, wolf, shark, crocodile, spider.

Creative Expression and Emotional Release

- Puppets that could express a range of expressions and emotions: googly-eyed monster (silliness), turtle or clam (shyness or fear), owl (intelligence), wizard (magic), butterfly (happiness);
- Various animals with no specific symbolism: cow, duck, lamb, and frog;
- Melissa & Doug Make-Your-Own Monster Puppet.

Practitioners can add to or change the sample set depending on the needs of the client or the client population with whom the practitioner works. For example, if a practitioner works primarily with military families, including a couple of military puppets into the sample set would be a good fit for this client population. Figure 6.1 presents a picture of a sample set.

There is a variety of ways to display and arrange puppets in the playroom. Types of puppet displays include wooden puppet trees, plastic shoe organizers hung on the wall or on the back of a door, and bookshelves that also display other toys in the playroom. Landreth (2012) recommends that toys be kept in a consistent place in the playroom after each session so that children do not have to search for the toy they need. This is true for puppet displays,

Figure 6.1 Sample Set of Puppets

as well. This author recommends that puppets be grouped and displayed in the toy categories listed above, so that children can readily find the puppet they need within a certain category.

CCPT Facilitative Skills

Ray (2011) presented nine categories of therapeutic verbal responses used in child-centered play therapy. These include tracking behavior, reflecting content, reflecting feeling, facilitating decision-making and returning responsibility, facilitating creativity, esteem-building, facilitating relationship, reflecting larger meaning, and limit setting. A description of each facilitative skill is provided below with a scenario and sample response.

1. ***Tracking behavior*** is reflecting what the child is *doing* in the playroom.

   Scenario: A child picks up a bat puppet and makes it fly through the air. *Tracking behavior response*: "That one is flying." (Note that the response does not name the puppet, so that the child can choose what he or she wants the bat puppet to be. This is based on Landreth's (2012) recommendation for counselors to not name toys in order to let children lead in the playroom.)

2. ***Reflecting content*** is paraphrasing what the child *says*.

   Scenario: A child picks up a kangaroo puppet with a joey in the pouch. The child says, "Look—this one has a baby inside!" *Reflecting content response:* "You noticed that one has a baby!"

3. ***Reflecting feeling*** is stating what the therapist believes the child is *feeling*, based on behavioral or verbal cues.

   Scenario: The child is holding a dog puppet in her arms and rocking the puppet back and forth. The child says with a frown, "The puppy hurt himself." *Reflecting feeling response*: "You're sad that the puppy is hurt."

4. ***Facilitating decision-making and returning responsibility*** is giving the child the opportunity and responsibility to make his or her own decisions and be responsible for choices he or she has made in the playroom.

   Scenario: The child takes all the puppets off the puppet tree and throws them on the floor. Then the child says, "Clean them up!" *Returning responsibility response*: "In here, that's something you can do."

5. ***Facilitating creativity*** is allowing the child to develop his or her own sense of creativity and expression (Ray, 2011, p. 87).

   Scenario: The child shows the dog puppet to the therapist, and asks, "What kind of puppy is this?" *Facilitating creativity response:* "It can be whatever kind of puppy you would like it to be."

6. ***Esteem-building*** is providing encouragement to the child for the effort the child has put into a task.

   Scenario: The child puts together a Melissa & Doug Make-Your-Own Monster Puppet. When he finishes putting the puppet together, he exclaims, "I did it!" *Esteem-building response*: "You made it just the way you wanted it to be!"

7. ***Facilitating relationship*** is a relational response that acknowledges the relationship between the child and the therapist (Ray, 2011, pp. 87–88).

   Scenario: The child gives the therapist a dragon puppet and says, "You are fun to play with! Let's make a story together." *Facilitating relationship response*: "You enjoy playing with me!"

8. ***Reflecting larger meaning*** is noticing and verbalizing patterns or themes in the child's play in order to increase the child's awareness of the significance or motivation for his or her play.

   Scenario: The child puts all the puppets back on the bookshelf. He has done this each session for ten sessions after he has finished playing with the puppets. *Reflecting larger meaning response*: "I notice that you always put them back on the bookshelf each time you finish playing with them."

9. ***Limit setting*** is setting boundaries in the playroom to promote safety and to help children develop problem-solving skills and self-control. Landreth (2012) recommends the ACT method for limit setting: A—Acknowledge the child's feelings, wishes, and wants; C—Communicate the limit; and T—Target acceptable alternatives (pp. 271–272).

   Scenario: The child grabs the dragon puppet from the therapist, appears to be ready to throw the puppet at the therapist, and says, "You're not doing it right!" The child waits and watches for the therapist to respond. *Limit setting response using the ACT method*: (A) "You're angry that I'm not doing the dragon the right way and you want to throw the dragon at me," (C) "but I'm not for throwing at." (T) "You can pretend the [stuffed bear] is me and throw the dragon at the [bear]."

The illustrative case study below demonstrates the use of all of these facilitative skills with a child using puppets in child-centered play therapy.

Case Study

The following case is presented as an illustrative vignette of a child using puppets in child-centered play therapy.

James is a 5-year-old boy who has been diagnosed with oppositional defiant disorder. His parents divorced when he was 2 and his mother remarried when he was 4. His mother and stepfather have a 5-month-old baby girl, who is James' new sister. His stepfather is an alcoholic. James has observed his mother and stepfather fighting on several occasions, some of which have gotten physical. James does not get along with his stepfather, and his stepfather does not make efforts to build a relationship with James. His mother has shared that James has explosive tantrums at home, does not comply with rules at home and at school, and has been in several fights with another student at school. While James does not get along with many of his peers or adults, James is particularly fond of his baby sister, Agatha. He often plays with her and asks his mom if he can hold her. The custody agreement between his mother and biological father states that James' father has regular visits every other weekend and one evening a week; however, James' father typically misses visits or cancels at the last minute.

Illustrative Vignette

James: (*Looking around the room*) I'm not sure what I want to play with today.

Counselor: You don't know what to play with. (***Reflecting content***)

James: (*Walks over to the puppet tower*) What are these?

Counselor: They can be anything you want them to be. (***Facilitating creativity***)

James: (*Picks up a shark puppet*) I know who this is.

Counselor: You've decided who that one is. (***Reflecting content***)

James: Yep—it's my stepdad.

Counselor: Oh—that one is your stepdad. (***Reflecting content***)

James: See—he's got big teeth and a huge mouth. He vomits a lot, just like this. (*James picks up some small cars and drops them so it looks like they are coming from the shark's mouth*)

Counselor: He's got big teeth and a big mouth that vomits a lot. (***Reflecting content***)
James: Yeah. (*James stands looking at the puppet tree for a while*) Hmm . . . .
Counselor: You're checking those out. (***Tracking behavior***)
James: I know what I want now. (*James takes the shark puppet and chooses the alligator, princess, and turtle puppets. He puts the puppets on the puppet theater.*)
Counselor: You found the ones you want. (***Reflecting content***)
James: I want to do a show with you, because you're fun!
Counselor: You enjoy playing with me. (***Facilitating relationship***)
James: (*Handing the turtle puppet to the counselor*) Here, you be this one.
Counselor: (*Takes the turtle puppet and puts it on her hand*) Okay.

Practice Point

The counselor has allowed James to decide with what toys he would like to play. The counselor also facilitated relationship by acknowledging that James enjoys playing with her. These skills of allowing a child to make choices in the playroom and acknowledging what the child says are important elements of child-centered play therapy.

Continued interaction:

James: (*Starts to put the shark puppet on his hand, but struggles a little to get the puppet on his hand. He doesn't make much of an effort, and the puppet falls to the floor. He looks at the counselor.*) Put the puppet on my hand.
Counselor: In here, that's something you can do. (***Facilitating responsibility***)
James: (*Tries again and gets the shark puppet on his hand. Then puts the alligator puppet on his other hand.*) I did it! I got both of them on!
Counselor: You got both of them on your hands all by yourself! (***Esteem-building***)
James: (*Puts both puppets on the puppet theater.*) [*Alligator to shark*] You think you're cool because of your teeth, but I have way more teeth then you! See? [*Alligator bites the shark's head.*]
Counselor: That one just bit him. (***Tracking behavior***)
James: Yeah—Crocky is going to hurt him bad. [*Crocky, the alligator, bites the shark's head again.*]
Counselor: Crocky wants to hurt him. (***Reflecting content***)
James: (*Takes his hand out of the alligator puppet and begins to try to rip the shark puppet's teeth out*) I want to hurt him! I'm going to pull out all his teeth.
Counselor: James, I can see that you want to hurt him by pulling out his teeth, but the teeth are meant for staying in his mouth. You can pretend to pull out his teeth. (***Limit setting***)

James: (*James thinks for a bit and then puts his hand back in the alligator puppet.*) Never mind. Crocky will get him. [*Crocky bites the shark in several places then throws the shark puppet on the ground.*] Yay—he's dead!
Counselor: You're happy that that one is dead. (***Reflecting feeling***)

Practice Point

Setting limits is an important part of keeping the child, the counselor, and the playroom safe. In this example, the therapist used the ACT approach to acknowledge the child's wishes, communicate the limit, and target an alternative behavior. James considered the limit and made a choice to follow the limit and continue using "Crocky," the alligator puppet, in the alligator/shark interaction.

Continued interaction:

James: Where is Turtle?
Counselor: (*Brings Turtle up to the puppet theater*) [*as Turtle with a special "Turtle" voice*] Here I am. (***Facilitating creativity***)
James: [*Crocky to Turtle*] Do you see what happened to Sharky? Sharky was mean and throwing up, so I killed him.
Counselor: [*as Turtle to Crocky*] You decided to kill him because he was mean and throwing up. (***Reflecting content***)
James: [*as Crocky*] I know Turtle was scared of Sharky.
Counselor: [*Makes Turtle nod to follow James' lead.*] I was scared. (***Facilitating creativity***)
James: [*as Crocky*] I was strong and I killed him so he can't scare you anymore. I won't ever let him hurt you again.
Counselor: [*as Turtle to Crocky*] It's important to you that he doesn't ever hurt me again. (***Reflecting larger meaning***)

Discussion

This case study illustrates the use of all nine facilitative skills with puppet play in child-centered play therapy. Throughout the vignette, the counselor allows the client, James, to lead by choosing toys and initiating play behaviors. The counselor uses therapeutic verbal responses to build a relationship with the child, acknowledge the child's behaviors, feelings, words, and meaning, and facilitate responsibility, esteem-building, and creativity. While each child will have a different way of interacting with puppets, this case study shows possible ways of responding to a client in a child-centered way.

Conclusion

Puppets can be an ideal resource for child-centered play therapy due to puppets' appeal to children and the usefulness of puppets in symbolic play. This author recommends a sample set of 15 to 20 puppets that include puppets from each of the three CCPT toy categories: real-life, acting-out aggressive-release, and creative expression and emotional release. Counselors should consider displaying puppets in a way that allows children to easily access the puppets, such as on a puppet tree, shoe organizer, or bookshelf. Ray's (2011) nine facilitative skills provide a framework for responding to children in a child-centered way in the playroom. This chapter described each of these facilitative skills, provided examples of each skill, and presented an illustrative vignette. The child-centered approach to puppet play provides a medium for relationship building and the use of facilitative skills to support the child in his or her own healing journey.

References

Axline, V. (1947). *Play therapy: The inner dynamics of childhood.* Oxford, England: Houghton Mifflin.

Ginott, H. G. (1994). *Group psychotherapy with children: The theory and practice of play therapy.* Northvale, NJ: Jason Aronson, Inc.

Landreth, G. L. (2012). *Play therapy: The art of the relationship* (3rd ed.). New York, NY: Routledge/Taylor & Francis Group.

Piaget, J. (1951). *The psychology of intelligence.* London: Routledge and Kegan Paul Ltd.

Ray, D. C. (2011). *Advanced play therapy: Essential conditions, knowledge, and skills for child practice.* New York, NY: Routledge/Taylor & Francis Group.

Ray, D. C., Lee, K. R., Meany-Walen, K. K., Carlson, S. E., Carnes-Holt, K. L., & Ware, J. N. (2013). Use of toys in child-centered play therapy. *International Journal of Play Therapy, 22*(1), 43–57.

Rogers, C. R. (1980). *A way of being.* Boston, MA: Houghton Mifflin.

Vygotsky, L. (1976). Play and its role in the mental development of the child. In J. Bruner, A. Jolly, & K. Sylva (Eds.), *Play: Its role in development and evolution* (pp. 537–554). New York: Basic Books.

7 The Use of Puppets in Psychodynamic Child Therapy

David A. Crenshaw and Jillian E. Kelly

Introduction

Psychodynamic child therapy enjoys a rich history and tradition. Among the luminaries that contributed in major ways to the early psychodynamic treatment of children include Anna Freud, Melanie Klein, and Donald Winnicott. In more recent decades Albert Solnit and Charles Sarnoff have made major contributions to psychoanalytic writings focused on children. *The Psychoanalytic Study of the Child* has been in continuous publication since 1945. The initial editorial board of this prestigious publication in the United States included such well-known analysts as Otto Fenichel, Phyllis Greenacre, Heinz Hartmann, Edith B. Jackson, Ernst Kris, Lawrence Kubie, Bertram Lewin, and Rene Spitz. In Great Britain, the initial editorial board included Anna Freud, Willie Hoffer, and Edward Glover. In the year 2017, the 68th volume of this distinguished journal for psychoanalytic treatment of children will be published.

The term "psychodynamic" refers to the interplay of forces or influences within the mind (Mordock, 2015). Mordock explains, "In contrast to the behavioral therapist, who connects behaviors to observable antecedents and consequences, the psychodynamic therapist considers the reasons for behavior as more complex than what is revealed by observable behaviors" (p. 66). Fundamentally, psychodynamic play therapists explore the painful or distressing feelings that underlie certain troublesome behaviors that are symptomatic of deeper, underlying problems.

Psychodynamic play therapy rests on four fundamental assumptions identified by Mordock (2015):

> (1) symptoms have meaning; (2) children's problems arise from internalized unconscious conflicts, failure to successfully assimilate overwhelming experiences, and failure to cope with developmental deficits, all of which they reveal in play; (3) children's play is symbolic, a projection of their inner feelings onto play materials in efforts to obtain mastery over both present and past experiences (their symbolic play provides the camouflage and distance needed for emotional control and psychological

> safety); and (4) transference-based thoughts characterize much of children's behavior, displayed in therapy sessions and elsewhere.
>
> (p. 66)

Neuroscience research (Gaskill & Perry, 2014; Porges, 2011; Schore, 2012: Siegel, 2012; Van der Kolk, 2014) strongly supports not only psychological safety but what Van der Kolk (2014) refers to as "visceral safety" (p. 79) for therapy to be effective. Thus, the distance provided by the symbolic haven created by the projection of the child's feelings onto puppets or other play materials is critical.

Implementation

It is well known that children growing up in environments that expose them to multiple adverse experiences and types of maltreatment suffer blows to their dignity consisting of the trilogy of shame, stigma, and silencing (Crenshaw, 2008). The damage to the sense of self is often evidenced by an insidious sense of "badness" accompanied by self-contempt and a high incidence of self-destructive behavior (Crenshaw, Rudy, Triemer, & Zingaro, 1986; Gil & Crenshaw, 2015). Play therapy allows for symbolization, externalization, and miniaturization of the problem a child is facing (Crenshaw & Kelly, 2015), thus enabling the child to gradually confront what might otherwise be overwhelming. The recent work of Daniel Siegel (2012), Bessel van der Kolk, (2014), and Stephen Porges (2011) emphasizes the neurobiological importance of play therapy by creating and maintaining conditions of safety to enable the work to be therapeutic and to reduce the risk of re-traumatization. The therapeutic challenge is to honor and be fully attuned to the affective "windows of tolerance" as children enact play dramas about their own internal experience. Children are resilient, and as therapists we have the unique opportunity to create a space and the time that allows for the uncovering of such resiliency in the context of therapy sessions. By using an array of puppets (hostile, docile, animal, persons, mythical creatures, etc.) in therapy, therapists provide children a developmentally appropriate means of sharing their inner worlds and constructing a narrative of what has happened, how they feel about it, and the meaning they have assigned to it.

The benefits of using puppets are numerous and present in all stages of treatment. Puppets enhance play therapy through relational engagement; allowing children to confront stress in small titrated doses (which enhances resilience); enabling children to develop a capacity for self-soothing and self-regulation; helping to break the cycle of secrecy and denial; correcting cognitive distortions; encouraging the expression of affect; facilitating the discovery of coping skills to return to healthy developmental functioning; reducing anxiety; increasing problem-solving; increasing self-esteem and self-efficacy; opening up opportunities and maximizing turning points; enhancing nurturing relationships beyond therapy; and enabling children to learn to make meaning of life's experiences. In the following sections the authors illustrate how to use puppets through various stages of treatment.

Beginning of Treatment

New and seasoned therapists alike have found puppets helpful partners in engaging children and developing rapport in the initial stages of treatment. I (JK) have had many a tender moment upon reuniting with former clients in the community, listening intently as they eagerly ask for updates about how my puppet "co-therapists" Cuddles, Cuddleito, and Biscuit are feeling! Puppets add a child-friendly atmosphere even to the most sterile of offices, and set the tone that our therapeutic space is a safe and playful one indeed. Puppets can be used to provide developmentally appropriate psychoeducation about the purpose of therapy and to normalize the child's feelings around starting treatment. For example, "*Cuddles (turtle puppet) feels nervous meeting new people. She uses her shell as a safe place to hide. She's inside there now. I wonder if you would like to say something to Cuddles to help her feel safe here?*" Puppets can also be used in gathering important information in a child-friendly manner as part of the initial assessment. The authors have obtained more information on attachment, feelings vocabulary, and social skills than would otherwise be available in the standard verbal directive in question-and-answer format.

Middle of Treatment

Puppets can be used as miniaturized representations of important parts of the child's world. In this way, the big problems they face can be reduced from their complexities into symbolic representations that are far more manageable to approach. When a child's inner world is externalized and shrunk down, they can show us what is truly happening. Puppets also create opportunities for relating metaphorically. Metaphor is a symbolized form of condensed but precise communication (Mills & Crowley, 2014) and creates a deep understanding indirectly and therefore at a safe distance. Playing it out with puppets creates an opportunity for seeking and finding mastery through play when experiences or emotions are overwhelming. The symbolism may be disguised to the degree necessary to allow a child to safely engage in repeated attempts at mastery without getting overwhelmed. Case vignettes to follow will further illustrate these concepts.

End of Treatment

Ending treatment can be bittersweet for both child and therapist. A special bond in the therapeutic relationship has been created, be it over weeks, months, or years. Puppets can help in the discussion of endings and in the creation of transitional items (such as making miniature/finger puppets with the child). The use of puppets at this stage of treatment provides a platform for role-playing, practicing, reinforcing, and maintaining learned social and problem-solving skills. The authors have found children respond positively to being asked to role-play as therapist with a puppet of their choice as client, to provide yet another opportunity for mastery through the experience of giving something—be it advice or guidance—and feeling valued and competent as they complete treatment.

Practical Considerations in Using Puppets

Puppets are available through specialized child therapy bookstores; our favorite is the Self Esteem Shop (www.selfesteemshop.com/), where Deanne Gruenberg and her husband Harry Gruenberg stand ready to advise purchasers on some of the best choices for the play therapist. Deanne is a registered play therapist and is uniquely knowledgeable about all the books and therapy supplies they carry. The Self Esteem Shop—along with other highly regarded therapy supply stores such as Child Therapy Toys (www.childtherapytoys.com), owned by Gary York, PhD, and Jane York, MA, two child mental health professionals—carries a wide range of puppets, including multicultural puppets, as well as human and animal puppets. Puppets vary in price and quality. Although somewhat more expensive, some of the best-quality puppets in our experience are made by Folkmanis (www.folkmanis.com/18/about-us.htm), a company founded in 1976 by Judy and Atis Folkmanis. The care and cleaning of the puppets is an important consideration. Detailed instructions for the Folkmanis puppets can be found on a webpage devoted to the care of the puppets (www.folkmanis.com/34/puppet-care.htm).

In terms of selection of puppets for the play therapy room, the authors find having an adequate array of multicultural puppets and several choices of human, animal, and mythical puppets to be helpful. With animal puppets, it is important to offer selections among aggressive puppets such as alligators, dinosaurs, and sharks as well as more vulnerable puppets such as rabbits, puppies, and kittens. With human puppets, diversity of selection would include mommy and baby puppets, daddy and grandparents, and a variety of role puppets including police officer, firefighter, doctor, nurse, teacher, and judge, to name a few. Mythical puppets, like dragons and fairies, add a magical dynamic to puppet play. The importance of puppets to the play dramas enacted in the play therapy room is revealed by the excited questioning of our child clients as to what new puppets we purchased upon our return from a conference. Most play therapists add to their collection when they attend conferences where vendors are present, and it is not necessary to have every puppet that a child might conceivably choose.

Case Vignettes

Children are remarkable in their ability to express their internal life through symbol and metaphor.

Figure 7.1 Parrot Incarcerated

The puppet in jail depicted in Figure 7.1 was powerful feedback to an intern therapist who was attempting to do child-centered play therapy in a disciplined way, but in the experience of the child, she overdid it. The child, a 7-year-old boy, communicated vividly his annoyance of her parroting his utterances while attempting to track and offer reflections on his play. She took the feedback to heart and reduced the frequency of such reflections.

While the authors tend to adopt a child-centered approach to play therapy, and thus the play scenes involving puppets and the puppets themselves are typically chosen by the children because of our faith in their resources for healing, an integrative approach (Drewes, Bratton, & Schaefer, 2011) to play therapy including the use of prescriptive play therapy (Schaefer, 2001) may be indicated with some children in certain situations that arise in therapy. Eliza, a 10-year-old girl, was depressed to an alarming degree. She and her little brother, age 7, witnessed their stepfather in a rage strangle their mother to death. The shock and the acute trauma blocked Eliza from externalizing her feelings of rage, and instead the internalization of these intense feelings led to her increasing degree of depression.

The therapist decided on a prescriptive approach with the goal of assisting her to voice her rage and externalize the suppressed anger to relive the internalized symptoms of depression. In Figure 7.2, the intervention is recreated with the help of a psychology student from Marist College at the time,

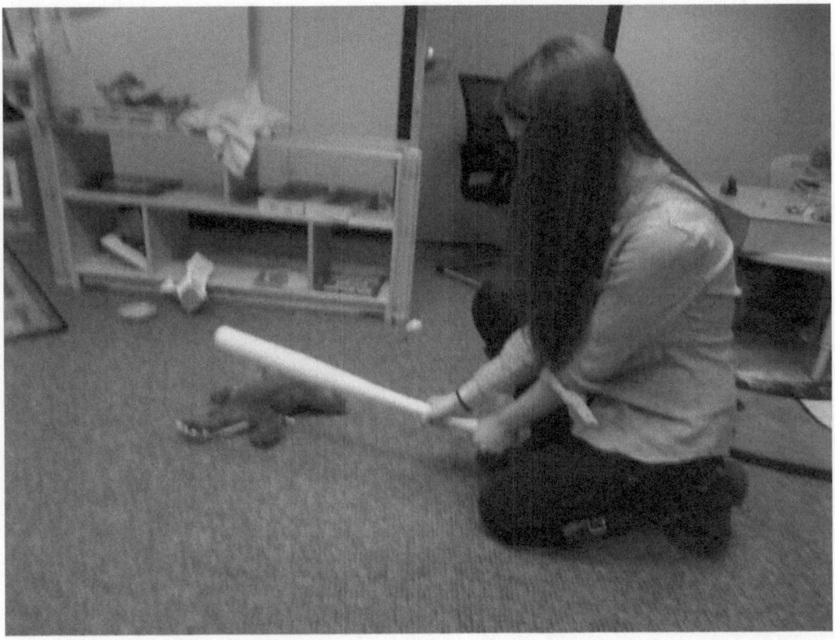

Figure 7.2 Alligator Pounded With a Bat

Stephanie Eick. Eliza was asked to consider the alligator puppet as a symbol of whatever makes her the angriest and to tell the alligator her feelings. She promptly picked up a plastic baseball bat and pounded the alligator puppet, while yelling at the puppet, "I hate your guts!" "You killed my mother!" "I hope you rot in hell!" The dramatic prescriptive intervention was successful, because a noticeable improvement in her depressive symptoms was observed in the weeks that followed and she was dramatically more verbal in the play therapy sessions that followed.

A favorite teaching case for the authors is "The Adventures of Frog and Turtle" (Crenshaw & Mordock, 2005). The puppet adventures began when Anthony was 5 years old. At that point Anthony suffered multiple fears and phobias, one of which was needles, which made going to medical visits and necessary immunizations for school a major ordeal for both him and his adoptive parents. Anthony projected his multiple fears onto Turtle (therapist) while the Frog puppet (Anthony) was fearless and heroic (see Fig. 7.3). Anthony had been adopted from a Caribbean island after abandonment by his birth parents, and abandonment themes were prominent, along with intense fears and phobias, in the adventures. The therapist was instructed by Anthony to play out with Turtle, a fearful, hesitant, and reluctant participant in these adventures. Clearly, Anthony projected his fears onto the Turtle puppet, which gave him the safe symbolic distance to work on these fears.

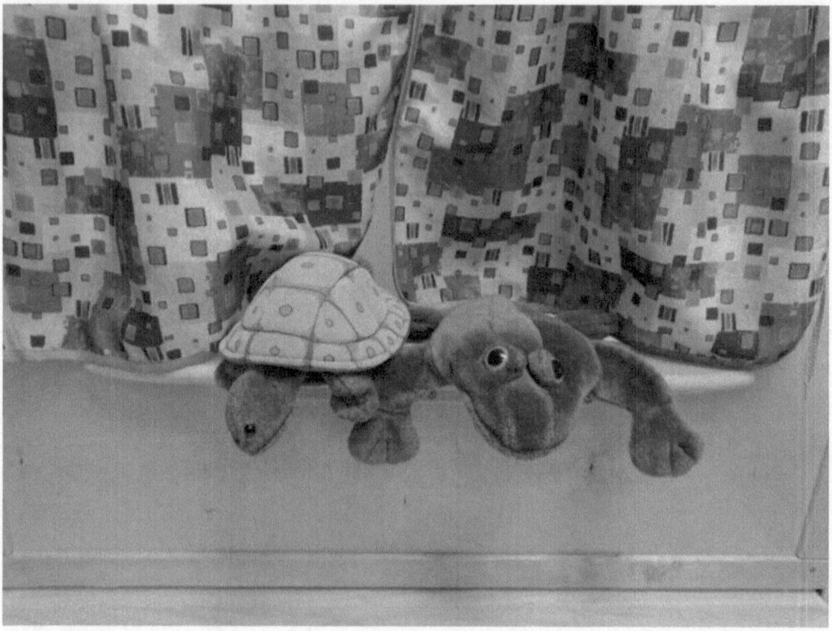

Figure 7.3 Turtle and Frog Puppets

In child-centered play therapy that extended over a three-year-period, the Frog puppet took the initiative under the direction of Anthony to coax the Turtle puppet to join in on countless daring and risky adventures involving hot-air balloons, landing in faraway places, attacks by natives, and barely escaping dire outcomes and eventually returning safely home. Among the adventures, Frog and Turtle met up with a bird named Woodstock, who came from a different planet, and talked Frog and an extremely reluctant Turtle into taking a trip to see his planet. Turtle's hesitation symbolized Anthony's fear of injury, separation, and loss. The spaceship taking them to planet Bird ran out of fuel, symbolizing Anthony's fear of further abandonment. Frog, working closely with Woodstock, however, discovered a spare source of emergency fuel in the spacecraft, and they were eventually able to return to earth. While on planet Bird, however, a fierce battle broke out with invading alien birds who tried to take over the planet, but the native birds fought back and sent the aliens away (emergence of rage/aggression symbolized by the violent fighting). Woodstock also took Frog and Turtle on a journey back to the land of dinosaurs and introduced them to each of the dinosaurs—two of the dinosaurs had initially thought the other was an enemy but became good friends and stuck together (symbolizing the longing for reunion with the birth mother, healing the rift and being reconnected forever). At the end of the session, Anthony was anxious that the baby animals be put on the shelf next to their mothers.

Anthony seemed to delight in the play drama of Frog terrifying Turtle by playing one trick after another on Turtle to entice him to join yet another high-risk daring adventure, including one across a desert involving multiple encounters with rattlesnakes. Anthony, represented by Frog, gained courage with each subsequent adventure and gradually encouraged Turtle to overcome his fears.

The story of how Frog and Turtle first met was interesting. Per Anthony, Frog stole Turtle's food. Thus, they had a big fight. While Frog tried escaping with the food, a log fell on him and Turtle saved his life. The story of their first meeting portrays Turtle as the hero who saves Frog's life. Perhaps it foreshadows Frog's projection of his fears onto Turtle (the therapist) knowing that he (the therapist/Turtle) would be strong enough to tolerate such projections. During the middle phase of the therapy, Anthony via his puppet (Frog) no longer taunted Turtle and instead encouraged him gradually to confront and face down his fears. Finally, the day arrived when Frog announced that it was time for Frog and Turtle to part. Anthony declared through Frog that Turtle no longer needed him and that Turtle was strong and brave enough to follow his own path.

The therapist was amazed that Frog, however, decided that before they would part, Frog and Turtle (in preparation for termination) would revisit the highlights of all the adventures they undertook together. One of the most dramatic of those adventures involved a hot-air balloon ride that Turtle was extremely reluctant to join in which they drifted way off course, requiring them to land on an isolated island. Promptly, Frog and Turtle were captured by the natives and hung upside down over a barbeque pit with the anticipation that they were going to be roasted. During this terrifying experience, Turtle complained to Frog about getting him into such a horrifying situation and that he would never follow Frog again if they could get off the island alive. Frog rose to the occasion and got free and then untied Turtle, and they both escaped the island in their hot-air balloon and finally arrived back home. At the end of the revisiting of some of their more dramatic adventures together, Frog and Turtle said a final good-bye and went their separate ways.

One of the remarkable lessons taught by the "Adventures of Frog and Turtle" was that when the fears or conflicts that drive the symbolic play scenarios are mastered, the play loses its compelling value. Anthony, because he was an unusually creative and imaginative child, instead of just losing interest altogether and seeking an abrupt termination built his preparation for termination right into the metaphor of the play drama by Frog and Turtle revisiting their past frightening adventures and celebrating their joint mastery before the final parting.

The authors consistently marvel at children's ability to work through complex scenarios and find meaning through play. The experience of having one's parent incarcerated is arguably among the most complex. A miniature jail in the playroom, along with props and puppets, may capture the focus and imagination of a child from the first session. The jail can represent such a wide range of meanings and feelings for a given child. Some children—for example, those who were directly harmed by the parent(s) in jail—may experience relief and safety in placing the miniature of the parent(s) behind bars and checking each session to make sure they are still there. Parents incarcerated because of substance abuse or commission of other crimes may have disappeared and reappeared in the child's life multiple times, and the jail may represent confusion, mystery, guilt, or self-blame for the child. In the case of Ralph, his incarcerated stepfather had physically and emotionally abused his mother during their two-year relationship, and terrified him and his younger maternal half-brother. Despite his stepfather's rages, at times he had also been a source of fun and attachment, thus creating a mix of feelings, especially anxiety, for Ralph regarding the absence/incarceration and the upcoming release back into the community.

Over several sessions, Ralph's play with the puppets, jail, makeshift rehabilitation center (using chairs), and props (including handcuffs) evolved. Initially, Ralph expressed his anger at his stepfather by assuming the role of policeman and "locking up the bad guys," which consisted of several puppets. Soon, one of the bad guys, a dragon puppet, was given special attention by Policeman Ralph. The other puppets remained in jail as Ralph began to engage in one-on-one teachings with the dragon about how to care for others, how to express his feelings through his words not through violence, and in exploring whether anyone could trust the dragon should Ralph decide to release him from jail.

Figure 7.4 depicts the jail Ralph created, in which the top level remained for the "bad guys" and the bottom level functioned as the area where the dragon learned new behaviors taught by Ralph. The dragon steadily moved and returned session after session to his lower level "closer to the street" as the release date approached. While treatment did not end here, the use of puppets during this phase enabled Ralph to begin his journey in processing his mixed feelings about his stepfather, creating an opportunity to reinforce that police officers in the community are available to help all children and families, preparing himself for the inevitable reunion, sharing his belief that people's behaviors can and do change, and attempting to understand that "badness" is not inherited. The latter especially helped Ralph in his attachment to his younger maternal half-brother, who was the biological son of his stepfather. Belief in rehabilitation, in goodness, and in a person's behaviors being "bad" but in the person having the overall potential for being "good" was a central and important theme in Ralph's play, and it all started with the help of puppets.

The authors have also used puppets successfully in working with children when words are either not available because of deep pain related to trauma (van der Kolk, 2014), or because of an actual language barrier. Dena was age 6 when she began therapy after having been referred by her pediatrician for

Figure 7.4 Scene of Jail/Rehabilitation by Ralph

an adjustment reaction. She suffered anxiety evidenced in an elevated heart rate when television news programs were playing in her home, and depressed mood evidenced in poor appetite, sleep problems, and crying daily. The child had recently moved to the United States, escaping her beloved war-torn country of Yemen. She had moved to the United States where her father had citizenship, but in doing so had to leave her mother behind. As her primary attachment figure, the loss was tremendous for Dena. Dena worried for her mother's safety and yearned for the comfort of routine and the life she once knew, to share meals with her mother as she had every night. Understandably, Dena was slow to warm to the idea of being in therapy, as she was adjusting to the new space, new language, and new person around her. The therapist placed plastic food toys, a small blanket, and several puppets in the room after learning from her father during the assessment that Dena yearned for the foods of her country, the companionship of her mother, and the routine she had followed every day for many years. Over several sessions, Dena created the same picnic scene with the puppets, and in her beautiful native language communicated with the puppets. She also communicated nonverbally, by gently stroking, feeding, and hugging each puppet throughout the meal. Figure 7.5 depicts Dena's final session, in which she prepared a meal for mother, daughter, and therapist using a pair of turtles (Dena and mother) and a deer (therapist). Through use of puppets, Dena could create a ritual that helped her to acclimate to her new home, and to connect and express the love she felt for her mother in Yemen.

Figure 7.5 A Brightly Colored Picnic by Dena

Concluding Remarks

Children are incredibly resourceful and make do with what is available, making puppets out of socks, gloves, oven mitts, and all sorts of materials found in the playroom! The authors hope you, too, consider inviting an array of puppet creativity into your practice. As evidenced in the stories of Eliza, Anthony, Ralph, and Dena, when puppets are added to a safe, nurturing, and warm play therapy environment, the opportunities for where the therapist and child can go together are truly boundless!

References

Crenshaw, D.A. (2008). *Therapeutic engagement with children and adolescents: Play, symbol, drawing and storytelling strategies.* Lanham, MD: Rowman & Littlefield Publishers.

Crenshaw, D., & Kelly, J. (2015). Dear Mr. Leprechaun: Nurturing resilience in children facing loss and grief. In D. A. Crenshaw, R. Brooks, & S. Goldstein (Eds.), *Play therapy interventions to nurture resilience* (pp. 82–106). New York: Guilford Press.

Crenshaw, D., & Mordock, J. (2005). *Understanding and treating the aggression of children: Fawns in Gorilla Suits.* NY: Jason Aronson Inc. Publishers.

Crenshaw, D, Rudy, C., Triemer, D., & Zingaro, J.C. (1986). Psychotherapy with abused children: Breaking the silent bond. *Residential Group Care & Treatment, 3*(4), 25–38.

Drewes, A. A., Bratton, S. C., & Schaefer, C. E. (2011). *Integrative play therapy.* New York: Wiley.

Gaskill, R. L., & Perry, B. D. (2014). The neurobiological power of play: Using the neurosequential model of therapeutics to guide play in the healing process. In C. A. Malchiodi & D. A. Crenshaw (Eds.), *Creative arts and play therapy for attachment problems* (pp. 178–196). New York: Guilford Press.

Gil, E., & Crenshaw, D. (2015). *Termination challenges in child psychotherapy.* NY: Guilford Publications.

Mills, J. C., & Crowley, R. J. (2014). *Therapeutic metaphors for children and the child within* (2nd ed.). New York: Brunner-Routledge.

Mordock, J. B. (2015). Psychodynamic play therapy. In D. A. Crenshaw & A. L. Stewart (Eds.), *Play therapy: A comprehensive guide to theory and practice* (pp. 66–82). New York: Guilford Press.

Porges, S. W. (2011). *The polyvagal theory: Neurophysiological foundations of emotions, attachment, communication, and self-regulation.* New York: Norton.

Schaefer, C. (2001). Prescriptive play therapy. *International Journal of Play Therapy, 10*(2), 57–73.

Schore, A. N. (2012). *The science of the art of psychotherapy* (Norton Series on Interpersonal Neurobiology). New York: Norton.

Siegel, D. J. (2012). *The developing mind: How relationships and the brain interact to shape who we are (2nd edition).* New York: Guilford Press.

Van der Kolk, B. (2014). *The body keeps the score: Brain, mind, and body in the healing of trauma.* New York: Viking Press.

8 Puppet Play in Adlerian Therapy

Kristin K. Meany-Walen

Adlerian theory is a popular approach to play therapy and is inclusive of many interventions that help children to move toward healing and adjustment. The use of puppets is one way play therapists intervene with children. This chapter provides a brief background of Adlerian play therapy (AdPT), followed by pragmatic approaches for implementing puppet play from an Adlerian perspective, and will wrap up with a case study in which the Adlerian play therapist uses puppet play throughout the play therapy process.

Adlerian Play Therapy Theory Overview

Adlerian theory was developed by Alfred Adler in the early 1900s to encompass his beliefs about personality development and the process of change. In the 1980s, Terry Kottman merged her beliefs about what is important and necessary for working with children with Adler's ideas, creating AdPT. Today, AdPT is an evidenced-based practice according to the Substance Abuse and Mental Health Services Administration (2017) and is a leading approach to play therapy (Lambert et al., 2007). The following explanation is a brief and simplistic overview of Adlerian theory and AdPT. For a more thorough explanation of theory and practices, I refer you to *Partners in Play: An Adlerian Approach to Play Therapy* (Kottman & Meany-Walen, 2016).

A few key concepts are the foundation for AdPT. First, people are socially embedded and have a need for belonging. They cannot be understood without understanding their social context. They function in relationships in ways that they believe (sometimes unconsciously) they belong (Kottman & Meany-Walen, 2016). For example, a child who gets "credit" in the family for being the smart kid will act in ways that get him or her attention for being smart (doing well at school, coming up with wise ideas, showing off grades, etc.). The child who gets attention by being the risk taker will act in ways that keep this status. Second, all behavior is purposeful. The purpose of the behavior is to secure belonging and significance, or get other needs met. Often, the purpose of the behavior is out of the client's awareness and not likely to change without intervention that increases the client's awareness. For example, if the risk-taking child gains attention or power from these types of behaviors, the child will continue to engage in these behaviors, which might become dangerous. If the child is able to get attention (or whatever is the identified need) in a different manner (being the helper, the creative one, or athletic), the child might reduce his or her need for risk-taking because it's no longer the only way to meet his or her needs. Third, people develop personality priorities, which are consistent ways of being and belonging that create predictability and security (Kfir, 2011). Fourth, Crucial Cs are defined by Lew and Bettner (2000) as assets children need in order to meet the demands of life; children who possess these characteristics are more likely to successfully adapt to challenges. The four Crucial Cs are connect, count, capable, and courage. Fifth, and the last concept described in this chapter, is *social interest*. Social interest is the sense of connectedness with others and behaving in ways that contribute to the betterment of society (Adler, 1927/1998).

AdPT follows four phases of counseling: (1) building a collaborative and egalitarian relationship, (2) investigating the child's lifestyle, (3) helping the child gain insight, and (4) reorienting/re-educating the child to think and behave in a more productive fashion (Kottman & Meany-Walen, 2016). In the first phase, the client and counselor work to build a relationship that is characterized by trust, collaboration, and equality. The counselor works to create an environment in which the child feels prized and valued. Before moving into subsequent phases, the counselor ensures the relationship has a steady foundation.

In the second phase of AdPT, the counselor works to understand the unique qualities of the child's lifestyle. According to Adler's successors, Maniacci, Sackett-Maniacci, and Mosak (2014, p. 66), "Lifestyle is the use of the personality, traits, temperament, and psychological and biological processes in order to find a place in the social matrix of life." In sum, it is the way in which people believe they belong and their actions that accompany those beliefs. The lifestyle is fairly consistent. The goal of the therapy is not to necessarily change the lifestyle but to understand the lifestyle so that interventions and goals of change can be adapted to meet and respond to the child's individual way of being. With the information learned during the second phase, the therapist conceptualizes and develops a treatment plan for the client.

The third phase is dedicated to helping the child gain insight (Kottman & Meany-Walen, 2016). The play therapist is active and directs the play and activities in ways aimed at igniting the child's insight and understanding into his or her patterns of thinking, feeling, behaving, and interacting. The therapist uses developmentally responsive and specifically designed interventions to help in this process. Helping the child understand these patterns allows the child to make informed decisions about if and how to make changes.

Lastly, the play therapist and child engage in reorienting the child in healthy, adjusted, and socially acceptable ways of being. The therapist might teach new skills, role-play, have the child join a play therapy group, or engage in other play activities that help provide opportunity for the child to learn and practice new skills. Eliciting feedback from parents, teachers, or other important people in the child's life is also used to monitor the child's progress and change.

Throughout the entire process, Adlerian play therapists include adults or family members of the child. They follow the same phases of therapy with the others in order to help understand the child from multiple perspectives, create optimal environments and relationships for the child's positive changes, and assess changes made. Moreover, because Adlerian theory holds that people are socially embedded, with every person making meaning and connection in relation to one another, as the child changes, all other relationships change. The constant adjustments within the family or teacher-child relationship are processed and assessed for progress.

Implementation

The nature of AdPT allows for an infinite number of ways in which to implement and use puppets in the therapeutic process. The flexibility of the intervention within this theory insists on the therapist's and child's creativity. However, for some play therapists, the nebulousness of specific and exact interventions can feel overwhelming. As I outline several important considerations and ideas for implementing puppet play in the Adlerian play therapy session, I encourage readers to think of how they might use puppets with their current or future clients. The following ideas can be adapted and manipulated to meet clients' unique needs.

The therapist's collection of puppets should elicit a variety of feelings and allow for a range of creative expression. See Table 8.1 for a list of categories. Remember that clients are not required to use the puppets in any particular sort of fashion, but the categories help therapists to be sure they have a range of puppets available for their clients.

Adlerian play therapists' interventions are designed purposefully with a desired goal in mind. The four overarching goals of a puppet interventions are to (1) help build or strengthen the collaborative relationship between

Table 8.1 Puppet Categories

People	*Animals*	*Fantasy*	*Safety/Protection*	*Characters*
Males/Females Young/Old Variety of skin shades	Dinosaur Bear Bird Skunk Puppy/Cat Snake	Three-headed dragon Wizard King/Queen Prince/Princess Joker Unicorn Witch	Firefighter Doctor Police officer Teacher	Scaredy Squirrel Harry Potter Peppa Pig Elmo

client and counselor, (2) investigate or gather more information about the child's lifestyle, (3) help the child gain insight into his or her lifestyle, and (4) teach or practice new skills, attitudes, or beliefs. Within each phase, different puppet interventions are employed. Adlerian play therapists also use various degrees of directedness in the puppet play.

In phase 1, building the egalitarian relationship, the counselor might introduce himself or herself to the client by using puppets. For example, "Hi, Marcus, I'm Penguin and I'm so happy to meet you. I notice you're wearing a monster truck shirt. I really like monster truck shirts." The therapist can instruct the client to pick a puppet and have a conversation between the puppets. The therapist can notice things about the puppet, the child, the reasons for coming to therapy, and so forth. The child can also ask things of the therapist or the therapist's puppet.

- *Introductions.* The client can introduce himself or herself to the counselor or the counselor can introduce himself or herself to the client through/as the puppet. An example of a therapist introduction could be, "Hi, Rachel, I'm Zoey Zebra, and I have lots of stripes. Sometimes I use my stripes to blend in and other times I use my stripes to be different and stand out. Did you know that all zebras have different stripes?" The therapist might invite the child to pick a puppet and introduce the puppet to him or her. Although not necessary, it can be helpful to remind the client to introduce the puppet, not himself or herself (similar to the example of Zoey Zebra).
- *Description of the presenting issues.* The therapist can use puppets to describe, or engage in a conversation with the client about, the presenting issue. For example, the therapist chooses the turtle puppet and says, "I'm Timothy Turtle and lately I've been feeling sad and confused because my mommy and daddy don't live together anymore. I used to always be out of my shell but lately I've been scared and I just want to hide in my shell. I get bored and I cry a lot. When I'm in play therapy, I can play and talk with Ms. Kristin and it helps me to feel better."
- *Explanation about the play therapy process.* Similar to the descriptions above, the explanation comes from the puppet. The therapist engages the child in dialogue or simply gives information. Using the wizard puppet (and a mythical, magical voice), the therapist says, "I am Wizard McWizardson and I am here to tell you all about the playroom and play therapy. There are three things you must know: (1) You can play with the toys in many of the ways you would like, (2) sometimes you will get to decide what we do in here and other times Ms. Kristin gets to decide, and (3) Ms. Kristin's job is to make sure you're safe, so if you tell her that someone is hurting you, she will have to talk with people who can help you. (A developmentally appropriate description of confidentiality can also be described here.) What do you think about those rules?" If there

is discussion, the therapist can decide when to use the wizard to communicate and when to respond as the therapist.

In phase 2, exploring the child's lifestyle, the therapist is interested in knowing about the child's mistaken beliefs (Kottman & Meany-Walen, 2016; Mosak & Maniacci, 1999), goals of behavior (Dreikurs & Soltz, 1964), personality priorities (Kfir, 2011; Kottman & Ashby, 1999), Crucial Cs (Lew & Bettner, 2000), and family atmosphere/constellation (Kottman & Meany-Walen, 2016). The counselor aims to know how the child makes decisions and solves problems, the child's assets and perceived assets, and how the child functions in various situations (i.e., with other children, at school, with adults, etc.). The counselor might be less directive during this phase, with his or her primary role being setting up or suggesting a topic for a puppet show. The therapist might direct the client to conduct a show independently, with siblings or family members, or with the therapist. The decision will depend upon what the therapist wants to know and what the therapist already knows about the child and his or her circumstances.

- *Family communication.* The therapist directs the client to identify a puppet for each member of the family and have discussions between two or three puppets at a time. The therapist notices which puppet the child assigned to which family member and if any family members were left out. The therapist also attempts to understand *how* the different members communicate and *what* they communicate about. It may be particularly noteworthy to identify who argues, who supports one another, who are allies, who are leaders, who gets his or her way, or who has power/doesn't have power in the house, and so forth. In family sessions, each family member can choose his or her own puppet and have discussions with one another.
- *Puppet creation.* In this technique, the client doesn't choose a puppet that is already available, but rather he or she makes a puppet to represent himself or herself or another person, or someone who can make everything better. This puppet can be used to do one of the other puppet interventions and/or can make reappearing cameos throughout the play therapy process.
- *Creating a story.* The client is instructed to create a story with a beginning, middle, and end (younger children have more difficulty completing this task), or a story where there is a problem that needs to be fixed. The child is responsible for the development of the plot, and the therapist might collaborate when asked. The play therapist looks for examples of how the client identifies problems, how he or she attempts to solve problems, what assets he or she has and employs, and who else might be involved in the problem or solution.

In phase 3, helping the child gain insight, the therapist's main objective is to create interventions that help bring about an increased awareness on the part of the client about his or her ways of functioning. These include his or her assets, goals of behavior, and other dimensions of the lifestyle described earlier. During this phase of therapy, the counselor is more directive and will sometimes interject ideas or plots, or plot twists, into the stories in order to help the client overcome or address particular issues.

- *Fellow traveler/wise wizard.* The fellow traveler or wise wizard can accompany any story without being the main figure. The therapist introduces this puppet as someone who can offer advice when requested or when the puppet believes he or she has something valuable to offer the story characters. In a story with a problem that the child is unable to solve in a healthy manner, the wizard could join the story and say, "Ellie, I remember that you are really good at solving puzzles. I bet if you see this situation as a puzzle, you'll be able to put together clues in order to come up with a solution." Or "Leo, when you jumped over the river, you forgot about your pals, skunk and bear. You seem to forget your friends a lot and they feel sad about that."
- *Alter ego.* The alter ego is similar to a sportscaster or story narrator who expresses underlying feelings, motivations, or concerns of the client (or others in the client's life) and verbalizes them in the session. The alter ego may or may not be a part of the play. The main objective is to metacommunicate to the client. An example is a peacock puppet who says to a child who frequently makes crafts to give to her mother, "I'm guessing you like to take these with you because you like to make your mom happy." The puppet could talk to the client, to another puppet, or to the therapist. The therapist and puppet could have a brief conversation. In the previous example, the therapist could respond to the peacock, "I know her mom loves her so much no matter what AND sometimes kids get worried that they will disappoint their parents and so they work really hard to make them happy."

The final phase of Adlerian play therapy, reorienting/re-educating, focuses on helping the child think about things differently and behave differently in various situations. To assess the child's changes, the counselor can rely on feedback from the client and important people in the child's life (e.g., family and teachers); observe the child for changes in behaviors, attitudes, and feelings in session; and/or observe the child in other settings (e.g., waiting room or school).

- *Game show puppets.* The client picks a puppet who will compete in a game show challenge. The therapist can act as the game show host or can have a puppet play this role. The therapist also chooses a puppet who will be a contestant. The therapist's puppet is used to provide correct answers in the event the child cannot, encourage the child, and occasionally provide incorrect answers to the host. It can also be fun to have game show music to start the game or some kind of buzzer to indicate a puppet's readiness to answer a question. The questions should be tailored to the client's circumstances. The following is an example of a child who misbehaves in school. Host: "Welcome contestants! I am going to ask you questions and you will do your best to provide a correct answer. If you provide an incorrect answer, you will work as a team to come up with a correct answer. Here we go! Name one positive way to behave when you see a classmate do something mean to another kid." Or "Describe a positive way to act if you are cut in line by another kid."

- *Preemptive puppet play*. In this technique, the therapist (or parent or teacher) uses puppets to play out or tell a story that is similar to the child's experience or situations in which the child experiences difficulties. The goal is to help the child see new ways of doing things and to metaphorically prepare for events (e.g., going to a new school, visiting mom or dad, staying with a new babysitter). If the child is staying with a new babysitter, the adult (therapist, parent, or teacher) enacts a play in which one puppet is the mom and/or dad, another puppet is the child, and another puppet is the babysitter. Mom and/or dad puppet reinforce to child puppet that they are going to dinner and a movie. They will check in between 7:30 and 8:00 and be home when the child is sleeping. The babysitter puppet knocks on the door, mom and/or dad puppet answer the door excitedly and help the sitter and child begin to play. The child puppet acts excited and nervous (or however they think the child will act/feel). Mom and/or dad puppet say good-bye, give hugs and kisses, and remind child of the plan. Mom and/or dad leave, and the child puppet and sitter puppet play happily. Mom and/or dad puppets call to check in, child puppet goes to bed, parent(s) come home, and sitter puppet leaves. Child wakes up happy. This role-play can be repeated several times to reinforce the process. The child can take over the role of the child puppet or other puppets. The adult facilitating this technique uses the other puppets to reinforce the behavior that is desired of the child and help reduce the child's anxiety.
- *Role reversal*. This isn't a specific technique per se; rather, it is the reuse of any of the above described interventions or any other strategies a therapist might particularly like. The goal is for the child to be able to express how he or she reacts to particular situations or demonstrate a change in attitudes, beliefs, and behaviors. The therapist assesses the child's changes, gives information, encourages, or acknowledges changes the child has made. For example, the client could *describe the presenting issue* by having a conversation about how the issue has changed. In the *puppet creation*, the therapist might make note of any changes that were made in the creation or description of the puppet. A child could *create a new story* or be the *wise wizard* in a story where the therapist presents a problem.

Case Study

This case is a compilation of multiple cases and fictional details used to mask identities. Tiffany, a 6-year-old, first-grade, European American female, came to counseling at the decision of her father (Jeremy) due to family dynamics he feared were contributing to Tiffany's aggressive and erratic behaviors. Jeremy is Tiffany's adoptive father. Tiffany is an only child. Her biological mother (Lauren) and he separated six months ago, after Lauren was caught having an affair with a woman. Jeremy moved Tiffany to a new house within the same city. According to Jeremy, there was no yelling or aggression in the home when Tiffany was present. Lauren does not want to raise Tiffany but does expect occasional visits with her daughter.

In my (KMW) first meeting with Tiffany, I used a puppet to introduce myself and invited her to do the same. I used a sheep puppet because I had learned that she really likes farm animals. I said, "Hi, Tiffany, I'm feeling a little baaaashful (playful sheep sound) but I'm soooo glad you're here and I'm happy to meet you. I am going to tell you a little about play therapy and a little about Ms. Kristin. You can choose to use a puppet or be yourself to introduce yourself to me!" Tiffany watched timidly and uncertainly as I continued. "Lots of kids come to play with Ms. Kristin when they feel sad, angry, confused, scared, or hurt. Sometimes I feel those things too, and I play and talk in here. Lots of times, I feel better when I leave the playroom. Ms. Kristin is a nice grown-up who sometimes lets me choose what to play and sometimes she decides what to play. She has lots of fun ideas for us to try. Tell us a little bit about you."

Tiffany chose the three-headed dragon and said, "I'm Tiffany the Terrible Dragon. I'm in first grade, I'm really smart, and I have blonde hair."

"Bahhhh," said the sheep, "Tiffany the Terrible Dragon, I notice you and Ms. Kristin have the same color hair. You two probably have lots in common." Dragon and Sheep briefly continued this type of conversation and then moved into other play activities aimed at building the therapeutic relationship.

During the third session and in phase 2, Tiffany asked to play puppets again. Together, Tiffany and I decided to make up a story about what it's like to be a three-headed dragon.

Tiffany: I look really scary and sometimes I get angry. People always think I'm bad and I get in trouble a lot. Most of the time it's not even my fault! I get blamed for other kids being naughty!

Sheep: I bet you feel really angry when you get blamed for other kids' behaviors.

Tiffany the Terrible Dragon: Yep. And, my teacher is so mean! She just hates dragons and that's why she's mean to me.

Sheep: Even dragons feel sad when they are not treated fairly. I wonder if dragons get in trouble at home too?

Dragon: Nope. Dragons don't get in trouble. Mommy and daddy dragons love their kids, even when they burp smoke and blow fire.

Sheep and Dragon carried on this dialogue with the puppets being the characters. That is, I stayed in the metaphor with the child and didn't directly apply the play to Tiffany's life. In my regular meetings with her dad, I learned that Tiffany behaved more erratically at school than at home. Her teacher was a woman who had some similar physical features to her mom. The behaviors were more pronounced after spending a day with her mother, which was infrequent and inconsistent. We discussed the importance of consistency and ways he could support her upon her return.

Over the next several sessions and into phase 3, Sheep became a regular figure in the playroom activities. Tiffany frequently asked for her and talked directly to her. Sheep acted in the role of an *alter ego* and often the voice of reason who meta-communicated throughout the session. Some examples of statements used by Sheep were: "Dragon [notice, the dropping of 'Terrible'], sometimes you feel angry and then you blow out fire. It can be hard to know when it's going to happen and how to control yourself." Or "When you miss your mommy, your tummy feels upset like a volcano. The only thing that feels better is to explode." Or "You're glad to have your daddy and you still miss your mommy." Or "You're worried your daddy will leave you too." Or "I wonder if when you're mean to your friends, you think you don't have to worry about them being mean to you."

I continued to work with her dad in order to help him honestly, and developmentally appropriately, process Tiffany's feelings and the circumstances between him and Lauren. We discussed ways to help Tiffany in school and ways to communicate with the teachers about what is going on for her, and strategies that might be helpful in her classroom and with her peers. I taught him to do *preemptive play* with Tiffany. Jeremy also began his own counseling, which helped him to take care of himself during this process.

As we moved into the final phase of Adlerian play therapy, Sheep was able to teach Tiffany and Dragon with helpful strategies. For example, Sheep said, "Hey, Dragon, I learned something that helps me when I feel sheepish. I slowly breathe in through my nose and then I breathe out through my mouth. Let's try it! Smell the cake (breathe in) and blow out the candles (blow out)." They practiced this several times and then used this strategy throughout subsequent sessions to emphasize the technique. I also talked with Jeremy about using it at home and at school. Sheep also commented on Tiffany's improvements, "I noticed you used to give up and throw things when you got frustrated. Most of the time, you don't do that anymore. Give me a high hoof (sheep talk for high-five)!"

Because Tiffany and Jeremy really liked the *preemptive puppet play* and Jeremy became the firefighter puppet, I invited Dragon, Firefighter, and Sheep to have a final session together. They took turns telling stories and interacting. Each puppet also had a chance to tell the other puppets what they liked and appreciated about the other puppets.

Conclusion

Adlerian play therapy allows for interventions that are creative, are responsive to individual clients, and are directive and nondirective. The therapist decides when and how to use puppets in the therapeutic process based on the phase of therapy and interests of the client. The suggested interventions outlined in this chapter are suggestions and not recipes. The intent is for readers to use these as a launching pad of ideas, and to integrate their own creativity and clients' uniqueness into the puppet interventions.

References

Adler, A. (1998). *Understanding human nature.* London, England: Oneworld Oxford. (Original work published in 1927).

Dreikurs, R., & Soltz, V. (1964). *Children: The challenge.* New York, NY: Hawthorn/Dutton.

Kfir, N. (2011). *Personality and priorities: A typology.* Bloomington, IN: Author House.

Kottman, T., & Ashby, J. (1999). Using Adlerian personality priorities to custom-design consultation with parents of play therapy clients. *International Journal of Play Therapy, 8*(2), 77–92.

Kottman, T., & Meany-Walen, K. K. (2016). *Partners in play: An Adlerian approach to play therapy* (3rd ed.). Alexandria, VA: American Counseling Association.

Lambert, S. F., LeBlanc, M., Mullen, J. A., Ray, D., Baggerly, J., White, J., & Kaplan, D. (2007). Learning more about those who play in session: The national play therapy in counseling practices project (phase 1). *Journal of Counseling & Development, 85*, 42–46. doi:10.1002/j.1556-6678.2007.tb00442.x

Lew, A., & Bettner, B. L. (2000). *A parent's guide to understanding and motivating children.* Newton Centre, MA: Connexions Press.

Maniacci, M., Sackett-Maniacci, L., & Mosak, H. (2014). Adlerian psychotherapy. In D. Wedding & R. J. Corsini (Eds.), *Current psychotherapies* (10th ed., pp. 55–94). Belmont, CA: Thomson Brooks/Cole.

Mosak, H., & Maniacci, M. (1999). *A primer of Adlerian psychology.* Philadelphia, PA: Brunner/Mazel.

Substance Abuse and Mental Health Services Administration (SAMHSA). (2017). *Adlerian play therapy.* Retrieved from http://nrepp.samhsa.gov/ProgramProfile.aspx?id=160

9 Puppet Play in Solution-Focused Brief Therapy

Elsa Soto Leggett

Solution-focused brief therapy, also called solution-focused counseling, has revealed the ability to be flexible, brief, and effective in working with children, adolescents, adults, and families in various settings that include school, agencies, and hospitals. It recognizes the client's strengths and capabilities to access change and create changes to develop a more satisfying life (Bond, Woods, Humphrey, Symes, & Green, 2013; Corcoran & Stephenson, 2000; Leggett, 2009). Solution-focused brief therapy (SFBT) uses signature questions to help focus on the change a client wants to create. The counselor listens to the client's words and absorbs their meaning, and then formulates these signature questions using the client's key words and phrases. This exchange creates collaboration between the counselor and the client that leads to new thinking and co-constructing new and/or alternative meaning. This new thinking creates an avenue toward change and solutions (Leggett, 2017; Trepper et al., 2008). The various components of SFBT are built over time. The description of the problem invites the client to tell his or her story. While little time is devoted to the exploration of the problem, this allows the counselor opportunity to (a) reorient the client to the problem, (b) search for clues as to how others perceive the problem situation, and (c) notice changes (Gillen, 2011). During this give-and-take, clear goals are articulated. The miracle question helps the client to look beyond the present, beyond the problem, and into the future. The client opens up his or her imagination to a time when the problem is gone. Relationship questions reveal who and what is important to the client. They add clarity to what the miracle looks like, what is different, and who notices these differences, thus helping the client to visualize the future without the problem or when the situation is better. The exploration for exceptions to the client's problem or situation is another key component. Exceptions are those moments in the past when the miracle was already happening, already taking place in the client's life. These are moments when the problem did not occur or occurred less frequently. To help a client recognize these exceptions, Murphy (1994) suggests these five methods: (a) elicit times when the problem was absent, (b) elaborate on the features and circumstances of these times, (c) expand the exception to other contexts, (d) evaluate the exception based on the goals and details of the miracle, and (e) empower the client to maintain that change over time. The solution message is the final step of the SFBT process. This final step provides a take-home message for the client (Nims, 2011).

Solution-Focused Play Therapy

As a *talk therapy* SFBT may include limitations on a child's or adolescent's tendencies to express one's self through nonverbal means. Likewise, a young client may not be capable of cognitively understanding some abstract concepts such as *miracles* and *goals*. At times, the ability of a young client to respond to therapeutic interventions may be found in the context of his or her level of developmental function. The counselor should not push a client beyond this current developmental level. A counselor working with a young client, while searching how to best serve this population, oftentimes makes the client's needs fit the particular counseling model. To facilitate a client's verbal and nonverbal expression of thoughts, feelings, and behaviors, it becomes necessary to consider therapeutic approaches designed especially for children and adolescents and the use of a combination of talking and play. By expanding on the basic SFBT model with a more therapeutic flexibility, the needs of a young client can be adequately managed (Leggett, 2017; Nims, 2011). The use of solution-focused play therapy (SFPT) provides an effective integration to meet the need of a young client. While considering the flexibility of SFPT, the counselor can recognize how the signature components of SFBT can be successfully integrated with play.

Solution-Focused Play Therapy

SFPT therefore expands the basic solution-focused model and provides both verbal and nonverbal tools for expression. SFPT uses signature SFBT questions and experiential activities to help focus on how a client can change. It allows adjustments according to the needs of the client. Furthermore, it increases the communications between the counselor and client while facilitating the relationship (Leggett, 2009). The experiential activities basic in play therapy include books and literature, drawing, prescribed selection of toys, puppets, and sandtray to serve as the medium of this dialogue (Leggett, 2017; Nims, 2011). The use of these mediums helps the client to establish the groundwork for new thinking while co-constructing with the counselor movement toward change and solutions (Trepper et al., 2008). SFPT is crafted with the client's specific details in mind: needs, situation or problem, developmental level, and culture and diversity.

SFPT Process With Puppets

The use of puppets in SFPT allows for an emotional distance to be created between the problem or situation and the client. This distance can diminish

Table 9.1 Puppets With Solution-Focused Play Therapy

Solution-Focused Play Therapy	*Describing the Problem*	*Miracle Question*	*Exploring Exceptions*	*Scaling Question*	*Solution Message*
PUPPETS	✔	✔	✔	✔	✔

the fear, guilt, timidity, and various other feelings the client may be experiencing. This will also allow the client to project his or her feelings about the conflicts outwardly, externalizing the problem (Alter, 2001). A variety of puppets should be available for the client. Some counselors make their own hand or mitten puppets; various accessories such as spoons, pencils, and handmade paper creations can add to puppet presentations. As well, an assortment of sizes should be included. Of course, a good assortment can be purchased commercially. Table 9.1 clarifies areas in SFPT where puppets have been helpful to this author. Keep in mind the counselor is only limited by his or her own imagination and creativity.

Describing the Problem and Establishing Goals

"What brings you here today?"

This initiation step invites the client to tell his or her story. The client identifies what he or she wants different or to change, which leads to establishing a goal. This goal should (a) fit the young client's needs; (b) be relevant, meaningful, and specific to the situation; and (c) be concrete, behavioral, and measurable. At times a young client has difficulty explaining or expressing the problem he or she is facing, and the use of puppets can be very helpful.

Problem Puppet

A puppet can provide important elements with the onset of counseling. It can help the client identify the problem or situation and also help in externalizing it. As always, a variety of puppets and/or stuffed animals should be available for the client's selection. This initial session will allow the client to describe a current problem. Begin by asking the client to select a puppet that could represent the problem or situation being described. *I was wondering if you could find a puppet that matches the problem you want to describe.* A name can be given to the puppet selected and be used for future conversation about the problem or situation. Allow the client to use the puppet to share the details of the problem. If the client is describing a situation that involves others, then additional puppets may be used, each with its own identity. In order to keep the description of the problem confined to a small portion of the session, it may be best to only have two or three key persons/puppets.

It can also be helpful to use a puppet to externalize a problem. Once the client has described the problem and given it a name, the puppet can be removed from the presence of the client or even the room. Once the puppet is gone from sight, the exchange would then change to how life will look without the problem. *Now that (problem's name) is gone, how do you feel? What will your day look like now that (problem's name) is gone*? Furthermore, without this puppet present a smooth introduction to the miracle question of a day without the problem can be presented.

Miracle Question

> *"If a miracle happened tonight while you were asleep and you woke up tomorrow to find that the problem that brought you here today was solved by magic, what would be the first small thing you would notice that told you this miracle has happened?"*

The miracle question is intended to help the client look beyond the present into the future. It helps the client to visualize how life will be different when the goal is achieved. This step can prove to be the most difficult for the youngest of clients due to its abstract nature and the developmental level of each client. Sometimes a change in wording or a question format is sufficient; for example: "*Imagine that tomorrow was a perfect day and the problem you are having today is gone. What would that perfect day look like?*" Moreover, puppets can be used to contribute to the facilitation of this stage.

Miracle Day Puppet

A new puppet should be selected for the miracle day if a problem puppet was previously used. This one will help the client describe this day without the problem or issue present. A variety of puppets should be available to the client. However, if the client used a puppet selected to represent him or her, then the client may choose to use the same puppet or a new puppet. This is something the client can decide. Once the client has decided or selected a puppet, it can be used to role-play or describe this perfect day. *Can you find a puppet that can help you describe your perfect day? The puppet that could be you on this day? What are some things you might be saying differently on this day? What else would you be doing differently on this day? Use your puppet to show what you would be doing.*

The miracle day question allows the client to see beyond his or her world and gain other perspectives. This type of puppet play in the miracle day permits the client to share or demonstrate how other important or key people might interact on this day. Therefore, other puppets might be added to this puppet play. *Can you use other puppets to show who would be around to notice this day? What would they be noticing that was different about you? What would they say to you that would let you know they noticed this difference?*

Exploring for Exceptions

> *"Can you think of another time when you did not have a problem with _____________?"*

The exploration for exceptions includes the search for times when the problem is not happening or is less severe. It can also include times in the past similar to the miracle picture. Additional questions provide insight to action taken or behaviors and choices that contributed to the exceptions that occurred. The recognition of these exceptions, even the smallest ones, is important and contributes to the hope that comes from SFPT.

Miracle Day Puppet

The client should be encouraged to consider exceptions. Allowing the client to use puppet play to role-play the exception may allow him or her to contemplate the actions or behaviors that contributed to the exception. Begin by asking the client to consider a time in the recent past when he or she may have experienced a small part of his or her perfect day or miracle. For some young clients it may be simplest to concentrate on only one exception rather than the exploration of several. Allow the client to consider which puppet to use for this puppet play. The client may want to use the miracle day puppet, one self-identified as the client, or he or she may decide on a new puppet. This is a decision the client can make. Keep in mind that if the client selects a puppet that has been named to use this name in the questions. *Can you use __________ to show me the time you were talking about, that time when the problem wasn't so bad?* Once more, it is important to allow the client time to both conceptualize the details of the exception and to describe or role-play those details to the counselor. The idea is for the client to become aware of his or her contributions to making the exception occur. This time spent on the exploration should not be rushed and should create the opportunity for self-awareness and empowerment.

Scaling Questions

> *"On a scale of 0 to 10, with 10 meaning you have every confidence that this problem can be solved and 0 meaning no confidence at all, where would you put yourself today?"*

These questions allow a client to evaluate his or her own progress. A tangible representation of the scaling question can make this step concrete and more meaningful to a young client. The use of puppets can bring valuable meaning to this question. The format of the question may be altered to fit the selection of the puppet and scaling question. An example of such a rewording might be: *On a scale of 0 to 10, with 10 being your miracle picture/perfect day, and 0 being the worst day, where would you say you are today, right now?*

Miracle Day Puppet

The client may believe it is easiest to place his or her puppet on the scale. A physical response to the scaling question can provide a unique format. On the floor designate a location for a number line marking off the locations for 0 through 10 if space provides. If not, then 0, 5, and 10 will work as well. Then when asking the client the scaling question, ask him or her to place his or her puppet on the number line. If the client has given the puppet a name, it would be important to use that name when using the puppet in this activity. If a floor scale is too large for a smaller setting, a simple number line can be used. The scaling question can be used to ask various assessment questions. *If 10 is the miracle day you are hoping for and 0 is a day without that hope, where do you see ___________ (puppet's name or yourself) today? If 10 shows how much you believe the change is coming and 0 means you don't believe, where do you see _________ (puppet's name or yourself) today?*

Follow this up with questions about how this decision was made and what needs to be different to be closer to 10. Always use small increments to encourage small changes. *How did you know that ___________ (puppet's name or you) was at a 6? What needs to be different for ___________ (puppet's name or you) to move from a 6 to say 6 ½?*

0 1 2 3 4 5 6 7 8 9 10

Solution Message

The final step of the SFPT process is the solution message. This time offers the opportunity to summarize the details of the session in a way that is meaningful for the client. There are three parts to this message: compliments, the bridge, and the task or suggestion. The compliments are affirmations of strengths about the client that were revealed in the participation and efforts communicated through play in the session. Past successes, exceptions, and attempts at reducing the problem or changing the situation are acknowledged. For the client it may be helpful to create a list of these. A drawing of one such intentional act could also be created by the client. The client could keep either of these so that he or she can recall his or her thoughts, feelings, and actions that contributed to the outcome. This is followed with the bridge that connects the past success or exception to the task or suggestion. Therefore, the bridge acts as an explanation for the task or suggestion the counselor will offer. The solution task or suggestion should be something small and simple the client can aim for in the near future. For a client, the task should also be directly relevant to the goal and is likely to be more successful when it is something the client has already achieved a level of success with. Therefore, the solution task might easily be selected from the compliments list or drawing. Keep in mind that with SFPT the notion is that small tasks lead to experiencing more success, and small changes lead to big changes.

Puppets

In the solution message, a puppet can be used by the client to demonstrate how the task or suggestion might be carried out or how it will look. The client can use the miracle day puppet or a puppet already self-identified by the client as himself or herself. This puppet play may help the client visualize what his or her actions or behaviors might look like outside of the counseling office. *Using your puppet, can you show me what that might look like when you decide to ___________?*

Additional Considerations

This SFPT approach may be used with children and adolescents. It allows the counselor to make the selection to use one or more of the solution-focused techniques described to meet the client's needs and the counselor's comfort level. This SFPT with puppets can be used with children as young as 4 through adolescence, with consideration given to the client's emotional and cognitive development. Age and developmental level will also impact the amount of time it takes for a client to progress through this counseling process. The time needed for the client to discuss the details of a problem or situation, the details of the miracle day, an exception, and so forth will vary. This can be especially true with the use of puppets and other experiential activities. Therefore, it would not be unusual to have a client of any age progress through the session slowly, sometimes only progressing through one or two steps during one session.

Ruby's Case

Ruby is a young Latina girl in third grade. Her parents and teacher were concerned about the anxiety she was displaying. She is increasingly having difficulty getting to school, and on some occasions when she has already arrived at school she does not want to change classes. Ruby has no diagnosis nor has she been identified for special education services.

Session One

It was important to begin our counseling relationship by creating a safe and accepting environment for Ruby and to allow her to build her trust in me. It was also important to begin exploring her perspective of her world. I began by sharing the book *The Way I Feel* by Janan Cain (2000). With this book, Ruby would be better able to describe, understand, and identify various feelings she has experienced. I read the book to her, taking time to enjoy the contents and illustrations. Then I asked Ruby to identify three feelings she had recently. This portion of the session took time as she flipped back and forth through the pages of the book selecting her most recent feelings.

Of the three feelings Ruby identified, *scared* caught my attention. I decided to focus on this feeling. First I asked Ruby if this was a feeling she would like to change. Ruby gave this some thought and decided that it was. We agreed to make this the focus, the goal for our time together.

Next I asked Ruby to select a puppet that to her best resembles this feeling of *scared*. Ruby selected a green and purple dragon finger puppet made of felt. She also decided to name this puppet *Mr. Roar*. Ruby slipped this puppet on her finger and we explored her feelings. The following questions helped her to describe Mr. Roar, the problem, and how she was experiencing her time when he was with her.

How do you know Mr. Roar is with you? Does your body feel different when Mr. Roar is there? What kind of things do you say when he is with you? What do you say to your family or teachers that lets them know Mr. Roar is present?

This exchange allowed me to understand her situation and perspective.

I indicated to Ruby our time today was almost over. I let her know when we would be meeting again. At this time, I also provided a solution message to end this session. I summarized what feelings she identified from the book. I also restated the goal she identified: Change her feeling of scary. I talked about Mr. Roar and the comments she made about when he is with her. I wanted to amplify her ability to recognize Mr. Roar and his impact on her. Then I let her know that in our next session we would talk about what it is like when Mr. Roar has less control, less impact on her. I wanted her to prepare for the miracle question, and I wanted her to give thought to how life will be different when Mr. Roar is gone or under her control. This idea brought a small smile to her face as she began to consider what that would be like.

Session Two

This session focused on the miracle question and creating the image of Ruby's miracle day, or her perfect day without being scared. During the time between our first and second session, Ruby's anxiety had remained the same. When Ruby returned, it was evident that her level of comfort and trust in me had increased. She entered the room with ease and had a small soft smile.

We began with a short summary of the previous session. Ruby immediately looked for Mr. Roar, her problem puppet. Then I reminded her that we were going to talk about a time when Mr. Roar was not with her. Because the miracle question can be too abstract for some young clients, a change in the wording or presentation can be helpful. *Think about a day when Mr. Roar is not with you. He is gone. Is it okay for me to put him out of the room?* With this suggestion, I placed Mr. Roar outside the door. With the problem puppet gone, this young client could begin to consider what this day would be like. *Now, think about this day without him, your perfect day. Can you find a puppet that can help you describe your perfect day? The puppet could be you on this day*. Ruby returned to the bucket of puppets, returning to the collection of felt finger puppets. With time, she found a yellow chick finger puppet and claimed it as her miracle/perfect day puppet. Ruby named this puppet *Sunshine*, to match the color. She placed Sunshine on her finger and wiggled it around as she responded to my questions. *What are some things you might be saying differently on this day? What else would you be doing differently today? Use Sunshine to show what you would be doing. Who might notice Sunshine is with you today instead of Mr. Roar? What are some things they will see different about you?*

This give-and-take took time, and it was important to allow Ruby time to ponder her responses and to add details as she thought of them. It gave her the chance to see a day without being scared to leave her parents or when changing classrooms and activities at school. We closed this session with a solution message that touched on what Ruby noticed would be different when Mr. Roar was gone and Sunshine was with her. I also reminded her when we would see each other again. I explained at that time we would be looking for times when her perfect day with Sunshine was already happening. I asked her to notice times when she saw these things happening, to look for exceptions when her perfect day was already happening. She agreed.

Session Three

As previously discussed with Ruby, this session focused on exploring exceptions, those times when the problem was less evident or not present. Again, there was no report of change in Ruby's anxiety in a positive or negative way since our last session. In preparation for this session, I made sure my table scale was ready and accessible. This scale is a paper number line that displays 0 through 10. While it is generally displayed on a wall about four feet from the ground, for this session it would be placed on the table. Ruby entered the room with the same amount of comfort displayed in the last session. I started by asking Ruby what she recalled from our previous session. I filled in any gaps with details. This allowed her to recall the important and noteworthy details of the session. Then I drew her attention to the paper number line and explained this would be used for a scaling question. I asked her to find Mr. Roar and Sunshine. Mr. Roar was placed on the 0 and Sunshine on the 10. *I want you to think about what we talked about earlier. Remember when you described what it was like to have Mr. Roar. And remember how you described the day when he was gone and you had Sunshine for your perfect day. I want you to think of this end of the scale (the 0) to be that feeling with Mr. Roar, and this end (the 10) with Sunshine. Now take some time to show me on this scale where you are today between Mr. Roar and Sunshine.* Since this was Ruby's first time answering a scaling question, I knew it would take a few extra minutes, and that with time this question would become easier and faster to answer. To add meaning and depth to her answer, additional questions were needed. *How do you know that this is your number? What do you think needs to happen to make you move from this number a little closer to Sunshine?*

This prepared Ruby for the exploration of exceptions, moments since our last session when she might have seen some of these things already happening. I reviewed portions of the perfect day she had described in the last session along with what helped her know her place on the scale. *Now can you think of a time this past week when some of these things were already happening? Think about maybe just one time. When that happened did you know what you were doing to make that happen, were you thinking about what you were doing?* To make this moment more concrete for Ruby, I asked her to use Sunshine, her perfect day puppet. She quickly found Sunshine, slipped the puppet on her finger, and began using it to slowly elaborate the exception that happened recently. Through Sunshine, Ruby was able to describe one occasion during the past week when she moved from one class to another with Sunshine rather than Mr. Roar. As the session came close to ending, I asked Ruby to draw a picture of that moment, of the exception she had experienced. This drawing became the focus of the solution message. It was something for her to take with her to recall a piece of her perfect day, what she had done to contribute to it, and what she could do again.

Follow-up Sessions

Once Ruby recognized and understood her exception experiences, the subsequent sessions looked at what had been different since the last session. The scaling questions were always helpful to her in determining who was in control of that day, fear and anxiety or Ruby (Mr. Roar or Sunshine). Then we would focus on what needed to happen to move to the next higher number on the scale. Within these sessions, we also took some time to learn how to be mindful and use breathing to reduce anxiety. Drawing and books were commonly used as well. But often Ruby would return to her finger puppets, Mr. Roar and Sunshine, to play out her struggles. Returning to school after weekends was sometimes still a challenge, but following an extended break it was expected for her to be more scared or anxious than other times. She began to accept that her anxiety might always be a part of who she was and that she had resources within her to cope with it. She also realized she had fewer moments of anxiety and more of her perfect day.

References

Alter, M. (2001). Play therapy behaviors of sexually abused children. In G. Landreth (Ed.), *Innovations in play therapy: Issues, process, and special populations* (pp. 119–130). New York, NW: Brummer-Routledge.

Bond, C., Woods, K., Humphrey, N., Symes, W., & Green, L. (2013). Practitioner review: The effectiveness of solution focused brief therapy with children and families: A systemic and critical evaluation of the literature from 1990–2010. *Journal of Child Psychology and Psychiatry, 54*(7), 707–723. doi:10.1111/jcpp.12058

Cain, J. (2000). *The way I feel.* Seattle, WA: Parenting Press.

Corcoran, J., & Stephenson, M. (2000). The effectiveness of solution-focused therapy with child behavior problems: A preliminary report. *Families in Society, 8*, 468–474.

Gillen, M. (2011). Solution-focused therapy. In S. Degges-White & A. L. Davis (Eds.), *Integrating the expressive arts in counseling practice: Theory-based interventions* (pp. 29–33). New York, NY: Springer Publishing Company.

Leggett, E. S. (2009). A creative application of solution-focused counseling with children's literature and visual arts. *Journal of Creativity in Mental Health, 4*, 191–200.

Leggett, E. S. (2017). Solution focused play therapy. In E. S. Leggett & J. Boswell (Eds.), *Directive play therapy: Theories and techniques* (pp. 59–80). New York, NY: Springer Publishing Company.

Murphy, J. (1994). Working with what works: A solution-focused approach to school behavior problems. *School Counselor, 42*, 59–68.

Nims, D. R. (2011). Solution focused play therapy: Helping children and families find solutions. In C. Schaefer (Ed.), *Foundations of play therapy* (2nd ed., pp. 297–309). Hoboken, NJ: Wiley & Sons Inc.

Trepper, T. S., McCollum, E. E., De Jong, P., Korman, H., Gingerich, W., & Franklin, C. (2008). *Solution focused therapy treatment manual for working with individuals research committee of the solution focused brief therapy association.* Retrieved from www.sfbta.org/Research.pdf

Section IV

Puppet Therapy Techniques

10 The Use of Puppets to Externalize a Child's "Problem"

Brie Turns and Brandon Eddy

Introduction

Externalization is the concept that a problem experienced by a client is not a part of who he or she is, rather, it is the process of a client attributing a problem into an external factor (White, 1995, 2007; White & Epston, 1990). The goal of externalization is to help an individual realize that he or she is not the problem—the problem is the problem (White & Epston, 1990). The usefulness of externalization has been explained as creating distance between the problem and the client (Butler, Guterman, & Rudes, 2009; Turns & Kimmes, 2014). Externalization is also helpful for clients because it allows them to view problems from a different perspective (Freedman & Combs, 1996).

Parents often mandate their child to attend therapy (White, 2007) due to the belief that the child is the "identified patient" (Berg & Steiner, 2003) and has a problem that needs to be fixed. This message can cause the child to feel shame and to believe there is something "wrong" with him or her. Mental health clinicians can use externalization to begin helping a child, and his or her parents, view the "problem" as an external factor, rather than a trait of the child. One way to help children to externalize problems is to use tangible objects, such as puppets.

Nuts and Bolts of Technique

Age Range

When using puppets to externalize a problem, a clinician must first consider the child's chronological and developmental age. Typically developing children should be between 5 and 12 years of age. Children who are diagnosed with a developmental or intellectual disability can also benefit from this intervention, but clinicians should consider the child's intellectual ability. For example, I (BT) commonly externalize children's diagnoses because parents often view the symptoms as a "problem."

An important consideration when deciding the appropriateness of using a puppet to externalize the child's problem is the child's ability to pivot

(Vygotsky, 1978). Pivoting is the ability to distinguish between concrete objects and their meanings. Children are usually around preschool age when they are able to begin pivoting (Vygotsky, 1978). In order to use this intervention, children must be able to see an object (the puppet) and view it as something else (themselves). During this intervention, the therapist will be asking questions about the "problem" in an effort to externalize it from the puppet. The ability to pivot will allow the child to apply the conversation about the puppet to himself or herself.

Materials

After considering the child's intellectual ability and age, clinicians should equip themselves with numerous puppets for the clinician, child, and family members to use during the activity. Depending on their environment and experiences, the child and other family members may be attracted to certain puppets. We recommend clinicians have an assortment of animal puppets such as alligators, rabbits, dogs, elephants, and sharks.

Practical Aspects

We recommend therapists designate a whole session to externalizing a problem. Before beginning the conversation, lay out all the puppets on a table or the floor and ask each family member to select a puppet he or she likes. The therapist should also select a puppet. Some older family members, such as parents or older children, may feel the puppet activity is childish or immature. Therapists are advised to encourage members to participate and model how to play with the child. Discussing the activity and explaining the usefulness of playing with children to parents ahead of time can prevent their resistance to the activity.

The first step in externalizing the problem is typically done with the child naming the puppet's problem (Ramey, Tarulli, Frijters, & Fisher, 2009). The following statement is an example of how to begin the conversation: "[Name the puppet the child is holding], I heard that you often struggle with [problem]. Can you tell me more about [name the problem]?" Altering the language by stating the problem as a noun gives the assumption that it is not the puppet's problem, but rather it exists outside of the puppet. It is vital that the therapist always uses his or her puppet to ask questions to the other family member's puppets, not the child.

Another option to assist in externalizing the problem is to begin altering the language the family uses to describe the problem (Ramey et al., 2009). For example, a parent may state, "I'm very worried about Tommy's anger." The therapist can alter the language toward the parent's puppet, "[Parent's puppet], what time of day does anger seem to bother [name of child's puppet] the most?" Using this language provides the assumption that anger is not a characteristic of the child, but rather an external entity that comes in and out of the child's life.

The following questions can help the child and family further describe the puppet's problem. For example, "[Dad's puppet], what does [name of the problem] feel like for [child's puppet]?" or "[Child's puppet], how does it feel when the [name of problem] comes and bothers you?" Other questions can include how the problem interferes with the puppet's hobbies, relationships with the other puppets, and other activities. The following page provides a list of questions that clinicians can use to ask the child and family members.

Examples of Questions Clinicians Can Ask the Child and Family Members

1. What can we call the problem bothering you [child's puppet]?
2. What does [name of problem] look/sound/feel like?
3. How do you [family member's puppet] see the worry monster bothering [child's puppet]?
4. When does the [name of problem] come and bother [mom or dad's puppet]? How do they handle the problem? Who helps them with the problem?
5. How would [mother's puppet] see the [name of problem] bothering [dad or child's puppet]? How could you help them? How could they ask you for help?
6. Where does the [name of problem] bother [child's puppet] the most/least?
7. What can I [therapist's puppet] do to help [child's puppet] when you're bullied by [name of problem]?
8. Are there times where [name of problem] goes away and doesn't bother you?
9. Does [name of problem] ever help or protect you?
10. Does [name of problem] ever come and bug you at school? How do you get rid of [name of problem] when you are at school?
11. Does [name of problem] ever bother your friends? Have you helped your friends get rid of [name of problem]?

Case Illustration

Joey was diagnosed with autism spectrum disorder (ASD) when he was 6 years old. He is currently 14 and recently began his freshman year in high school. His mother and father, Alice and Peter, brought him to a family therapist in hopes of "fixing Joey's anxiety and the amount he worries." During the intake session, Alice described Joey as being a "10-year-old boy, mentally," who struggles making friends and managing his fear for the future. Peter described Joey's main "problem" as being worried about his schoolwork, where to sit in class and at lunch, and how to make friends. The family's clinician, Tara, decided to externalize Joey's "anxiety" in hopes of helping the family see it as an external factor rather than a characteristic belonging to Joey. After Joey selected a dinosaur, Alice chose a dolphin, Peter selected a penguin, and Tara picked a parrot, the following externalization conversation occurred. Throughout this brief clip, each participant used his or her puppet to communicate.

Tara: Dinosaur, I heard the worry bug comes and bothers you a lot lately.
Joey: Yeah, I tend to worry about school a lot.
Tara: Is there a name that we can give this worry?
Joey: Uh . . . I think it's like a big worry monster that keeps me up at night.
Tara: The worry monster sounds scary! Hey, Penguin and Dolphin, how do you see the worry monster bothering Dinosaur?
Mother: Well, gosh. I know Dinosaur needs to get his schoolwork done, but then worry monster tells him he isn't doing it right.
Father: Dinosaur's teachers also said that the worry monster is mean to Dinosaur at school by telling him he can't sit anywhere at lunch.
Tara: Wow, this worry monster seems so mean. Dinosaur, what does the monster look like?
Joey: He's big and black and has really sharp teeth.
Tara: Oh my! So I know the monster gets Dinosaur in trouble at school and at home; does he get in the way of Dinosaur having fun?
Joey: ALL THE TIME!! Even when I try to watch TV at night, I start to worry.
Tara: (*Noticing the personalization of the worry, Tara alters the language.*) Man, I wonder if the worry monster ever bullies Penguin or Dolphin when they watch TV?
Father: Come to think of it. Just last night the worry monster reminded me of work I had to do tomorrow and my chest got heavy.
Tara: The worry monster makes your chest heavy, Penguin! Dolphin and Dinosaur, does the worry monster make you feel anything too?

Although this is a brief conversation, make sure you notice the language that the therapist is intentionally using with each of the puppets. She is asking numerous questions about the externalized problem, worry monster, and allowing the puppets to build on the problem's identity.

This chapter provided a brief explanation for externalizing children's problems, the benefits it can have in the therapy room, and practical questions that therapists can use when conducting this intervention. Although the clients are not directly discussing the child's experiences with the problem, the use of the puppet allows the child to communicate more openly and not be in the spotlight.

References

Berg, I. K., & Steiner, T. (2003). *Children's solution work.* New York: W.W. Norton & Company.

Butler, S., Guterman, J., & Rudes, J. (2009). Using puppets with children in narrative therapy to externalize the problem. *Journal of Mental Health Counseling, 31*(3), 225–233.

Freedman, J., & Combs, G. (1996). *Narrative therapy: The social construction of preferred realities.* New York: W.W. Norton.

Ramey, H., Tarulli, D., Frijters, J., & Fisher, L. (2009). A sequential analysis of externalizing in narrative therapy with children. *Contemporary Family Therapy, 31*, 262–279.

Turns, B. A., & Kimmes, J. (2014). "I'm NOT the problem!" externalizing children's "problems" using play therapy and developmental considerations. *Contemporary Family Therapy, 36*(1), 135–147.

Vygotsky, L. (1978). *Mind in society: The development of higher psychological processes.* Cambridge, MA: Harvard University Press.

White, M. (1995). The narrative perspective in therapy. In M. White (Ed.) *Reauthoring lives: Interviews and essays* (pp. 199–213). Adelaide, Australia: Dulwich Centre Publications.

White, M. (2007). *Maps of narrative practice.* New York: W.W. Norton.

White, M., & Epston, D. (Eds.). (1990). *Narrative means to therapeutic ends.* New York: W.W. Norton.

11 "Mr. Fox Is Sad"

Puppets as Symbolic Clients in the Playroom

Susan M. Carter

Puppets are a staple in children's toys worldwide and are commonplace in the tools of play therapists. Their scope is international and their appeal to children is without cultural or socioeconomic bounds. The usefulness of puppets for play therapy lies in how they facilitate projection of a child's inner world, to communicate their concerns and externalize emotions. It is a way of engaging the child in the therapeutic process and enhancing the therapeutic relationship (Prendiville, 2014; Bromfield, 1995; Carter & Mason, 1998). Puppets allow children to express themselves in an active yet nonverbal manner, fostering communication of the unspeakable. When we speak of puppets as the symbolic client, we refer to this process of natural projection, encouraging self-expression from a safe perspective (Bromfield, 1995; Narcavage, 1997). At the start of therapy, particularly with anxious, traumatized, or highly defended children, the use of puppets to represent the child's limitations can be freeing and empowering (Narcavage, 1997). The fearful distrust of others from trauma can be projected onto a puppet along with the sharing of a complicated, emotional, and confusing narrative made safer and possibly more explicit via the action and dialogue created through the puppet. Acting out a carefully chosen or crafted story through a character puppet gives life and meaning to the issues of the child client.

Practical Considerations in Choosing and Using Puppets as Symbolic Clients

A child can be engaged and participate in the play therapist's manipulation of a puppet-client at any age. However, to participate actively, the child needs to be capable of the physical manipulation of the puppet on his or her hand, generally around age 3 (Carter & Mason, 1998).

As puppet play knows no cultural or ethnic limits, if human puppets are chosen for this intervention, they should have various skin tones to entice many cultures of children into play (Irwin, 1993). The multicultural puppets can facilitate cross-cultural understanding, serve to lower defenses, and naturally draw a child into the play. The actual puppets used in these interventions can be of various materials, sizes, shapes, and styles (Prendiville, 2014;

Bromfield, 1995). Puppets come in several forms: hand puppets, Muppets, marionettes, and ventriloquist dummies (Carter & Mason, 1998). Most play therapy settings opt for hand puppets because of their ease of manipulation and the soft, nurturing, and often colorful materials from which they are made. Muppets, however, are also useful because more than one person may operate the speaking and gesturing, and can either allow the child more options for self-expression or provide for inclusion of the play therapist in collaboration (Bromfield, 1995; Carter & Mason, 1998).

For purposes of these play therapy interventions, a varied puppet collection is suggested, and should usually contain an aggressive puppet (shark, alligator, wolf), a nurturing or friendly puppet (bear, dog, rabbit, owl), a magical puppet (dragon, fairy, witch, or sorcerer), a beautiful/ugly puppet (bird, dinosaur), and a puppet family (various ethnicities, regular people, royal family; Carter & Mason, 1998). Puppets should be openly displayed and easily accessible, numbering about 15–20, noting that enough puppets allow for creativity and imagination, but too many might overwhelm the child and result in an inability to choose any one puppet or an avoidance of puppet play altogether (Bromfield, 1995; Carter & Mason, 1998).

Having an open, visually positive display for the choices of puppets can expand the child's self-expression, creativity, and imagination. It also affords the therapist a platform for staging an intervention with the puppets that is developmentally and prescriptively appropriate.

Techniques Using a Puppet as a Symbolic Client

"The Hidden Puppet Technique" (Bow, 1993) requires that a container (sack or box) be available in which to hide a puppet, or that a puppet can hide itself (such as a turtle or rabbit-in a hat). The resistant (shy, anxious) client is then engaged (directed) to assist the play therapist in coaxing the puppet out of hiding. By addressing the puppet's anxiety, the child is afforded a safe avenue to express his or her own fears and needs (Prendiville, 2014) and to become engaged in play therapy through the purpose of helping the puppet.

I employ another intervention in the playroom in initial sessions with an anxious or resistant client. I choose two puppets, one acting as the client and the other as the play therapist. Through the puppets, I explain the process of play therapy and the rules of the playroom; the puppet-client asks many questions that the child may be thinking, which are answered by the puppet-therapist. The puppets then participate in a tour of the playroom, one identifying to the other the activities available. The intervention serves to give the child a predictable map of the world of play therapy, helping the child to move through his or her emotions by observing the interaction of the puppets. As interest builds, the play therapist may offer to transfer one of the puppets to the child's control.

A third intervention I employ combines the use of bibliotherapy with puppet play, acting out the part of the identified characters, one of which would be the symbolic client. Several children's books already come with puppets included: *Brave Bart* (TLC, 1998) is the story of a little cat (Bart) recovering from trauma with the help of Helping Hanna; *Stellaluna* (Cannon, 2007) is the story of a young bat, accidentally separated from its mother; *The Kissing Hand* (Penn, 2009) is the story of a little raccoon afraid of leaving his mother to attend school. Through the story of the character that mirrors their own story, children seem to feel empowered by an unconscious sharing of the journey with a knowing other. Bibliotherapy is a tool for the play therapist to normalize the child's experience, to amplify and identify the emotional response to certain experiences, and to provide a plausible resolution and positive outcome to a situation like their own (Perhsson, 2011). Coupling bibliotherapy with puppet play brings the client's story to life in the form of the symbolic client. The role of the play therapist as narrator creates an empathic witness to the drama unfolding within the story, the puppet's reenactment, and within the child. Finally, these interventions integrate both directive and nondirective techniques into a prescriptive, individualized treatment potential, still allowing the child to mold the play to express his or her own needs.

Case Example

Emily, a precocious 5-year-old child, was referred for play therapy by her pediatrician, with whom her parents had consulted at the request of her prekindergarten teacher. She was identified with emotional dysregulation, irritability, sensory defensiveness, and negative externalized behaviors (verbal outbursts, opposition to authority, antagonistic to peers, controlling of situations, and at times physically violent). In early assessment of family dyads, I noted Emily's attraction to puppet play, along with dominant, noncollaborative behaviors and an attitude resistant to challenge or structure. I determined to use the two-puppet technique and introduced her to the playroom and its structure. I engaged the puppets in a tour of the playroom, asking questions about play therapy that were answered in metaphor. I decided that creating the symbolic client through the puppets would be a positive treatment avenue for Emily. Not finding a published story to draw upon, I wrote a story entitled, "Mr. Fox Is Sad." I used a specific puppet in the playroom—Brer Fox—as the main character. The story closely mirrored the behaviors that Emily's teacher and parents found unacceptable. In the story, Mr. Fox feels sad and lonely because no one understands that he really wants to be friendly and nice. Wise Owl resolves his difficulties by helping him name his feelings and learn new ways to manage them.

Emily showed interest in Mr. Fox, listened to his story, and watched as I then acted it out using various puppets. Although Emily refused to participate, I was encouraged by the attention she paid to the process. Several nondirected play therapy sessions passed, and although the puppets were present in the playroom, Emily did not choose to play with them. However, in our fifth session, Emily announced she had decided to do a puppet play. She directed me to use the fox puppet; she selected several other animal puppets and roles in the play. Emily proceeded to reenact "Mr. Fox Is Sad," directing my role as Mr. Fox and interacting sequentially with the other puppets one by one. In our seventh session, Emily returned to the puppet play, this time deciding to portray the sad Mr. Fox herself. She engaged Mr. Fox in telling the others [puppets] that he was sad and that made him say mean things. Emily used the fox puppet as a symbolic client to express that she was ready to learn to identify her feelings and to better manage her behaviors with others, a turning point in her play therapy.

In the coming sessions, we continued to use stories and puppets to identify feelings and to introduce coping strategies. Emily maintained a dominant role—choosing the puppets and nominating me as narrator of the stories—but through the puppet play her demeanor softened with others, she was more kind and more predictable, and she was able to return to school with fewer incidents.

References

Bow, J. N. (1993). Overcoming resistance. In C. E. Schaefer (Ed.) The *Therapeutic Powers of Play* (pp. 17–40), Northvale, NJ: Jason Aronson.

Bromfield, R. (1995). The use of puppets in play therapy. *Child and Adolescent Social Work Journal, 12*(6), 435–444.

Cannon, J. (2007). *Stellaluna.* New York: Houghton Mifflin Harcourt.

Carter, R. B., & Mason, P. S. (1998). The selection and use of puppets in counseling. *Professional School Counseling, 1*(5), 50–53.

Irwin, E. C. (1993). Using puppets for assessment. In C. E. Schaefer & D.M. Cangelosi (Eds.), *Play Therapy Techniques*, (pp. 83–90). New York: Jason Aronson.

Narcavage, C. J. (1997). Using a puppet to create a symbolic client. In H. Kaduson & C. Schaefer (Eds.), *101 Favorite Play Therapy Techniques*, (p.199). New York: Jason Aronson.

National Institute for Trauma and Loss in Children. (1998). *Brave bart.* Albion, MI: National Institute for Trauma and Loss in Children.

Penn, A. (2009). *The kissing hand.* Terre Haute, IN: Tanglewood Publishing.

Perhsson, D.-E. (2011). Utilizing bibliotherapy in play therapy for children with anxiety and fears. In A. A. Drewes, S. Bratton, & C.E. Schaefer (Eds.), *Integrative Play Therapy*, (pp. 207–224). New York: Wiley.

Prendiville, S. (2014). The use of puppets in therapeutic and educational settings. In E. Prendiville & J. Howard (Eds.), *Play Therapy Today*, (pp. 97–112). London: Routledge.

12 Teaching Children to Problem-Solve Through Puppet Play Interactions[1]

Carolyn Webster-Stratton and M. Jamila Reid[2]

Young children often react to their problems in ineffective ways. Some cry, tantrum, and yell, others hit, bite, and become destructive, and still others tattle or lie to their parents or teachers. These antisocial, but normal, responses do little to help children find satisfying solutions to their problems. In fact, they create new ones. Research shows that children continue to use these inappropriate strategies either because they have not been taught more appropriate ways to manage their emotions and to problem-solve and/or because, in the short term, their inappropriate strategies work to get what they want.

The Incredible Years Dinosaur small group treatment and classroom prevention curriculum for young children have been shown in randomized studies to show increases in children's emotional language, social skills, school readiness, and appropriate problem-solving (Webster-Stratton, Reid, & Stoolmiller, 2008) as well as reductions in conduct problems, hyperactivity, and inattention at home and school (Webster-Stratton & Hammond, 1997; Webster-Stratton & Reid, 2016, 2005; Webster-Stratton, Reid, & Beauchaine, 2013; Webster-Stratton, Reid, & Hammond, 2001, 2004). This curriculum has been described in detail in a book entitled *Incredible Teachers: Nurturing Children's Social, Emotional, and Academic Competence* (Webster-Stratton, 2012) as well as other articles (Webster-Stratton & Reid, 2003, 2005, 2008a, 2008b).

In this chapter, we will focus on how we use puppets in the Incredible Years Dinosaur Program to teach children emotional management and problem-solving skills. The puppets in this curriculum are large, child-size puppets dressed according to the different cultures and gender they are working with. Moreover, like children they regularly change their clothing according to the climate and local customs and to represent different developmental issues. For example, some child puppets may have glasses or a hearing aid if that is an issue being addressed with the group. However, for a limited budget clinicians can use smaller puppets and in fact almost any puppet with a moving mouth. Young children, ages 4–8 years, are enthralled with puppets and will talk with them about painful or sensitive issues more easily than an adult.

The Feeling Literacy and Identification Combined With Emotion Regulation Are the First Steps of Problem-Solving

The beginning steps of problem-solving focus on the link between feelings and problems. Clinicians can use puppets to help children understand that an uncomfortable feeling such as anger, frustration, sadness, fearfulness, or loneliness is a "signal" that they have a problem that needs to be solved. Because children this age are visual thinkers and love imaginary play, one of the ways to promote a child's emotional language and self-regulation skills is through stories and puppet play. Puppets can facilitate pretend play that helps children experience the feelings of other characters (early empathy development). Puppets act out stories with children and explore feelings and ways to cope with uncomfortable feelings. Puppets model feeling talk and tell children about times they are feeling left out, teased by other children, frustrated because they have difficulty learning to read, anxious about inviting a friend over, angry because their parent won't buy them new shoes, or worried about their parents fighting. Puppets also talk about positive feelings such as being proud at learning to ride a bike, happy playing the drums, pleased at getting a compliment for sitting still, or excited to have learned to read. For example, the puppet Wally (a character used in the Incredible Years Dinosaur Child Social Skills Program) might share his feelings by saying, "*I am angry because my brother took my airplane and broke it.*" The clinician replies by asking Wally if he used one of his secrets to calm down. Wally replies, "*Yes, I realized I needed to take three breaths. Can you help me take those three deep breaths?*" The child and puppet take some deep breaths together and practice using calming self-talk, "*I can calm down. I am going to think of my dog who makes me feel happy.*" After they practice this several times, the clinician praises Wally and the child for practicing how to stay calm. The clinician says, "*You have helped Wally stay calm by taking deep breaths, counting, telling yourself you can stay calm, and thinking of your happy place. Do you think you could use this idea when you get mad with your sister or a friend?*"

Many scenarios with puppets can be used to help children practice talking about their uncomfortable feelings and then practicing using calming thoughts, positive images, and deep breathing. Here are some sample scripts that the puppet can use to model positive and negative feeling talk. The puppet says to the children:

"*I am frustrated building this tower, but I take a deep breath and try again when it falls down.*"
"*I am so proud of how I finally built that.*"
"*I am excited about playing in the bath. Are you?*"
"*I am having fun playing with my friend, Molly. Who do you have fun playing with?*"
"*I am disappointed that I can't go to the playground with my mom. I will think of my happy place.*"

"I feel left out and lonely when other kids won't let me play with them. Do you ever feel that way?"

"I am sad that my fish died. Have you had a pet die?"

Problem Identification and Brainstorming Solutions

After teaching children emotional language and calm-down strategies, clinicians begin to use the puppets to teach children basic problem-solving steps. It is important that this teaching be done first at a time when the children are actually calm and not when they are engaged in conflict. The first steps focus on problem identification and solution brainstorming:

1. What is my problem? (Define the problem and feelings involved.)
2. What is a solution? What are some more solutions? (Brainstorm.)

For children between the ages of 3 and 8, the steps of identifying the problem and generating possible prosocial solutions are the key skills to learn and practice. Later they will learn subsequent steps of evaluating consequences and implementing solutions. The ability to think ahead to possible outcomes for each solution is a big cognitive developmental step and will be particularly difficult for hyperactive, impulsive, and very young children.

Puppets are an extremely effective teaching technique for modeling these first problem-solving steps and for engaging children in practices that bring problem-solving discussions to life.

A fun way to begin problem-solving discussions with children is to ask them to pretend they are "detectives" who are trying to solve a problem that

1 What is my problem?

their puppet friend has. The puppet tells them about a particular problem he or she wants help solving. These problem scenarios are selected to be similar to the child's actual problems. Sample problem scenarios that can be acted out by puppets include the following:

Wally and Molly and Their Friends Ask Children for Help Solving These Problems

- Wally is afraid to bring home his behavior chart from his teacher because he hasn't done well.
- Wally has had a fight in the school yard with other children who won't let him play with them.
- Molly fights with Wally over what channel to watch on TV and ends up being sent to time-out.
- Molly is not invited to a party when most of her friends are going.
- Wally takes his friend's baseball glove because his parents won't buy him one.
- Oscar the Ostrich hides his head in the sand and is afraid because his parents fight—he is sure they are fighting because of him.
- Tiny Turtle is afraid of an adult who gets angry at him.
- Wally tells a lie because he is afraid he will get into trouble.
- Wally is teased and doesn't want to go to school anymore.
- Freddy Froggy is hyperactive, impulsive, and jumps around a lot. He finds other children are annoyed with him.

Defining the Problem: The puppet tells the children about the problem. The children guess how the puppet is feeling and then say the problem in their own words. For example: "*Wally, I think you are sad because your mom is going out and you don't want to stay with the babysitter.*"

After the problem has been defined, the next step is for the clinician to invite the children to help the puppet think of solutions. The idea is to encourage them to generate as many different solutions as they can in order to solve the puppet's problem. This brainstorming process is fun and teaches children flexible thinking while encouraging them to realize that there is often more than one reasonable way to solve the problem. It is important to avoid criticizing or editing any of the children's ideas, no matter how silly they may seem. Instead, encourage imaginative thinking and try to use the puppet to model creative solutions. Be sure to praise children for their attempts to solve Wally's problem. In particular, it is helpful to praise them for their *different* solutions (e.g., "*Good, that is a different idea*") because it will encourage a broader variety of solutions.

If children are having difficulty finding a solution, Wally might suggest some ideas or ask them to check *Wally's Solution Kit* for other ideas. In this kit there are pictures of a variety of solutions such as: walk away, wait, say

2 What is a solution?

3 What are some other solutions?

please, do something else, trade, share, offer to help, ask for help, talk about your feelings, ignore, ask politely, calm down, think of happy place, take deep breaths, admit mistake, apologize, give a compliment, or forgive.

What Happens Next?

Acting Out Solutions

Once children have discussed a variety of solutions or chosen a solution from the Solution Kit, then the parent or teacher asks them to show Wally what these proposed solutions look like (see Fig. 12.4 and 12.5). It is fun for children to act these solutions out with hand puppets or toy characters. For example, if the children have suggested saying "please stop" and ignoring as possible solutions to the problem of being teased, then ask them to show Wally how they would do this. The puppet would act out the role of the teaser (children are never asked to act out negative behaviors). The child would show how she could say, "Stop teasing me," and then walk away. Children will love participating in these "plays," and the practice helps them to experience what behaviors and words are involved in carrying out the solution. Behavioral practice is far more important to a child's actually learning and using new problem-solving behaviors than theoretical cognitive discussions.

It is important to keep problem-solving practice paced to the child's developmental level and attention span. Most young children will be happy to help the puppet with one or two solutions in a session and then will be ready to move on to another activity. After a problem-solving practice with the puppet, it may be useful to have the puppet just play with the child in a free play setting and to comment on all the friendly solutions that the child uses with the puppet. For example: "*Wally wanted that block and you gave it to him.*

That's such a friendly solution." Or *"I see that you want the car that Wally is using and you are waiting. That's a great solution."*

Sample Problem-Solving Scripts

The following script is one that would work well for early elementary school children who have had practice with identifying feelings, problems, and generating solutions.

Sample Script for Puppets: "Wally Gets Teased"

Wally: Today the kids at school were teasing me and calling me a monkey face!

Clinician: How did that make you feel?

Wally: I felt so mad, I called them names back!

Clinician: How did you feel about that solution?

Wally: Not so good, because they called me a dummy and said I couldn't play with them.

Clinician: I wonder if there was a different solution that might have worked better? Do you want to ask these kids for their ideas?

Wally: I guess so—but I bet they never get teased.

Clinician: Oh, I think all kids get teased sometimes.

Wally: Really? Well, how do you kids feel when you are teased?

Clinician: *(Encourages students to label their feelings)*

Clinician: Well, I guess those feelings are clues there is a problem. Right? So, Wally, how would you state the problem?

Wally: The problem is I feel really mad because they are teasing me.

Clinician: That's right, so now what can you do to solve that problem? What are some solutions or choices of what to do? *(Encourages students to generate solutions—such as ignoring, walking away, being humorous in response, taking a deep breath and calming down, explaining feelings)*

Clinician: Wally, these kids are great problem-solving detectives, look at all the solutions they came up with.

Wally: Can we practice some of those ideas, because I'm not sure I know how to do that?

Clinician: Okay, let's pick two children who will show you how to react when someone teases you. And Wally, you can be the one to tease, okay? *(Two students volunteer)*

Wally:	Neaner, neaner, you are a monkey face!
Students:	(*Role-play some of the solutions that were discussed*)
Wally:	Wow, that was cool—I didn't get any reaction from either of you when I teased—it wasn't much fun. I'm going to try that next time someone teases me. I'll let you know what happens.

Is your solution fair?

Evaluating the Consequences of Solutions

After children understand how to identify problems and brainstorm solutions, they can begin to evaluate their solutions by thinking through the consequences. The puppets and children learn that a consequence is "What happens next?" and solutions can have good or bad consequences.

What Happens Next?

There are three questions that are used to decide whether the solution is a good one: Is my solution safe? Is it fair? Does it lead to good or okay feelings?

4 What happens next? (consequences)

The following script adds in the evaluation step of problem-solving to Wally's teasing scenario.

Next Session

Wally: Hey, you know what, someone was teasing me again and saying I was stupid and couldn't even kick a ball, and you know what I did?

Clinician: Tell us, Wally.

Wally: *(Wally demonstrates)* Well, I was feeling really mad, and I knew I was supposed to say how I felt about the teasing, but I just couldn't do it, so then I took some big breaths so I could calm down. And I thought to myself, "I'm not going to pay any attention to him, I can be stronger than him." I walked away and found someone else to play with.

Clinician: How did you feel about that?

Wally: Oh, it was so cool, I felt so powerful.

Does Your Solution Lead to Good Feelings?

Clinician: *(to students)* How do you think Wally did? Was his solution fair? Did it lead to good feelings? Was it safe?

Many young children will not be ready to evaluate consequences until they have had considerable practice with the earlier steps. When children are ready to evaluate solutions, the puppet asks what would happen if he tried one of their solutions. For instance, if a child suggested "grabbing" or "hitting" in order to get a toy back, clinicians help the child to consider the possible outcomes by asking, "*Imagine what might happen next if you did grab the ball away.*" Children will likely picture such things as losing a friend, getting into trouble with the teacher, or getting into a fight. This discussion should be carried out in a noncritical way even though the solution proposed is inappropriate. If children feel criticized for their solutions, they may avoid suggesting ideas in the future.

Next, children are asked to imagine the possible consequences of a different solution, such as asking the friend politely to have the toy back or offering to share. This might result in getting the toy back. It's also important to consider that even a prosocial solution might not work (maybe the child won't give the toy back even if asked nicely). Often, children are surprised or upset when things don't go according to their plan, and learning to predict possible outcomes can help a child cope with disappointment. Solution evaluation is an important part of problem-solving; however, be sure that this does not become a burdensome or compulsive activity. Children do not need to discuss the consequences of every single solution.

Sample Script for Puppets: "Felicity Steals Something"

Felicity (a puppet): Well, I came today because I have a problem. I need your help.

Clinician: These kids are great problem-solvers; I bet they could help.

Felicity: I did something at school this week. My friend Ruby had this stuffed animal, and she had it in her locker. And I really wanted one like that, so I just took it! She was really upset because it was her special animal.

Clinician: What happened then?

Felicity: Well, the teacher asked, "Who took Ruby's animal?" and I didn't want to tell so I lied and said, "Not me." I really thought I would get in big trouble if she found out it was me. I knew I shouldn't have taken that animal but I thought I would lose Ruby as a friend if she found out it was me. And the teacher would send a note home, and I would definitely get in trouble from my parents.

Clinician: Well, you know Wally says you're supposed to pick solutions with good consequences. Sounds like you had two solutions—first you took the stuffed animal because you wanted one so badly, and then you lied because you were scared. So let's think about the consequences of those two solutions.

Students: (*Brainstorm why students think her solutions might not be the best ones in terms of safety, fairness, and good feelings*)

Felicity: I see, so I see that I used two bad solutions and I made one problem into two problems because I lied. What should I do now?

Students: (*Generate solutions such as admit mistake, tell teacher and Ruby, apologize, give back animal*)

Felicity: Are you disappointed in me? Do you think I'm really awful because I did that?

Clinician: Well, you know, Felicity, everyone makes mistakes sometimes. How do you students feel about Felicity now?

Students:	*(Tell her how they feel)*
Felicity:	Well, I'm worried I won't be strong enough to admit my mistake. Can we practice doing that?
Clinician:	Sure, let's have someone be the teacher, another person Ruby, and another person be Felicity. *(Student role-plays admitting mistake to Ruby and teacher and experiencing consequences)*
Felicity:	Okay, let me try it now and see how I do. "Ruby, I am really sorry I took your doll, here it is back. I shouldn't have taken it, and I want to make it up to you. Would you like one of my toys for a while? Do you think we can still be friends?" Well, how did I do?

In this sample scenario, the clinician and puppet encouraged thinking about another's perspective and feelings, admitting a mistake, apologizing, and forgiving. Be sure to have the children only practice prosocial solutions, not inappropriate solutions. If the consequences of an inappropriate solution are to be role-played, the puppet should be the one to demonstrate the bad choice, not the children.

To Sum Up . . .

- Use puppets to present hypothetical problem scenarios to engage children in problem-solving practices.
- Use puppets to model talking about feelings and help children clearly define the problem and to recognize the feelings involved.
- For preschool children, use the puppet to help children focus on generating many different solutions.
- Help children practice the solutions and show the puppet what the solution looks like.
- Use the puppet to demonstrate how he or she used one of the solutions a child came up with.
- For primary- or elementary-age children, use the puppet to help them focus on thinking through to the various consequences of different solutions so the puppet or child can make the best choice.
- Use the puppet to help children anticipate what to do next when one solution doesn't work.
- Make these problem-solving scenarios fun and engaging, and praise children for their ideas/solutions.
- Model effective problem-solving yourself and with your puppet.
- Remember it is the process of learning how to think about conflict that is critical, rather than getting the correct answer.

Notes

1 The figures in this chapter were drawn by David Mostyn and have been reused with permission of the Incredible Years program.

2 Carolyn Webster-Stratton has disclosed a potential conflict of interest due to the fact she provides training and instructional materials for these Dinosaur Programs and therefore stands to gain financially from a positive review. This interest has been disclosed to the University of Washington and has been managed consistent with federal and university policy.

M. Jamila Reid also trains clinicians in Dinosaur small group and classroom curriculum and works for the Incredible Years Inc.

References

Webster-Stratton, C. (2012). *Incredible teachers: Nurturing children's social, emotional, and academic competence.* Seattle: Incredible Years Inc.

Webster-Stratton, C., & Hammond, M. (1997). Treating children with early-onset conduct problems: A comparison of child and parent training interventions. *Journal of Consulting and Clinical Psychology, 65*(1), 93–109.

Webster-Stratton, C., & Reid, M. J. (2003). Treating conduct problems and strengthening social emotional competence in young children (ages 4–8 years): The Dina Dinosaur treatment program. *Journal of Emotional and Behavioral Disorders, 11*(3), 130–143.

Webster-Stratton, C., & Reid, M. J. (2005). Treating conduct problems and strengthening social and emotional competence in young children: The Dina Dinosaur Treatment Program. In M. Epstein, K. Kutash, & A. J. Duchowski (Eds.), *Outcomes for children and youth with emotional and behavioral disorders and their families: Programs and evaluation best practices* (2nd ed., pp. 597–623). Austin, TX: Pro-Ed, Inc.

Webster-Stratton, C., & Reid, M. J. (2008a). Adapting the incredible years child dinosaur social, emotional and problem solving intervention to address co-morbid diagnoses. *Journal of Children's Services, 3*(3), 17–30.

Webster-Stratton, C., & Reid, M. J. (2008b). Strengthening social and emotional competence in socioeconomically disadvantaged young children: Preschool and kindergarten school-based curricula. In W. H. Brown, S. L. Odom, & S. R. McConnell (Eds.), *Social competence of young children: Risk, disability, and intervention* (pp. 185–203). Baltimore: Paul H. Brookes Publishing Co.

Webster-Stratton, C., & Reid, M. J. (2017). The incredible years parents, teachers and children training series: A multifaceted treatment approach for young children with conduct problems. In A. E. Kazdin & J. R. Weisz (Eds.), *Evidence-based psychotherapies for children and adolescents* (3rd ed.) (pp. 122–141). New York: Guildford Publications.

Webster-Stratton, C., Reid, M. J., & Beauchaine, T. P. (2013). One-year follow-up of combined parent and child intervention for young children with ADHD. *Journal of Clinical Child and Adolescent Psychology, 42*(2), 251–261.

Webster-Stratton, C., Reid, M. J., & Hammond, M. (2001). Social skills and problem solving training for children with early-onset conduct problems: Who benefits? *Journal of Child Psychology and Psychiatry, 42*(7), 943–952.

Webster-Stratton, C., Reid, M. J., & Hammond, M. (2004). Treating children with early-onset conduct problems: Intervention outcomes for parent, child, and teacher training. *Journal of Clinical Child and Adolescent Psychology*, *33*(1), 105–124.

Webster-Stratton, C., Reid, M. J., & Stoolmiller, M. (2008). Preventing conduct problems and improving school readiness: Evaluation of the incredible years teacher and child training programs in high-risk schools. *Journal of Child Psychology and Psychiatry*, *49*(5), 471–488.

13 Storytelling Through Puppets

The Turtle Technique[1]

Pam Dyson

Introduction

Stories and puppets are powerful learning tools that can open doors to conversations with children. Child therapists often have a variety of puppets available in their playroom, yet they have not explored the valuable potential of those puppets in helping children identify emotions and resolve problems (Irwin, 1993). Therapists sometimes overlook the fact that when children tell stories, insights can be gained into the child's frustrations and inner conflicts (Gardner, 1971) and how you can support them. In this chapter I will describe how the turtle technique can be used in conjunction with storytelling to help children learn self-control and develop social-emotional skills.

The Nuts and Bolts of the Turtle Technique

The turtle technique uses the metaphor of a turtle going inside its shell when feeling threatened. A child can be taught to go inside an imaginary shell when feeling overwhelmed by strong emotions or frustrating situations (Robin & Schneider, 1974). The turtle technique involves three steps: (1) going inside your imaginary shell when you are feeling angry; (2) relaxing while inside of your shell; and (3) coming out of the shell to think of solutions for the problem (Schneider, 1974). In my experience, the turtle technique is best suited for children 4 to 8 years of age and is best taught with the use of a turtle puppet.

Puppets can engage young children, strengthen their social skills, and play a significant role in managing frustration (Feindler, 2009). Whether you use puppets with an individual child or with a small group of children, it's important to model for children how to engage with a puppet. This can be accomplished in three basic steps: (1) talk to the puppet; (2) talk for the puppet; and (3) have the child talk with the puppet (Sharapan, 2016). Children are more willing to talk to the turtle puppet if they see you talking to the turtle puppet. When you ask the turtle a question and have the turtle respond, a child will be drawn into the dialogue. Having the turtle talk

Figure 13.1 Folkmanis Tortoise Puppet
Photo by John Dyson

directly to the child should be considered after the child appears comfortable with the first two steps.

Once a child is at ease with the turtle puppet, the mutual telling of a story can unfold. The basic story line includes: (1) here is what happened to me; (2) here is what I did; (3) here is what I could do next time. Children will often share things with a puppet that they may not be comfortable sharing with an adult.

Folkmanis Puppets is a company that sells a variety of puppets, including a realistic tortoise puppet with a head that can retract into its shell. (See Figure 13.1.)

This tortoise puppet is the most popular puppet in my play therapy room. Turtle puppets do not need to be purchased. They can also be handcrafted using inexpensive and easy-to-find materials. I often have children create a turtle puppet from a Dixie cup, jumbo craft stick, stickers, and adhesive wiggly eyes. (See Figure 13.2.)

Scissors are used to cut a small slit in the bottom of the cup after it is wrapped with construction paper. A sticker, with a face drawn on using a marker and wiggly eyes, is attached to one end of the craft stick, and the other end is inserted into the slit. The child can slide the craft stick up and down, inside the cup, to represent the turtle going in and out of its shell. (See Figure 13.3.)

Figure 13.2 Puppet-Making Materials

Photo by John Dyson

Figure 13.3 Turtle Stick Puppet

Photo by John Dyson

Children treasure things they make themselves. When they craft their own turtle puppets, they are more likely to use them creatively in storytelling and problem-solving.

The turtle technique is not limited to anger management. I've successfully adapted the technique for children to use in anxiety-producing situations. One child used the turtle technique when her parents argued with one another. Another found it helpful during thunderstorms.

Case Illustration

John, a 6-year-old boy in kindergarten, was referred to me by his parents, at the suggestion of his teacher, because of his angry, aggressive outbursts toward peers in the school setting. His inability to manage his frustration and his lack of social skills made him a candidate for group play therapy.

I had an initial, individual play therapy session with John to assess him developmentally. When he entered my play therapy room, he immediately walked over to the puppets. He picked up the tortoise puppet, handed it to me, and said, "Make him talk." I slid the puppet onto my hand and said, "Hi, my name is Tucker. What's your name?" John's eyes lit up and he replied, "My name is John!" Tucker replied, "I'm happy to meet you. How old are you, and where do you go to school?" John replied, "I'm six and I go to Clark Elementary." Before Tucker could say anything else, John started telling Tucker about his family, his school, the names of his classmates, and the activities he enjoys doing. Tucker responded, "You sound like a boy who knows a lot about a whole lot of things. I'm wondering if you can help me with a problem I have." John leaned toward Tucker and with a big smile on his face replied, "Sure! What's your problem?" "Sometimes," Tucker said, "I get mad when a kid at school calls me a name and I hit him. The teacher sends me to the office and the principal calls my mom. Then my mom, my teacher, and the principal are all mad at me for making a bad choice. I just don't know what to do instead of hitting kids when they make me mad. Do you have any good ideas?" Without hesitation, John said, "I have the same problem! Here's what you can do. You can take deep breaths. You can tell the teacher you need a break." Tucker excitedly responded, "Those are terrific ideas! It reminds me of what my Grandmother Lucy Turtle tells me to do when I'm feeling angry and want to hit someone. She tells me I can pull my head inside my shell, take three deep breaths, and then come back out of my shell to think of something I can do instead of hitting the person who made me angry. She calls it doing the turtle. It really works for me. Would you like to try it?"

John nodded his head and Tucker continued. "Let's pretend a kid at school says you are dumb. It makes you really mad and you want to hit him, but instead you do the turtle. Since you don't have a real shell like I do, you can put your head down on your chest and put your hands on top of your head." John follows Tucker's directive as Tucker continues: "Now you take three deep breaths. Let's take them together. Ready? One, two, three! Now, you pull your head back out of your shell and come up with an idea that would be better than hitting that kid." John paused for a moment, then replied, "I can tell my teacher I need a break. She will let me get a drink of water." "That's a great idea," replied Tucker. "Next week when you come back to the playroom, we can make a turtle puppet that you can take home so you can practice doing the turtle."

The second session was a group play therapy session that included two additional 6-year-old boys. They struggled to share toys and were easily angered. I put Tucker on my hand and asked John if he would like to help me show the other two boys how to do the turtle. He agreed, and the two of us demonstrated the technique. I then pointed to a bag of supplies and suggested they create turtle puppets using Dixie Cups, craft sticks, stickers, and wiggly eyes. They eagerly crafted their puppets and we practiced doing the turtle, with each boy sharing a story of a time he felt angry. Collectively, the boys offered solutions for problem-solving.

The third session found John feeling frustrated when one of the other boys in the group called him a name. He paused, took a deep breath, and began to cry while saying, "He makes me so mad. I just want to hit him. But if I hit him I'll get in trouble." The crying turned to sobs and he began taking deep breaths and slowly rocking back and forth repeating, "I want to hit him but if I do I'll get in trouble." John was wearing a hooded shirt and he pulled it over his head, simulating going into a turtle shell, while continuing the deep breathing. I positioned myself near John and commented, "You're doing the turtle. You're taking deep breaths. You didn't hit him. You made a choice to take deep breaths instead of hitting." I repeated those phrases until John stopped crying and his breathing became more regulated. Once he was calm I told him he could be proud of himself for remembering to do the turtle and calming himself down. John smiled at me through his tear-stained face.

The effective use of the turtle technique requires practice. It's important for parents, teachers, and other caregivers to be instructed on the turtle technique so they can review the technique with children and remind them to use it when struggling with self-control. When storytelling is integrated into the turtle technique it provides children with the opportunity to share their own stories and come up with creative resolutions to problems.

Note

1 The case described in this chapter is a composite of several cases. Details have been changed so that no detail corresponds to any actual client.

References

Feindler, E. L. (2009). Playful strategies to manage frustration: The turtle technique and beyond. In A. Drewes (Ed.), *Blending play therapy with cognitive behavioral therapy* (pp. 401–422). Hoboken, NJ: Wiley & Sons.

Gardner, R. A. (1971). *Therapeutic communication with children: The mutual storytelling technique.* New York: Science House, Inc.

Irwin, E. C. (1993). Using puppets for assessment. In C. E. Schaefer & D. M. Cangelosi (Eds.), *Play therapy techniques* (pp. 69–81). Northvale, NJ: Jason Aronson, Inc.

Robin, A., & Schneider, M. (1974). *Turtle manual.* Retrieved January 10, 2017, from http://files.eric.ed.gov/fulltext/ED128680.pdf

Schneider, M. (1974). Turtle technique in the classroom. *Teaching Exceptional Children*, 7, 21–24.

Sharapan, H. (2016). *The power of puppet play—it's not just make-believe.* What we can continue to learn from Fred Rogers. Retrieved January 10, 2017, from www.fredrogerscenter.org/2016/01/20/the-power-of-puppet-play-its-not-just-make-believe

14 Finger Puppets in Play Therapy

Jo Ann L. Cook

All the world's a stage,
And all the men and women merely players:
They have their exits and entrances;
And one man in his time plays many parts . . .

William Shakespeare, *As You Like It*

Introduction

Finger puppets may be an extension of the original fingerplays with Thumbkin, Pointer, Longman, Index, and Pinkie initiated during the sensorimotor period when eyes and hands first meet in play. This tiny stage will set in motion a future option upon which to direct and express emotions, thoughts, and actions. The fingers themselves may enact characters just as they are, with painted faces, or shrouded in miniature puppets that allow distance and objectivity for enactment, observation, and the process of change to begin. The directness and simplicity derived from and observed by the player entwine in finger puppetry.

Description

The use of finger puppets provides a viable option for applications with children from preschool through elementary ages and older children who function within these developmental levels. The ease of fit and manipulation allows ready access and choice of materials with which to initiate their story-making work (see Figure 14.1). Through the use of multiple and simultaneous figure involvement the process can flow uninterrupted, encouraging a ready stream of ideas and sequence of events. Personalized puppets can be constructed from wooden dowels (Cook, 1997), rubber balls as puppet heads (Jenkins & Beckh, 2002), and family groups drawn on glove fingers. Small props can easily be submitted or constructed as needed (see Figure 14.2). A miniature stage can be formulated through the introduction of an adapted shoebox or strawberry crate and decorated with a backdrop that can be changed if desired. A spotlight can be shone on the scene to

Figure 14.1 Finger Puppet Collection

Figure 14.2 Child-Made Finger Puppets

illuminate characters or raised and lowered to depict the setting of the moon and rising of the sun on a new day. The setup is well suited and contained to engage the child's attention and involvement within a small space at eye level and within arm's length. The entire stage can be covered with a box top or drape to preserve a scene at the point of the departure, for reenactments or subsequent scenes for an upcoming visit. The process involves the child totally and specifically as director, participant, and observer within his or her own personal space.

Rationale

Children within preoperational to concrete-operational stages of development benefit from use of representational objects that encourage projection and identification toward enactment and mastery of their situations. The direct physical involvement and manipulation of finger puppets puts this task within their easy reach. The option to immediately use multiple figures with ease of activation enables fluid storytelling, which moves their narrative along. The need to master manipulation skills of larger hand puppets and more frequent need to halt the play to search for and acquire additional puppets is minimized. The field of view and action sequence is maximized for the child's involvement. Children are drawn to the wide variety of puppets available for their choosing and are not limited in that they can devise additional characters as they construct their story. Having been able to observe their thoughts and feelings in action, they are better able to problem-solve and predict potential options and outcomes that would not have been available to them before. This provides a vehicle with the benefit to propel them forward from a previously cemented circumstance into a future in which they experience greater control and mastery. This all occurs within a three-dimensional diorama, which reflects a world that they operationalize and encourages the mental constructions of thoughts and ideas they can take forward to more adequately address new situations.

Applications

Given the multiple finger actors upon which to build, the applications of finger puppets are amplified. Frequently the hand grouping is seen to represent the family unit, which can provide further information regarding relative size, order, and proximity in which the roles are introduced as well as their puppet identities and how they present in the dynamics of the process. Facets of the self are also seen but may more likely be presented as animals with distinct personalities and behaviors. While the one hand may engage in the puppet play, the other can be free to introduce props or stage changes. Children often engage the therapist to operate lighting, provide props as

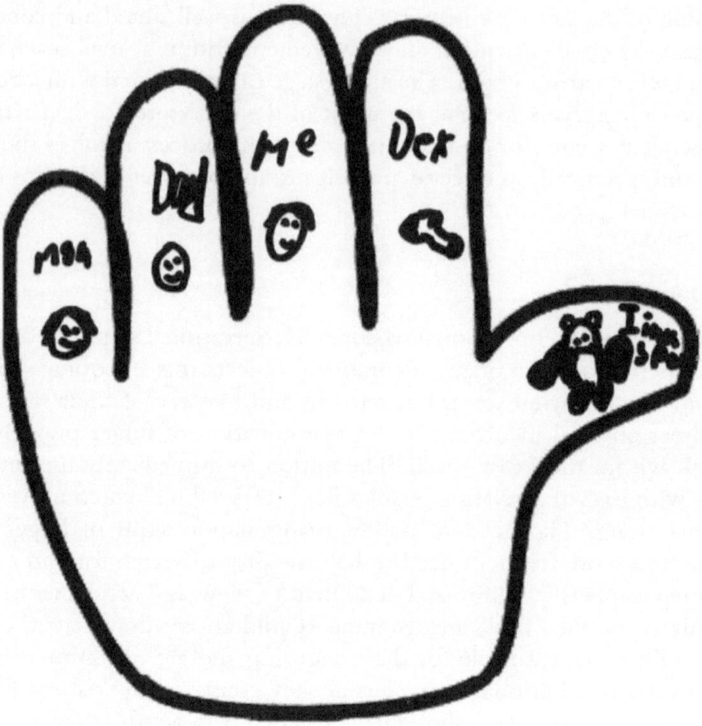

Figure 14.3 Glove Finger Puppet Family

needed, or act as an observer along with other finger puppet audience members. Simple filming for later review and stop-action descriptions has been found to be useful, particularly for children with selective mutism. These scenarios were later shared with parents, teacher, or selected classmates if given permission. The act of reviewing and observing their puppet shows would generally be followed by subsequent applications with increased volume and length of utterance and, at times, increased verbal participation in small classroom group activities. Additional applications have included the use of two scenarios, using one hand and then the other, to signify process and change (see Figure 14.3 and Figure 14.4). These have included real/ideal situations, pre- and post-observations such as current and future self (me/best me in future, old/new me), or with blended families by joining the two family hands in a scenario. The puppets have also been found to be useful as movers during game play, as they are easily applied in the role-plays involved in practicing new skills.

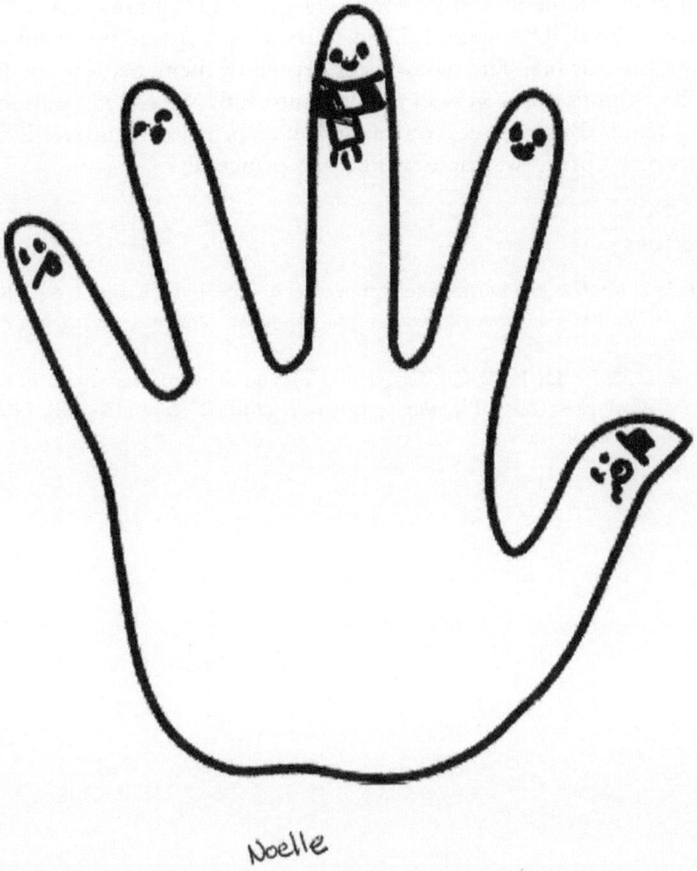

Figure 14.4 Hand Finger Puppets

Case Illustration

A first-grade girl, Sophie, had a history of speech/language delay, learning, attention, and anxiety disorders. She often compared herself unfavorably with her older talented sister, frequently escaped the classroom by going to see the nurse, and spun highly exaggerated stories for attention. Her puppet story, which was told within swift order, portrayed an improved understanding of her strengths and weaknesses, a more hopeful outcome, and a reframe of her identity within the family. The story unfolded with successive members of a royal family and depicted the transference of a grand celebration within the kingdom. The story was told by a wizard puppet affixed above the family.

The princess is at the castle with a large collection of jewels. She is the big sister. All the people are royal. They have a tradition every 500 years. They collect all the special things in the kingdom and put them next to the castle for her. The oldest sister gets all of them, because she likes to collect things so she gets all the precious stuff. We call it "Village Princess Land." But you see, you can also be a princess. Whoever lives here becomes a princess. There will be two princesses.

References

Cook, J. A. L. (1997). The Dowel finger puppet technique. In H. Kaduson & C. Schaefer (Eds.), *101 favorite play therapy techniques* (pp. 191–193). Northvale, NJ: Jason Aronson Inc.

Jenkins, R. L., & Beckh, E. (2002). Finger puppets and mask-making. In C. E. Schaefer & D. M. Cangelosi (Eds.), *Play therapy techniques* (2nd ed.) (pp. 115–122). Northvale, NJ: Jason Aronson Inc.

15 Play Therapy Puppet Techniques for Childhood Sexual Abuse Trauma

Athena A. Drewes

Introduction

Often the norm for childhood sexual abuse trauma treatment is cognitive behavioral therapy (Deblinger & Heflin, 1996). Treatment is usually through an evidence-based approach, such as trauma-focused CBT, which is structured, educational, and follows a manualized approach (Cohen, Mannarino, & Deblinger, 2012). While the core value of TF-CBT is flexibility, which allows the clinician to utilize a playful approach, the success of TF-CBT, as is true for most child treatment, whether or not for trauma, is through the "creativity, adaptability and playfulness of the clinician" (Briggs, Runyon, & Deblinger, 2011, p. 174). CBT works best with children 8 years and older who have developed abstract thinking skills and are able to verbalize and respond to verbal directions and psycho-educational teachings by the therapist. Younger children do not have the cognitive nor verbal capacity to understand some of the abstract concepts such as the "feelings triangle" or being able to come up with a complete narrative of their trauma.

Challenges exist in implementing TF-CBT with young children who are verbally and/or cognitively limited and have more difficulty grasping the TF-CBT components. Using developmentally appropriate play to implement TF-CBT components allows for children and parents to feel more relaxed, become engaged, and maintain interest and attention, as well as process and comprehend each of the components through a multimodal approach that taps into the natural learning style and life experiences of the child. Blending play and play techniques, specifically puppet play, allows effective delivery of CBT, as well as supporting engagement and enhanced participation, while not affecting theoretical underpinnings nor jeopardizing protocol fidelity (Drewes, 2009; Drewes, 2011; Drewes & Cavett, 2012; Knell & Desari, 2011). Without a playful aspect to the components, young children may view treatment activities as though they were formal, academic tasks and may become disinterested or refuse to participate.

Over the 20-plus years that TF-CBT was developed (Cohen & Mannarino, 1996), it has become "clear that children respond very differently to therapy than adults, and the element of play became a crucial ingredient in engaging children in the therapy process as did the important involvement of parents" (Briggs, Runyon, & Deblinger, 2011, p. 169). Indeed, difficult and emotionally laden trauma material can be more easily digested, with the use of puppets and play-based techniques becoming a sort of "enzyme" (Goodyear-Brown, 2010) that dissolves the painful connection to traumatic memories. In turn the healing power of play (Schaefer & Drewes, 2013) results in the child's diminishing discomfort and resistance to treatment, along with an increase in the child's sense of control and confidence. Therefore, the applications of puppet play and play-based techniques into TF-CBT are consistent with and have been increasingly incorporated into this approach for use with young children to assist in engagement, as well as with psycho-educational and skill-building components that make up TF-CBT.

Use of Puppets

Puppet play, in general, has been utilized in cognitive behavioral play therapy (Knell, 1993; Knell & Desari, 2011; Meichenbaum, 2009) along with utilizing stuffed animals, bibliotherapy, and other toys with which cognitive strategies could be modeled. Puppets are most effective when used to enact scenarios common for the child, such as peer conflict, fears related to being in their bedroom, and being able to say "no" and be assertive, as well as those addressing defiance and other behavioral issues. Role modeling in play is often met with less resistance than simple discussions or enactments. The clinician's playfulness allows for the message to be heard while adding details and alternative solutions. The child can feel empowered while rehearsing and enacting scenarios and practicing assertiveness skills. Both finger puppets and regular hand puppets can be used. Younger children may prefer the use of finger puppets, as they are smaller and much easier to manipulate than the larger hand puppets.

It is important to note that young children have a poor fantasy-reality balance, and often may respond to puppets as though they are alive and literally "talking" to them. This can often be seen by how children visually fixate on the puppet and not the therapist or "puppeteer" manipulating it, even though the therapist's regular voice may be used. Thus, younger children may become overwhelmed by a hand puppet that is especially scary or aggressive, believing it has come alive and is threatening them.

Trauma Puppet Techniques

Three-Headed Dragon

Learning what a thought is and its connection to feelings and behaviors is often too complex for a young child to understand. The use of a three-headed dragon puppet (available through Folkmanis; see Figure 15.1) (Drewes, 2009,

Figure 15.1 Three-Headed Dragon

Photo by Athena A. Drewes

2011; Drewes & Cavett, 2012) can visually show a child that what we think, feel, and do are interconnected.

The goal is to help the "thought" dragon head to slow down or go to sleep so that the "feelings" and "acting" dragon heads can be heard or calm down; or in contrast, calming the feelings, and helping the thought dragon to understand what is happening, so that the behavioral dragon doesn't need to act out. It can also show how a thought or perceptual distortion, such as "that boy is staring at me," can immediately lead to the child hitting the boy, with the feeling dragon head feeling scared that it will be hit and needing to protect itself. But by becoming aware of and changing the thought, the behavior will also change.

All three dragon heads are on the same body, just as all thoughts, feelings, and actions all belong to the child and may emerge one at a time or feel like they all come out at once in a blur in reaction to situations the child faces. The therapist can use particular scenarios with the child and see what corresponding thought, feeling, and/or behavior might then ensue. The particular triggers or antecedents to the situation can be explored and put into a hierarchy of events, and then a variety of solutions can be created.

The three-headed dragon can also be utilized to help explain how we all have more than one feeling at a time within us, sometimes feeling ambivalent—having two or more feelings simultaneously, such as feeling angry and loving at the same time toward someone. Sometimes one feeling can become so strong that it can hide the other feelings, or the other feelings seem to "go to sleep" and aren't felt, which makes people feel confused and unsure about their feelings, or that they only have one feeling (e.g., anger). But if we are able to calm down the angry dragon feeling, letting it rest or go to sleep, then the other feelings can come out and be felt and experienced by the child.

Use of Puppets in Trauma Narrative Work

Puppets can be utilized to show how the child felt before disclosing the trauma event versus how the child felt afterwards, using a cloth puppet that has various interchangeable facial features—mouth, eyes, nose shapes—that stick with Velcro and are easily removed (Goodyear-Brown, 2010). The child can show the before and after feelings through changing the facial expression of the puppet. Puppets whose mouths open wide, or even have zipper mouths, can also become depositories for secrets written on paper and inserted into the mouth for safekeeping until the next session. The child writes down a secret he or she is afraid to verbalize openly and folds it up and puts it into the puppet's mouth, or zippered animal, to safely hold onto for when the child feels able to take it out and share it with the therapist (Goodyear-Brown, 2010).

Holding and handling puppets can also be soothing during treatment times when difficult subject matter needs to be addressed or spoken about. And because a trauma can create horrific images and thoughts of the event, a multimodal intervention can ease the discomfort and inability to talk about the event. Use of puppets in trauma work can help allow children to use a multisensory approach to access their traumatic memories and create their trauma narrative, which is a necessary healing component of TF-CBT (and all trauma treatments). Thus playful interventions structured to achieve the goals of the TF-CBT components, especially the narrative creation, are engaging and inviting to children. They will more readily and easily allow for communication of the child's experiences with the therapist, and help to overcome common difficulties encountered during treatment. By using puppets, the therapist is also helped to feel comfortable in directly addressing trauma while simultaneously being playful in order to be authentic and believable.

The old adage of "See No Evil, Hear No Evil, and Speak No Evil" is often associated with statues or images of three monkeys each standing with their hands on either their eyes, ears, or mouth. The following technique utilizes a playful monkey puppet. The therapist can utilize it to demonstrate, or the child could use it instead and make the monkey's hands move to cover its eyes, ears, mouth, nose, and body to explore the sensory experiences that occurred during the sexual abuse. The goal of getting the narrative out is to bring up as many memories as possible that are often encoded within the amygdala of the brain and hidden from verbalizations, but are impacted by feelings and sensual reminders that may in turn result in PTSD behaviors. Often the narrative is reviewed two or more times with the client, each time going "deeper" to explore not only the initial story that is remembered, but seeing if embellishments can be added about time of day, month of year, sensory reminders such as sounds that were heard, smells remembered, words said, or bodily sensations experienced. This repetition, but going deeper and deeper, allows for a more complete remembrance of the event, which ultimately results in a more complete healing and defusing of the related symptoms and triggers of the event.

This author utilizes an adaptation of Paris Goodyear-Brown's "See No Evil, Hear No Evil" technique (2010) whereby three monkey figurines, one with its hands over its eyes, another with its hands over its ears, and another with its hands on its mouth, are placed in the sandtray, and the child is asked to tell what bad thing happened that you wish hadn't (seen, heard, or said). If the child cannot say a response, he or she can draw a picture or write the response on a piece of paper and slip it under each of the monkey statuettes (see Figure 15.2).

Figure 15.2 Seeing, Hearing, Saying, and Feeling

Photo by Athena A. Drewes

Seeing, Hearing, Saying, Smelling, and Feeling Monkey

Children are asked to remember what they saw that they wish they hadn't seen (e.g., the perpetrator coming into their room), while having the monkey put its hands over its eyes; and then what would they have wished that they had seen (e.g., the parent coming in to stop things; police arriving at the house).

In turn, children are asked about what they might have heard that they wish they hadn't heard (e.g., the perpetrator opening their door; the sound of the person reaching orgasm); and what they wish they would have heard (e.g., police sirens coming nearer to the house; shouts by the parent for the person to get out). Similar questions are then asked about what children might have had said to them, and what they wish they might had said; as well as what they might have smelled or felt or wished they had smelled or felt, with the monkey's hands finally going to the mouth, nose, and across the body.

Being able to manipulate the monkey, or even imitate it, helps to empower the child and moves the horrific imagery to less intense expression. Having the tactile softness of the monkey puppet can also help to soothe the child's increasing anxiety and related physiological responses, such as increased heartbeat, breathing, and body temperature that may occur and signal dysregulation, which can result from pursuing such graphic details. The therapist may then need to also utilize some relaxation and deep breathing exercises intermittently during this phase, with or without the monkey puppet modeling the deep breathing together with the child, in order to help to lessen any possible emotional arousal or dysregulation.

Summary

Puppets have become a useful tool in helping children identify feelings, recall memories, and learn more difficult abstract concepts in CBT trauma treatments. Their healing powers should not be underestimated! Integrating play therapy with a cognitive-behavioral approach is crucial for ensuring a developmentally appropriate intervention for young children who experienced trauma.

References

Briggs, K. M., Runyon, M. K., & Deblinger, E. (2011). The use of play in trauma-focused cognitive-behavioral therapy. In S. W. Russ & L. N. Niec (Eds.), *Play in clinical practice: Evidence-based approaches* (pp. 169–200). New York: Guilford Press.

Cohen, J. A., & Mannarino, A. P. (1996). A treatment outcome study for sexually abused preschool children: Initial findings. *Journal of the American Academy of Child and Adolescent Psychiatry, 35*, 42–50.

Cohen, J. A., Mannarino, A. P., & Deblinger, E. (Eds.). (2012). *Trauma-focused CBT for children and adolescents: Treatment applications.* New York: Guilford Press.

Deblinger, E., & Heflin, A. H. (1996). *Treating sexually abused children and their nonoffending parents*. Thousand Oaks, CA: Sage Publications.

Drewes, A. A. (2009). *Blending play therapy with cognitive behavioral therapy: Evidence-based and other effective treatments and techniques*. New York: Wiley.

Drewes, A. A. (2011, April). *A skill-building workshop: Effectively blending play-based techniques with cognitive behavioral therapy for affect regulation in sexually abused and traumatized children*. Paper presented at the Annual Conference of the Canadian Association for Child and Play Therapy, Guelph, ON, Canada.

Drewes, A. A., & Cavett, A. M. (2012). Play applications and skills components. In J. A. Cohen, A. P. Mannarino, & E. Deblinger (Eds.), *Trauma-focused CBT for children and adolescents: Treatment applications* (pp. 105–123). New York: Guilford Press.

Goodyear-Brown, P. (2010). *Play therapy with traumatized children: A prescriptive approach*. New York: Wiley.

Knell, S. M. (1993). *Cognitive-behavioral play therapy*. Northvale, NJ: Jason Aronson, Inc.

Knell, S. M., & Desari, M. (2011). Cognitive-behavioral play therapy. In S. W. Russ & L. N. Niec (Eds.), *Play in clinical practice: Evidence-based approaches* (pp. 236–262). New York: Guilford Press.

Meichenbaum, D. (2009). Foreword. In A. A. Drewes (Ed.), *Blending play therapy with cognitive behavioral therapy: Evidence-based and other effective treatments and techniques.* (pp. xvii–xix). New York: Wiley.

Schaefer, C. E., & Drewes, A. A. (Eds.). (2013). *The therapeutic powers of play: 20 core agents of change* (2nd ed.). Hoboken, NJ: Wiley.

Section V

Populations and Settings

16 Puppets in Family Therapy With a Case of Trauma and Sexual Abuse

Eliana Gil and Quinn K. Smelser

Introduction

The youngest members of a family system should be able to actively engage in family therapy. To this end, the incorporation of play-based techniques is essential to inclusive family therapy. One such technique is the use of puppets in family therapy. Irwin and Malloy (1975) developed the Family Puppet Interview as an informal assessment tool for families struggling to communicate. The Family Puppet Interview allows the therapist to see the family's interaction patterns when accomplishing a goal together (Irwin & Malloy, 1975). Gil (1994) defined ways in which puppets could be used throughout family therapy outside of the assessment phase. Through puppets, the family is able to safely project problematic material, thereby symbolically revealing individual and group dynamics of the family (Irwin & Malloy, 1975; Gil, 1994).

Landreth (2012) outlines the symbolic nature of play as a child's form of communication. Further, Gil (2016) highlights the importance of the metaphors and symbols that children use in their play. Families also bring symbols or connect with metaphors in family therapy. Puppets can allow children and families "to participate in symbolic play that connects concrete experience to abstract thought" (Hartwig, 2014, p. 205). The puppets may symbolize family members, systemic issues, or specific problems in the family. In family sessions, the experiential use of puppets in family therapy helps alleviate the intensity of emotions by creating "therapeutic distance" (Pereira, 2014, p. 395). Puppet stories generate metaphors through which the therapeutic healing process begins.

When used in family therapy, puppets are the vehicle by which the family can externalize their problem. In work with children, Butler, Guterman, and Rudes (2009) point out how puppets can embody the problem, allowing that "therapeutic distance" to form (Pereira, 2014, p. 395; Butler et al., 2009). This space created between the family system, its individual members, and their battles moves the family to externalize their problem, which is a goal of narrative therapy (White & Epston, 1990). Sori (2011) further demonstrates the use of puppets in narrative therapy when puppets are included in reflecting teams. As a part of the reflecting team, the puppets relate what they see happening within the session, which can then be reflected by the therapist along with the maladaptive patterns that emerge (Sori, 2011). Reflecting puppets can be directed by family members as well as by the therapist (Sori, 2011). This frees the family from getting caught in patterns of blame and creates emotional safety for family members to realize their own relational issues (Sori, 2011; Karakurt, 2012).

Puppets are helpful for an array of presenting problems in family therapy. Nutting (2015) outlines a case in which puppetry allowed for the externalization of a child's illness. Because puppets rely on symbolism and metaphor, families can communicate material specific to their ethnic and cultural background as well as their familial traditions and nuances (Karakurt, 2012). In reviewing the literature, Johnston (1997) cited puppets as a popular and effective play therapy technique for therapists to use with children who have suffered sexual abuse. With cases of sexual abuse, there is often an extreme intensity of emotions and heightened visceral trauma. Puppets are especially useful in cases of trauma and sexual abuse since family therapy will trigger these intense feelings and upsetting content. With puppets, what comes out in therapy can be projected onto something the child and family can control (Johnston, 1997). The following is a case scenario that describes an example of using puppets in family therapy. In this family, there was a history of sexual trauma as well as a more recent traumatic event that caused the family to again seek out treatment.

Case Scenario

Nine-year-old Rihanna and her brother Sean, 6 years old, were brought into treatment by their parents, Monique and Sean Sr., after a fire displaced them from their house. A faulty wire led to an explosion in the basement, and the house was consumed in flames quickly. Fortunately, the entire family, including their dog Bullit, was away visiting extended family for the winter holidays. Even grandmother, Mrs. Esther, who lived in the basement, had traveled with them on holiday when her other plans fell through. Monique and Sean found out about the fire after the fact, when the Virginia (VA) Fire Department contacted them to tell them that their house had been burned to the ground. The parents were devastated to find out that they had lost everything they owned—old photographs, computers, paintings, furniture, clothes, everything. . . . They also rejoiced that they were safe and in the supportive home of extended family. Sean Sr. traveled back and forth from Virginia to North Carolina until he secured a small apartment in Virginia for his family while their house was rebuilt. Monique was able to keep her job remotely until she returned to Virginia to develop some semblance of a normal life.

This family was known to me (Gil), since Sean had been sexually abused in a preschool setting and required some specialized services due to his hypervigilance and anxiety. In addition, he was often aggressive and sexually preoccupied. At this time, Rihanna, the older sister, had developed night terrors and extreme hypervigilance, and her little brother was taking his cues from his older sister, crying and clinging in a regressed manner, and needing extra reassurance and comforting. In addition, he had started masturbating excessively, and the mother was upset that "he still wasn't over the sexual abuse." I reassured the mother that the masturbating could be the child's way of comforting himself, or he was remembering his past trauma because he felt helpless and confused, as he had when the abuse occurred (affective bridging). The parents were sensitive to their children and yet felt impatient at how long it was taking the children to settle down. They had told the children that they were lucky that they were all together, that no one was hurt, and that they had the resources to rebuild their house and replace their belongings. This seemed a rational explanation but may have not been appropriate for such young children.

I normalized the children's reactions quickly, stating that the family had been traumatized and displaced by this tragic event, and predicted that it could take up to six months for the children to stabilize and even longer, sometimes, to regain pre-trauma functioning, especially since there were so many changes taking place. In addition, Sean was a little more vulnerable since he had endured a traumatic experience when he was younger, and feelings of helplessness could be triggered for him. We talked about reintroducing family routines and schedules, trying to replace some of their most important lost objects, and trying to make their small apartment homelike as quickly as they could.

While in North Carolina, the children had not wanted to return to a temporary school, and since the mother was working from home, she felt it important to allow them to stay with her. This school avoidance had continued in Virginia, and I encouraged her to start a graduated return to school schedule with them, preparing them to answer a myriad of questions that could be asked by friends and teachers, since the fire had been very public. The mother was receptive to this idea and at the same time asserted that her children needed encouragement, "not coddling," in order to resume their lives. Monique reported that she herself was suffering the aftereffects of this traumatic experience: She said she frequently found herself itemizing lost objects, smelling smoke smells, and feeling worried about all the wiring in the new apartment. Her best response to this new stress was to busy herself with work, and she noted that she and her husband BOTH were eager to move forward, hunker down with their work, and get back to their house as soon as they could. It would be another 9–12 months before that could occur, so my advice to invest some of their energies in creating a warm and structured environment in the interim was well received.

Individual Conjoint Therapy for Rihanna and Sean

I met with Rihanna and Sean together since their symptoms appeared similar and they had experienced the same Type 1 trauma (external event). Their parents were struggling with specific worries and concerns related to losing all their material possessions and now rebuilding their home, but they were a resourceful and resilient couple, deeply imbedded with a Christian community, and doing the very best to provide a secure and stable environment for their children.

The children explored the room easily (Sean did not remember the room since it was a new one), communicated verbally and nonverbally, and mostly, seemed to be aware that their mother (or father) was in the waiting room and made a ton of excuses to go out and find them. In addition, shortly after they came into my office, the children found a way to bring the waiting parent into the room to play. It became clear to me quickly that the children would benefit more from family therapy than individual or conjoint therapy. In particular, they were needing more proximity with their parents, and longing for comforting and reassurance. The parents, however, were being challenged on many fronts, overseeing the construction site, negotiating work demands, dealing with insurance claims, and purchasing necessary furniture, household supplies, and clothing for them all. Everyone had their hands full, and at the time that the children needed consistency and time with their parents, those were in short demand. Thus, family therapy sessions seemed indicated sooner rather than later, and I came in to meet with the family on Saturdays in order to reduce the stress of their having to drive to our office during a weekday.

Family Therapy

I did a number of family therapy sessions designed to increase comfort, restore a sense of emotional connectedness, and facilitate a warm and comfortable time together. The family was able to relax quickly, and it was clear there was a strong foundation of prior positive joint experiences. Sean exhibited some sexualized behavior in the sessions, and I coached the parents to set limits, distract him, and speak calmly and clearly about their expectations that private touching is done only in private. Sean responded well quickly. Some of the exercises I did in the first few sessions were inspired by Theraplay and prioritized physical movement, energy, laughter, and fun (Booth & Jernberg, 2009). The children enjoyed themselves so much that they asked if they could come back more often and also invited their grandmother to join in the fun (which she did after the second joint session).

By about the fifth session, I opted to introduce puppets to give the family a way to create a collective metaphor through storytelling with puppets. The directive for family puppet therapy is simple:

> As you can see, there are a variety of puppets here for you to use. What I would like you to do is to make up a story (using the puppets), that has a beginning, a middle, and an end. There are only two rules: You have to make up a story (it can't be the retelling of a popular story like Cinderella), and you have to act it out, not just narrate the story.
>
> (Gil, 1994)

The children immediately started looking around and seemed gleeful as they identified an alien, a snake, a mosquito, a squirrel, a caterpillar/butterfly, a gorilla, and so forth. The children's very warm sibling relationship was on full display as they shared ideas with each other, gave suggestions to their parents and grandmother, and flitted around the room trying on the puppets and rehearsing voices. I told the family I would give them privacy by stepping into the background and remaining quiet, and that they should rehearse their story until they felt ready to perform it. The story came to life as each person gave their puppet a personality, a purpose, and a role in the story. Their laughter filled the room, and it was a joy-filled sound for us all. Their family dynamics were respectful and cooperative. The father's special role was to approve the story line or to suggest another. He always asked his wife, Monique, if she agreed, and she almost always did. The grandmother's role was to delight in everything her grandchildren did, and their positive attachment was also obvious. Both children made sure that the grandmother had very special puppets indeed and encouraged her to bring her chair closer to them so that she could participate more completely.

The Rehearsal for the Story

Sean Jr. first suggested the story of someone laying down a railroad track for the trains to connect between cities, "so families can visit each other faster!" This evolved into the families taking an inaugural ride from one city to another. Rihanna had offered to be the cook and provide the meals to the passengers, but she and her grandmother would be the "entertainment," performing for the guests, "if they ate all their food!" Rihanna quipped that she didn't want to work in a kitchen, which could get "too hot and explode!" Sean Sr. said that he would be the driver and that Monique would be his lookout, letting him know if there was anything strange on the tracks or if there was any unexpected danger. This story came together very quickly, and although many variations were made throughout the rehearsal, it stayed pretty much the same, with some notable exceptions. The train was to drop off and pick up passengers in a few cities, and Sean Sr. suggested that one time they would be "ahead of schedule," and he would be able to "lounge in" to the station without the pressure of being late. After about 35 minutes, the family seemed to feel ready to tell the story, and proceeded to signal me that they were ready.

The Telling of the Family Puppet Story

The family seemed excited to take their positions and start the story. The driver and the lookout were in the front, talking about starting the engines, checking the brakes and the whistles, and looking back to make sure that everyone was on board. The father had an "old gray hair, bearded puppet with a cap," and the mother had a puppet dressed in blue, similar to a police officer. Rihanna chose the gorilla and the mosquito while Sean Jr. picked a snake and an alien. Esther chose a butterfly, and all of them pretended to climb into the train. The story went as follows:

Rihanna began the narrative, "We are going on a family trip, ooops, we forgot our pet, just wait, we have to run and get our pet, he needs to go everywhere with us." The children ran to get a dog puppet to represent their pet; they also agreed to bring a kangaroo puppet with a small joey inside. Rihanna continued, "Whew, that was a close one, we almost left one of our important family people, and we would have been verrrrryyyyyy sorry if we'd forgotten him." Sean added, "Yeah, he could have become a crispy critter if we left him home."

The family pretended to have a bumpy ride, to walk through the train, almost falling over, and they pointed out swimming pools, parks, and roller coasters they saw along the way. Suddenly, the train came to a screeching halt and the conductor said, "Ladies and gentlemen, we have come to a complete stop, the track ahead is closed, a tree has fallen over the track, and we must wait until they remove the tree to proceed. Make yourselves comfortable, it will be a short wait."

Sean took his kangaroo to the driver (his father) and said, "The baby is afraid, he's worried that something bad is going to happen." The driver reassured him that nothing bad would happen, to which the baby said, "You don't know that, you never know that, maybe the tree hit a telephone line and it starts a fire!" This unscripted part of the story was very spontaneous, and the parents and sibs, in character, proceeded to address the issue at hand. Esther said, "I think I'll fly ahead and go see for myself if everything is okay," getting up and walking to the door. The kangaroo (Sean Jr.) asked to go with her, and they left the room together. Rihanna, using her mosquito puppet, went and stung the driver and the lookout, so they would "stay alert," while she used her gorilla puppet to make growling sounds and to show everyone how big a breath she could take and how big she could blow. "I'm practicing in case I'm needed to blow out any fires that might be around . . ." The lookout seemed confused, and said, "Looks like the tree has been removed, danger averted, we can resume our trip." Esther piped in as the butterfly, returning with the joey and kangaroo, to state that the "coast is clear for a long, long way."

But Sean Jr. needed convincing as he put his snake on the floor and started yelling, "Watch out, it's a python, it got out of its cage, and it's trying to bite us." The other puppets looked around and started jumping, trying to get away from the snake. Then Sean Jr. took the snake and started biting the other puppets, mostly between their legs. The conductor (Sean Sr.) fashioned a pretend snake-catching object and picked it up, throwing it out the window, but before he did that he set limits with the snake: "I know that you're worried and I know that you're scared, Mr. Snake, but it's not okay to touch other people's private parts, no matter how you're feeling." Sean Jr. looked up and said, "Sorry, Dad, I forgot."

"All engines go," he yelled. "Everyone take a seat and let's get home quick!!" The conductor then turned the train around and headed back home.

Processing the Puppet Story

The processing experience among family members, facilitated by clinicians immediately following their puppet storytelling, is a rich opportunity to explore the collective family metaphor. The clinician manifests therapeutic curiosity that seeks to magnify the family's exploration of their story. Inevitably, this type of amplification will redirect the family to look deeper into their story—reflect together about their story and possible meaning. Clinicians are encouraged to stay within the story metaphor, asking characters for their impressions, following the story line, wondering out loud about one thing or another (Gil, 2016). The originators of the use of puppets with families, Irwin and Malloy, developed a Family Puppet Interview, which was designed to obtain assessment information by drawing parallels between the family's story and their real-life situations (Irwin & Malloy, 1975). Family puppet therapy is an advancement of the interview technique, in which clinicians move beyond the assessment phase to conduct therapeutic interventions within the context of the family's metaphor. The clinical assumption is that the story line and puppet characters have underlying meaning to the family and that it is possible that they gain something from externalizing and then interacting with their story.

The family puppet story designed by Sean Jr. and Rihanna's family was deceptively simple and exposed some of the issues still in disarray in this family who had endured a Type 1 trauma. Consider, for example, that the family's house had been burned down while they were traveling: Their story is about a family's journey. Something is forgotten and must be retrieved, somehow an acknowledgement that they came very close to losing a family member had they chosen to leave the dog or their grandmother in the house.

The unpredictability of the fire was visible in the fallen tree on the track as well as the snake and mosquito that appeared to threaten the family. Sean used the snake puppet to show how intolerable feelings are often linked to sexual acting out, and although this behavior had ceased quite a while ago, it manifested itself in a moment of stress in the story.

The parents were put in a position of authority and served as a compass that guided the journey's outcome. The parents had been separated of late, so putting them in the same place, working as a team, seemed relevant. It also seemed to be a concrete representation of what the children needed: Their parents in charge, ready to face challenges or dangers, capable of providing safety and security. It was also clear in the story that the family was well bonded, that the children knew where to go to get direction or nurturing (the baby joey), and that they could express their thoughts and feelings to each other, even about feelings like fear. In addition, the father was quite calm and adept at setting firm and nonjudgmental limits about crossing boundaries and touching private parts—Sean Jr. responded well to reminders of the lessons he had learned previously about inappropriate sexual contact.

Both children raised the issue of fire: Rihanna when she talked about the kitchen getting hot and exploding, and Sean Jr. when he said the fallen tree could hit the telephone line and cause a fire to combust.

The grandmother's role was quite important as she set off to scout the rest of the journey, reassuring the family that there were no dangers from her vantage point. When she left to peruse the situation, she had a companion, the joey's mother, to help. The family faced several dangers and yet they also experienced joy and adventure, culminating with the parents forging ahead after reassuring the passengers on the train that all was safe.

Clinicians are listening and watching intently so that they can formulate questions designed to delve a little deeper into key concepts or issues. In this story, several questions were generated by the therapist (Gil) and posed to different family members:

> "What was it like for the joey to admit that he was scared?"
> "How did the joey feel when his father reassured him?"
> "How did everyone react when the train came to a sudden stop?"
> "What was it like to know that there was a crisis on board the train?"
> "How did everyone react when the conductor and his assistant knew just what to do in a crisis?"
> "What was it like when the butterfly flew ahead to see what was going on?"
> "I noticed that both a stinging mosquito and a dangerous python posed a danger to the family. What was that like?"
> "What was it like for the python for someone to set clear limits on his touching private parts?"
> "I noticed that the butterfly and the kangaroo went out as scouts to look over the rest of the road home. . . . What was it like when they left? What was it like when they returned?"

This family interacted openly in the discussion, and at one point Monique said, "Wow, seems like the passengers on this train are still pretty concerned that bad things could happen. I know why that's so. Because we had a bad thing happen without warning, and now we all have to develop trust that bad things won't happen again!" Sean hugged his wife at this point, and they left with a deeper understanding that it would take time to recover from this traumatic experience. We had another 12 sessions or so, and we utilized Family Play Therapy as a conduit toward relationship enhancement, exposure of underlying worries, and opportunities for the children to role-play asking and receiving support.

Summary

Using puppets in family play therapy is a useful and powerful experience during the therapeutic process. It has the potential to be disarming, allowing families a deeper look at hidden or unspoken concerns as well as a deeper understanding of difficult experiences that may need resolution. Puppets are often used in therapy with children; however, integrating puppets with family work is a less explored alternative. This family's puppet story is a useful example of what can be accomplished through incorporating puppets in family therapy.

References

Booth, P. B., & Jernberg, A. M. (2009). *Theraplay: Helping parents and children build better relationships through attachment-based play* (3rd ed.). San Francisco, CA: Jossey-Bass.

Butler, S., Guterman, J. T., & Rudes, J. (2009). Using puppets with children in narrative therapy to externalize the problem. *Journal of Mental Health Counseling, 31*(3), 225–233.

Gil, E. (1994). *Play in family therapy*. New York, NY: Guilford Press.

Gil, E. (2016). *Play in family therapy* (2nd ed.). New York, NY: Guilford Press.

Hartwig, E. K. (2014). Puppets in the playroom: Utilizing puppets and child-centered facilitative skills as a metaphor for healing. *International Journal of Play Therapy, 23*(4), 204–216. doi:10.1037/a0038054

Irwin, E. C., & Malloy, E. (1975). Family puppet interviews. *Family Process, 14*, 179–191.

Johnston, S. S. M. (1997). The use of art and play therapy with victims of sexual abuse: A review of the literature. *Family Therapy, 24*(2), 101–113.

Karakurt, G. (2012). Puppet play with a Turkish family. *Journal of Family Psychotherapy, 23*, 69–78. doi:10.1080/08975353.2012.654092

Landreth, G. L. (2012). *Play therapy: The art of the relationship* (3rd ed.). New York, NY: Routledge/Taylor & Francis Group.

Nutting, R. (2015). The strength of children externalizing the effects of chronic illness through narrative puppetry. *Journal of Family Psychotherapy, 26*, 9–14. doi:10.1080/08975353.2015.10002736

Pereira, J. K. (2014). Can we play too? Experiential techniques for family therapists to actively include children in sessions. *The Family Journal: Counseling and Therapy for Couples and Families, 22*(4), 390–396. doi:10.1177/1066480714533639

Sori, C. F. (2011). Using hip-hop in family therapy to build "rap" port. In H. G. Rosenthal (Ed.), *Favorite counseling and therapy homework assignments* (2nd ed.) (pp. 299–308). New York, NY: Routledge.

White, M., & Epston, D. (1990). *Narrative means to therapeutic ends*. New York, NY: Norton.

17 The Wonder Continues

Captivating and Engaging Adults Through Therapeutic Puppet Play and Puppet Therapy

Joanne F. Vizzini

Take the leap with me from childhood to adulthood, and notice the gifts we too often leave behind. As one who originally thought *only* of children when thinking of puppets both educationally and therapeutically, I vow to do my best in this chapter to restore you, as I have been restored: to wonder.

Take Time to Wonder

Do you have a vision of your puppet usage with adults? Is a need in your school, community, or clinical practice calling to you? Let my story inspire you, and notice how you identify with it. Take notes during this chapter and some time to "be with" your own story, your thoughts and feelings. Your adult participants will engage in the same practice with the stories of the puppets.

How to Begin? Try Teaching Through the Puppet's Voice

Jump in at whatever age you are! At age 18, I became a self-taught puppeteer who gave presentations to children, ages 2–12, demonstrating the idea of mainstreaming children with learning disabilities into regular classrooms. Within the scope of my Maryland State research grant (received 1980), I studied children and their responses to questions geared toward eliciting their knowledge of accepting differences after a specific regulated puppet presentation was given. Allowing puppets and dolls to return to their rightful place as objects for play at any age, I began to include adults, children, and their families who were hurting, where siblings were at odds and spouses were in disagreements. Soon after, I was called forth by school administrators to sensitize and instruct teachers, staff, and daycare providers about the special needs of children with learning differences, led by the "new law," Public Law (PL) 94–142 (1975) (Texas Council for Developmental Disabilities, 2013). *What are your targeted adult populations, topics, passions, and financial resources?*

At churches, fairs, school events, and parent nights, I presented getting along in relationships, coping with stressors and conflict within faith communities, navigating families' emotional dynamics, and activating positive behaviors in classrooms. Whether using therapeutic coping techniques, spiritual coping, or value-based cognitive-behavioral responses, there was interest and energy about facilitating learning in venues where there were intergenerational audiences with adults engaged (see Fig. 17.1). Librarians, teachers, school administrators, parents, and daycare providers captivated with my puppet troupe, "Sunny-sides Up," were educated about how to aid young people in self-regulation (Bernier & O'Hare, 2005). *What are your venues or potential venues? Who is your target audience?*

In many multicultural groups I encountered, the faith community or school was where guidance was acceptable for even getting close to sharing feelings outside of the family, if one were allowed to share, have, or express feelings at all. In many cultural groups, conflict was to be dealt with in a private and often hidden manner, or it was not acknowledged (Avent & Cashwell, 2015). Puppet play provides for a more socially acceptable format to learn, once removed from direct contact with a therapist (Notaras Murphy, 2010). *How will you be culturally sensitive?*

Figure 17.1 Practice Makes Permanent for Learning to Share the Passion of Puppets to Educate Parents/Adults About Children's Issues

Photo courtesy of the American Counseling Association

What then of the adult learner and the puppets? At my own Catholic church, many adults were sitting on the edge of their pews absolutely fascinated by the message of the puppets and the puppets themselves while observing their children participating. Adults called to say "hello" to Cool Eugene (one of my main puppets) after participating in church services focused on their children. Having the children present or as the focus of a training seemed to give the parents or trainees permission to enter their childlike wonder and engage in puppet play. *Notice how puppets captivate adults!*

Be Engaged and Engaging

How do you picture yourself in relationship to puppet use? Can you picture you and the puppet as one, like taking on a persona for a virtual game or being in a theatrical role? Think ahead to what kind of characters you might be attracted to if you were the adult receiving the puppet's message.

Choosing and Creating Puppet Characters to Speak Your Passion

I chose my characters by what was given to me, what I could afford as a teenaged adult, age 18, and what I thought would get the messages desired across to the listeners, at the time namely children. I suggest that you look for what attracts you, feels soft, and that your hand feels very comfortable in. I use all hand puppets. I have trained others who use marionettes or dolls and other types of puppets. *What kinds of puppets attract you?*

Elaine Meyers, muse and luminary, prophetically called forth the gift of puppeteering in me at age 17.5. She instantly became my "anam cara," soul friend. Together, we attended a performance of the Kids on the Block (KOB) (Aiello, 1977), a group of handicapped puppets. A strong suggestion for your own preparation for puppet use with adults is to attend workshops and performances (even if they are for children), especially of those who are presenting the same type of messages that you plan to deliver to your demographic. *Who calls forth your creativity?*

The puppets in my troupe each have a particular style of calling forth interaction from the audience, different from the KOB, which uses questions and answers throughout the educational program to aid in learning.

> Each puppet in the Vizzini Puppet Model has a distinct life-long personality with sustaining characteristics such as voice, dress, themes, and story . . . Just as in a 12-Step meeting, the puppets tell their narrative of recovery, passing on their "experience, strength and hope". The themes are reinforced in the [education or] therapy process through short, easy-to-remember sayings that allow [clients/patients/participants] to quickly recall appropriate behaviors in difficult situations.
>
> (Vizzini, 2003, p. 55)

Figure 17.2 Engaging Directly With the Puppet as a Helper for the Puppet Invites a Strength-Based Bond, Hand in Hand in Hand

Photo courtesy of Freedom Through Psychotherapy, LLC

I prefer puppets with mouths that move for my model, with any aged participant (see Fig. 17.2). For your puppet to be transformed into your client's therapist, a basic tenet of the Vizzini Puppet Model, the puppet becomes a messenger for all of the tools you know and use as a play therapist, clinician, or educator. Once your hand goes inside of that puppet, your mind, heart, and spirit breathe through that puppet and his or her voice comes from your wisdom, your strength, and your knowledge.

When designing my puppets' characters, I like to have them have funny sayings, sing songs, tell stories, and have difficulties with which the audience will identify. The puppets' way out of their difficulties is essential to the process. Captivating and engaging the participants by inviting them to help the puppet, giving the participant some object to hold, like the puppet that just spoke while another comes out, or singing along with the puppet is quite effective (see Fig. 17.3). *What characters come to your mind? Do you want creature puppets or people puppets? Choose puppets that have meaning to your demographic. Meet my first puppets—a man, Cool Eugene; the furry puppet with two red belly buttons; and many more acquired over years—at my website, www.drvizzini.com.*

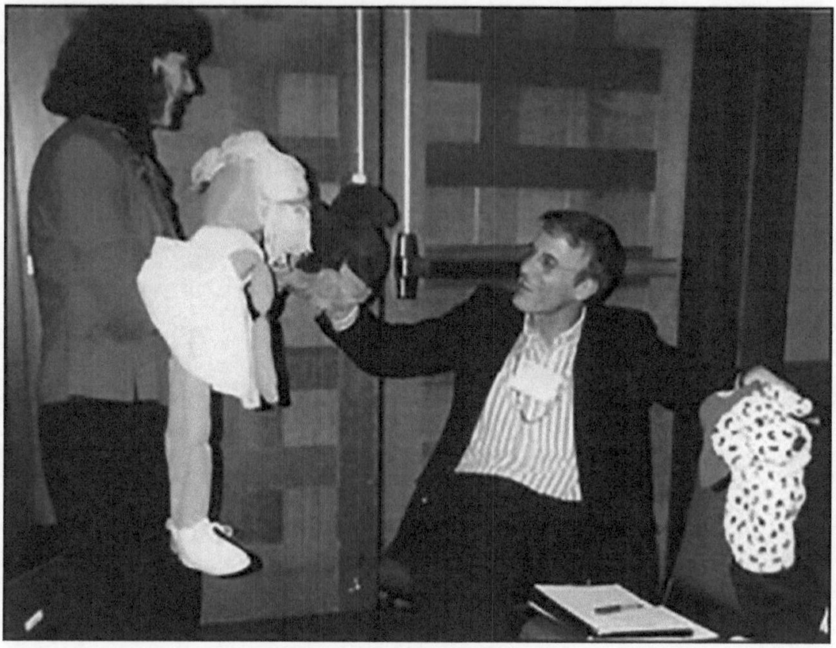

Figure 17.3 Become Captivated by Your Puppet and Your Life Will Breathe It Into Life

Photo courtesy of Freedom Through Psychotherapy, LLC

Activating and Engaging Adults With Puppets as a Therapeutic/Educational Tool

To practice puppet therapy, you must be certified or licensed in your state in the United States. According to this author, puppet therapy is the therapeutic use of puppets by a therapist with the intention of providing psychotherapy in a therapeutic setting (Vizzini, 2003). You can always share puppets for learning! I worked for 17 years providing therapeutic and psycho-educational puppets with great fervor and favor.

Puppets became a mainstay in my first- and second-grade classrooms, and in that venue, the troupe and I met regularly with adults about parenting and their children's issues. Also, and quite importantly, I engaged adults at friends' and families' parties, both for intergenerational events and for adult-only occasions. The latter became one of my best venues for practicing a puppet character's voice, style, and narrative. Becoming one with the puppet meant honing in on every detail that would make the puppet come alive. To be reminded of the specific ways to make a puppet appear more real, seek out the well-defined tenets in the beginning chapters of this text. The risk-taking idea of making an adult party more enjoyable by bringing your budding puppet personality to share is strongly recommended. You will get *in vivo* feedback immediately about voice, gestures, eye focus, and overall character. And, the hope is that you and others will be entertained. *With whom can you practice puppet characterization?*

Speaking Your Truth With Passion and Love

As a religious sister for 17 years—yes, I became what is called in common parlance, "a nun"—the puppets met families of mothers and their children at the Children's Center, Bedford Hills Maximum Security Prison, along with Ms. Jean Harris and Sr. Elaine Roulet. The puppets helped deal with their separation and loss, and family issues of addiction, abuse, and bullying. Ethics demand that we have enough support available to any population where we share puppets by having therapists on site or referrals to hotlines and therapists. Puppets can bring forth deeper emotion than an untrained person should handle. Even once you become a therapist, if doing a group that is not therapy, please be wise and provide resources. *What human service can you give voice to through the puppets? Are you willing to allow the powers of the puppets to speak?*

Moving Toward Your Use of Puppets in Therapy for Adults

Take time to know your story of learning useful therapeutic tools for your own recovery from any myriad of emotional, mental, or spiritual maladies. Will you dare to share these quips, these transforming moments and coping skills, from the context of your life and career? What outcome do you desire for the adults you choose to serve?

The usage of puppet therapy with adults has many faces. I carry them with me because they have honored me, privileged me, to walk their inner journey with them. There have been people of various colors, races, and socioeconomic wealth (see Fig. 17.4).

Figure 17.4 Dedication to the Human Spirit Being Freed and Becoming Whole Is Possible When Puppeteer and Puppet Join Together With a Troupe to Achieve What One Cannot Do Alone

Photo courtesy of Freedom Through Psychotherapy, LLC

When I was doing my own inner work, the puppets took on the frame for me that engaged my view of them as not only being therapeutic, but as therapy. As I grew as a person and a woman, as I grew as a healer and a teacher, the puppets grew as well.

Raising a child who was born with full-blown AIDS changed me. At age 3, G came to live with us, religious sisters, in our emergency shelter home. G had been living on the streets of the city, and at age 6.5, a parasite overtook her.

Medical use of puppets was born in me to support her living and dying. Still as an educator, not yet a therapist, and acting as "mother," I provided therapeutic relief on how to manage G's feelings or taught her about her next medical procedure. Days before G breathed her last breath, she asked to sing with her friend Cool Eugene.

Would You Take Puppets to a Hospital or Hospice Where You Could Do Work With Families?

Anyone who has lost a child knows that all of life's edges feel completely frayed, tattered. I turned to the puppets myself so that I could find the healing words that seemed buried deep inside. I was in a support group and shared the puppets, using the healing information I was gaining about trauma recovery. *What words need to come forth from your inner self?*

The puppets were so well received by the women in my support group that I wondered if they could be used at my clinical site (see Fig. 17.5). When I picked up those puppets, I picked my life back up.

Figure 17.5 Gather the Group. Share Your Truth. Watch the Puppet Power at Your Fingertips Transform the Room and You Along With It

Photo courtesy of Freedom Through Psychotherapy, LLC

The adult women in my group said it gave them hope, new ways of viewing the pain that they were going through, and at times joy. When a person is healing from grief, nothing seems funny for quite some time. We all knew we were healing when we could have a deep belly laugh together about something one of the puppets said. *When have you been able to get perspective through humor and the arts?*

Be Confident and Bold—Dare to Share Your Creative Juices With the World

Take notes in the next sections and create your own questions.

Populations: Homeless (Ages 18–60)

The homeless clients at my internship, mostly men, were never told they were having puppets for group. I prefer it that way. No adult in 22 years has ever left the room because we were using puppets. There have been people triggered by the power of the puppets who choose to leave to take care of themselves while they are sobbing.

When I first asked to use the puppets with the clientele, my boss was quite hesitant. If that occurs for you, do not lose heart. *Believe in what you can offer.* Go back and ask again. I got a chance to give birth to the Vizzini Puppet Therapy Model based on cognitive behavioral therapy tenets (Meichenbaum, 2017), mixed with narrative (Combs & Freedman, 1996) and humor therapy (Cousins, 1979).

In each puppet therapy session, I offered the clientele a specific means to help with the exact issue they were going through. Each puppet I shared was portrayed as in a recovery process. I designed a specific employment piece of therapeutic work to overcome the fears and hurts that kept self-esteem low.

Populations: People of Means (Ages 18–60)

The leader of a five-day residential therapeutic experience for people of means who wanted to overcome childhood hurts hired me. I became the Monday morning opening for the entire week, prepping the clientele to enter their playful, childlike selves who could be vulnerable and safe, while sitting on the floor enjoying the puppets. The training she provided me was in psychodrama, and all of the therapists had to experience the therapy program before beginning to work there. *Both ideas are excellent ones for you to consider to increase your skills and to recall that puppets and puppet therapy are experiential.*

Populations: Intergenerational Work and Young Adults (Ages 18–90)

Sharing your gifts may take more chutzpah than you are used to having; however, using puppets therapeutically with adults is a worthy cause. Young adults (18- to 24-year-olds) seem more at home holding the puppet themselves and being hidden to use the puppet. My puppets helped older teens regarding smoking cessation at a school for emotionally disturbed adolescents and with self-esteem at a juvenile detention center. I still own the camel puppet in a coffin that the aforementioned youth purchased for me as a gift to express their gratitude. Many of them were addicted to nicotine and ceased smoking or moderated their use.

An intergenerational format allows for the entire family to go home, use the puppet messages, and discuss the puppetry experience. Having some adults present for the puppet therapy can be helpful even if it is not the youths' parents.

The adults who participate when I am giving a presentation for therapeutic puppets in a grief camp setting have helped the experience be much deeper and acceptable to the children than if I were giving the presentation without them present (see Fig. 17.6). I call upon adults to enter into the puppet experience, and youth respond to "their counselor" participating, as if it hands the youth a permission slip to enter the puppet world. Adults are essential to help with management of youth in the room so that if a child is disturbed or is disturbing to other youth, an adult, not me, handles the child while I am "being" the puppet in my hand. If a youth becomes too out of control, then he or she is escorted to emotional safety and removed with a supportive adult helper. I prefer to have youth seated on mats on the floor and to have the mats all separated, not touching each other. Their adult

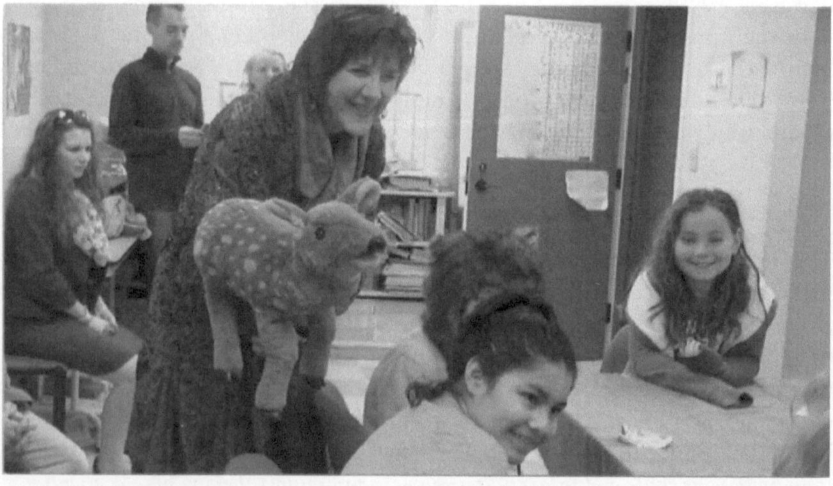

Figure 17.6 Intergenerational Puppet Experiences Allow Adults to Suspend Disbelief and Provide a Structure for All Involved to Have a Rich Time of Learning and Healing

Photo screenshot from video, "I Am Safe in My Space: Educating Adults to Help Children," Dr. Joanne Vizzini; Videographer: Ron Israel buddy getting on the floor too or being seated near them in a chair has helped many youth feel at home with their puppet participation. The adult volunteer receives the therapeutic experience as a "helper," which makes it more acceptable. I work on the floor best with young adults or adults. Often I am given a semicircle of chairs. Tables block the flow of the energy, so I have to work harder to engage the group. I do my best to set the stage for them to regress in service of their egos.

The Puppet Therapy Experience for Adults

What makes an adult client reach for a puppet? What makes adults more likely to be open to puppets or puppets used as dolls?

I have no empirical data to inform you. I do have 22 years of clinical experience using puppets with adults and 17 years as an educator. Notice the language of "evidence-based" may be slim here; however, anecdotally, the evidence of the effectiveness of using puppets with adults is profound. I have used puppets with every type of client/patient/participant. Ethically, caution must be used in cases of delusion, mania, severe depression, and some trauma. Use of additional supervision is recommended. As in all types of therapy, timing can make the difference between an acceptable or an inappropriate intervention. I have effectively used puppets with people who have schizophrenia when telling their story of losing their mind, which they generally would not share with me. And, for dissociative disorder, I have even given service at inner child do-over parties (see Fig. 17.7). Again, seek wise counsel, as the power of puppets is formidable.

A key difference between the Vizzini Model and other documented accounts of puppet therapy is the visibility of the therapist while he or she is manipulating and speaking through the puppets. Clients generally focus

Figure 17.7 Reaching for Freedom, Light, and Hope at a Time of Trauma, Despair, or Fear Is a Courage That Has Wings

Photo courtesy of Freedom Through Psychotherapy, LLC

on the puppet, not the therapist. I use a waist-high screen in front of me; a table with a cloth cover will suffice. The "stage" offers a means of hiding which puppets will come. The presence and visibility of the puppet therapist is thought to be significant for client safety and the conscious suspension of disbelief. The clients know that they are still working in a therapeutic setting, but they can disarm defenses and thus work on core therapeutic issues in a playful manner (Vizzini, 2003).

Preparing Scripts

You may desire more guidance than I am providing for your script. If so, please refer to the following websites: www.legendsandlore.com/puppetscript.html, www.puppetresources.com/#sthash.dA4aUhCG.dpbs, www.skits-o-mania.com/, and http://kidsontheblockottawa.ca/?page_id=150. These sites have many topics. They may seem too geared toward children, but they can give you a start.

All of my scripts are from my creative gift and my inner voice. The characters and their narratives flow from my experiences and my training as a therapist. Many of my characters use metaphors and short phrases, like, "Be a helper, not a hurter." Some of them sing familiar tunes. I ask about common tunes sung to children when I enter a culture to offer puppets. The adults relate well to what they were brought up hearing. Some of my puppets use rap songs and participants are chosen for the background sounds, "Puchoo. Puchoo!" Everyone stands, moves, and sings as they repeat back through song a healing rhyme in rap form, like, "You gotta feel, so you can heal, so you can deal, so you can become real."

Individuals

The sessions are usually in a group setting, but they can easily be modified for individual therapy. Populations other than those in a recovery program address human experiences of facing one's issues, soliciting help, releasing resentments, self-love, and the self-regulation of feelings and behaviors.

Have a puppet in the room, in the area where you meet the individual. I have Deerheart, a deer puppet who has particular spiritual meaning to me. You may choose a dog, a bear, or a lion. Individuals have at times asked to sit with Deerheart, and at times I have offered her. Perhaps it's when I'm giving a psycho-educational piece on how vulnerable or little they were when younger, as people tend to assess their past with an adult projection back as if they had all of the insight, skills, and size they have now. Perhaps it's when someone has done a regressive piece of work and they are crying. Trust your intuitive sense, like you do for introducing anything to another person. Perhaps you'll introduce the puppet like a doll, as a witness, or as an inroad to discover what kind of softness or dolls/puppets were available to your individual in the past. Be prepared to be surprised at the depth and breadth of the meaning attributed to "friends" who helped little ones to sleep, to animals/dolls who held secrets or gave comfort or who were their ONLY friends, to young people who gave shows for others, and even to adults who have used dolls or done puppeteering for their children, church, or other venue.

If used as a doll, the individual often sits with the puppet next to or on him or her. Frequently, both men and women stroke the puppet/doll.

If used as a puppet, the individual often uses the above-mentioned, and I ask if I can speak to him or her with that puppet or with another. In an Internal Family Systems (IFS) or a Gestalt manner, the individuals can talk to part of themselves. For example, an individual may want to hold Deerheart while talking to Wise Owl—a wiser, more mature part of themselves—or use Wise Owl or the oldest wise owl, Grandfather Hoo Hoo, to hear the voice of an outside wisdom figure known or brand new to the person.

Some individuals have benefited greatly from projecting a feeling, another person, or a part of themselves into the form of a creature puppet. Many individuals who could not express their anger get great benefit from making a puppet represent their anger or the situation of concern. Others have twisted, squeezed, thrown, or given loving, gentle touch to whatever the puppet represents.

I *always* ask if I can be nearer to the person. Do not assume that moving closer is a given, even with a welcomed puppet. I can either be the puppet therapist or support the individual in visualizing parts. Some individuals gather a group of puppets, or puppets used as dolls, and arrange them within sight (like a chair near them), placing them in significant places according to that part's role in their lives.

Search, Search, and Research

Firstly, search for your population, and then expect to search again as you discover what reaches you and the demographic you are called to serve. Add research to your to-do list. As a profession, our experiences and legacy deserve to be put forth, demonstrating an evidence-based clinical approach. My data produced a step forward in regard to puppet therapy being seen as feasible for adults. At a chemical dependency 12-step model facility, Hazelden, I went to the units at one of their sites to perform an experiment of comparing puppet therapy to regular therapy with adults. The outcome data demonstrated the patients favoring the use of puppets in therapy (ages 18–55, a men's unit and a women's unit, as well as an older adult unit of both men and women, ages 56–83); on average there was a greater satisfaction with puppet therapy versus regular therapy. And the strangest result was that the same older adults who chose the puppet therapy over and above the regular therapy were more anxious for both state and trait anxiety, while their younger counterparts, the men's and women's units, were less anxious following the puppet therapy. The upshot is if you are called to use the puppets for older adults, be aware

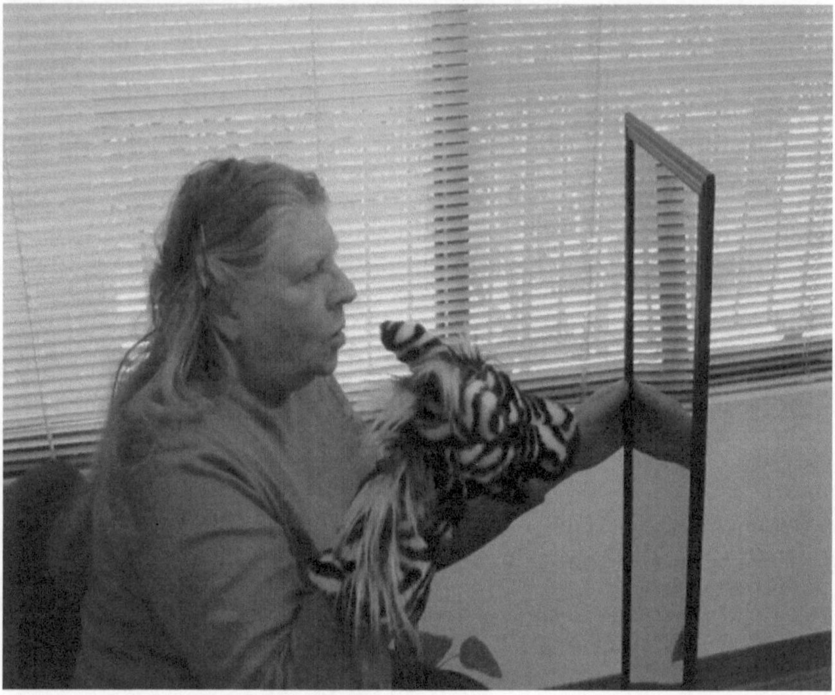

Figure 17.8 An Older Adult Can Look Forward to Being Less Anxious If Given the Attention Needed to Encourage His or Her True Self to Come Forward

Photo courtesy of Freedom Through Psychotherapy, LLC

that they are likely going to have some feelings about talking to and with the puppets (see Fig. 17.8). Use relaxation and give older adults time to adjust to the idea of working with puppets to allow them to participate more freely in the type of therapy they seem attracted to, puppet therapy (Vizzini, 2003).

Wonder With Wonder

At the close of this wondering chapter, please be sure to take a look at the handout, "Puppets 4 Adults." The basic premises of the chapter are included as a guide for you and as a reminder of salient points. The journey is yours, and hopefully you have taken the advice to journal along the route of the chapter so that you feel more prepared to launch into using puppets for adults. Start small if you must, but do start. Pick up the tools I have laid out for you and wonder, as I do, about the adventure of being captivated and engaged by using puppets for adults.

References

Aiello, B. (1977). *Kids on the block.* Columbia, MD: Author.

Avent, J., & Cashwell, C. (2015). The black church: Theology and implications for counseling African-Americans. *The Professional Counselor Journal, 5*(1), 81–90. doi:10.15241/jra5.1.81

Bernier, M., & O'Hare, J. (2005). *Puppetry in education and therapy: Unlocking doors to the mind and heart.* Bloomington, IN: Author House.

Combs, G., & Freedman, J. (1996). *Narrative therapy: The social construction of preferred realities.* New York: W.W. Norton & Company.

Cousins, N. (1979). *Anatomy of an illness as perceived by the patient.* New York: W.W. Norton & Company.

Michenbaum, D. (2017). *The evolution of cognitive behavior therapy: A personal and professional journey with Don Michenbaum.* New York: Routledge.

Notaras Murphy, S. (2010, February 14). Remembering play. *Counseling Today.* http://ct.counseling.org

Texas Council for Developmental Disabilities. (2013). Project ideal: Informing and designing education for all learner. *Special Education Policy.* Retrieved from www.projectidealonline.org

Vizzini, J. (2003). *A comparison study of puppet therapy to regular therapy in a chemical dependency twelve-step treatment model.* Baltimore: Loyola Library.

Appendix

Handout: A Basic Guide for the Therapeutic Use of Puppets 4 Adults

P ICTURE THE PUPPET AND YOU AS ONE. HAVE A VISION OF YOUR PUPPET USAGE.

U NDO YOUR BELIEF THAT PUPPETS ARE JUST FOR CHILDREN.

P LAN WELL FOR YOUR GROUP/INDIVIDUAL SESSION.

P URPOSE. ASK, "WHY THIS TOPIC?" AND "WHY THIS GROUP OR INDIVIDUAL?"

E VENT. ASK WHAT EVENT IS BEST? MORE THAN ONCE? IF SO, SEQUENTIAL?

T AKE TIME TO PREPARE.

S PEND TIME ON THE . . .

4 BASIC TOOLS. MAKE YOUR PUPPET BELIEVABLE (LIP SYNCH, EYE FOCUS, VOICE, AND GESTURE).

A CT AS IF YOU KNOW EXACTLY WHAT YOU ARE DOING. YOUR ATTITUDE AND CONFIDENCE SPEAKS VOLUMES.

D ARE TO DESIGN FROM YOUR HEART AND YOUR CREATIVITY. TRY SOMETHING NEW AND SPONTANEOUS.

U NDERSTAND YOUR GOAL(S).

L OVE WHO YOU ARE AND WHO YOU ARE BECOMING. THEN, THOSE YOU SERVE CAN DO THE SAME.

T RUST YOUR INSTINCTS AS A CLINICIAN OR EDUCATOR.

S TAY FOCUSED ON THE FUN. PASS ON THE FAITH YOU HAVE IN HEALING.

18 Puppet Play in Medical Settings

Judi Parson

Puppets may be used as agents to facilitate playful forms of communication, distraction, and education between children and professionals in medical settings. They are used for the purpose of providing health care information and procedural simulation as well as for therapeutic care. To explore puppet play in this environment, specific puppetry techniques are required. One such technique is called Pup-Ed (KRS simulation), developed by Reid-Searl (2012). It provides practical steps and an educational framework to teach professionals on how to engage children in various forms of puppet play in the medical setting. To engage in procedural education, this framework advocates wearing a two-handed puppet, also called a living puppet, which transforms the puppet into a pseudo health care professional. However, the characteristics assigned to a given puppet are done so that either single or multiple users can wear the puppet. Choice of puppet is important in the health care settings because the puppet should be fit for the purpose in relation to type, style, size, and according to infection control protocols. This chapter provides an overview of puppet play in medical settings with consideration given to procedural puppets with the inclusion of medical equipment, such as a nasogastric tube or venous access devices, and used by health care professionals to demonstrate the medical or nursing interventions. The chapter concludes with a therapeutic puppet play activity where the child may decorate and create his or her own puppet, which in turn provides a resource to facilitate communication.

Defining Puppet

Puppets can be made of virtually anything. Blumenthal (2005) states that they could be idols, idiots, or worms. Historically, puppets have been used for religious ceremony, teaching purposes, and entertainment. The art of engaging the audience through puppets occurs with not only the specific details and characteristics of the puppet structure but the actions of the puppeteer in moving and positioning the puppet. Thus, whenever someone creates an individualized scenario and projects the scenario onto the puppet, the puppet appears to be "brought to life." Projections allow for both conscious and unconscious parts of the self to be brought out into the open, as Bernier and O'Hare (2005, p. 125) state:

> Puppets are sometimes made as conscious self-representations or representations of others, but more often, puppets emerge that embody unconscious dynamics or parts of self that are not as easily or openly expressed.

Puppets are used therapeutically in both directive and nondirective play therapy practice and with consideration to a range of theoretical approaches. The puppet is an object, like other toys and creative tools in the playroom, which provides an extension of the self (the child-self and the therapist-self). As a result, puppet play may be aligned with all four major categories found in the therapeutic powers of play, namely to facilitate communication, foster emotional wellness, enhance social relationships, and increase personal strengths (Schaefer & Drewes, 2014). Therefore, with these categories in mind, puppet play may also be used therapeutically in various environments including medical and hospital settings. Medical puppet play draws on both theatrical and educational puppetry in conjunction with therapeutic interpersonal skills to amplify therapeutic change.

Setting the Medical Scene

Children accessing medical services do so for a range of pediatric health care problems, including a variety of illnesses and diseases, accidents and injuries, and/or for medical procedures or surgery. Children being admitted to an emergency room or pediatric ward in a hospital may experience a range of emotions due to the uncertainty of the environment and because they are worried or fearful about their health status, potential medical procedures or surgery, or even death and dying (Parson, 2009). Inherent in the strange medical environment is a barrage of sensory information that may or may not be familiar to the individual child. Hospital smells, lighting, and sounds are very different to everyday home or school life (Parson, 2009). Haiat, Bar-Mor, and Shochat (2003) state that play can help children make sense of hospital language, sights, and sounds. However, it is not uncommon to hear the sounds of pain and suffering in a children's ward, and this can be overheard by other children nearby, which may amplify fears and concerns.

In the medical setting today, the scene is changing, as children tend to experience themselves as more active and competent health consumers compared with previous generations, and are given more responsibility to manage their own illness (Ekra, Korsvold, & Gjengedal, 2015). One factor that may have led to this change is an increased awareness of children's rights with the United Nations Convention on the Rights of the Child (CRC) (United Nations, 1989) and responding to those rights within organizations, such as hospitals. This requires that health care professionals in the hospital be cognizant of children's rights and in particular the following UNCRC articles, which state:

> ***Article 12:*** *Parties shall assure to the child who is capable of forming his or her own views the right to express those views freely in all matters affecting the child, the views of the child being given due weight in accordance with the age and maturity of the child.*
>
> ***Article 13:*** *The child shall have the right to freedom of expression; this right shall include freedom to seek, receive and impart information and ideas of all kinds, regardless of frontiers, either orally, in writing or in print, in the form of art, or through any other media of the child's choice . . .*

To uphold the CRC in the medical setting requires that children give and receive information about their health care and indeed about any medical procedures or surgery. Most importantly, information must be communicated to the child in a way that is developmentally appropriate for the individual child. Ekra et al. (2015) state that finding ways to balance children's vulnerability and agency seems to be the best way to care for children in hospitals. Therefore, to find this balance one must enter the world of the child in and through play, because play is the child's most natural way of communicating (Landreth, 2012). Engaging in play, especially puppet play, may enable therapeutic and educative ways to communicate and connect with children in the medical setting to optimize the health care experience.

Types of Puppets

Puppets may be classified in many ways, including character style, size, and purpose. The size of the puppet may be from very small finger puppets, to hand and glove puppets, to large and wearable life-size puppets. In traditional play therapy a range of 20 to 30 puppets are usually available for children and/or family members to access in the playroom (Irwin & Shapiro, 1975). The range of puppets vary, including human figures or character puppets; aggressive, friendly, or shy puppets; wild or domestic animal puppets; mythical, fantasy, and fairy puppets; and the list goes on and is almost limitless in the types and styles of puppets available. It is not feasible to have such a large range in the hospital context due to multiple staff users and child patients, which may breach infection control protocols. Therefore, specifically designed and washable puppets are used in the medical setting.

When purchasing puppets, or even when they are made on the ward for the child to take home, the design may allow the user to operate the puppet's mouth or hands. Puppets with mouths, such as a sock puppet or a living puppet, may enhance verbal expression as well as the playing out of oral interests, including eating, sucking, biting, and licking, whereas puppets with hands allow for holding, hugging, wrestling, and fighting (Parson, 2016).

However, a living puppet, which is designed to be operated by the mouth and/or hands, or a procedural puppet have been more commonly used with children in the pediatric ward.

Puppets in Medical Settings

Puppets have been used to creatively enhance communication, to educate and support children in medical settings, and to simulate child patients for nursing students (Reid-Searl et al., 2016). Procedural puppets have been used to demonstrate specific procedures for the purpose of educational or medical puppet play. Living puppets are a particular type of two-handed puppet (see Figure 18.1) that may reside on the pediatric ward to help "talk" to children

Figure 18.1 Living Puppet

Puppets from left to right include Hamish (standing), Carlos (hiding face), Maggie, and Rosie

Table 18.1 The Pup-Ed (KRS Simulation) Framework (Reid-Searl, 2012)

The Pup-Ed Framework	
P	**Puppet preparation phase:** Users are taught how to create the puppet history and use the puppet.
U	**Understanding the learner:** The user considers different learning styles.
P	**Play in action:** Users learn how to use the puppet with the child in spontaneous situations without rehearsed scripts.
E	**Evaluation:** The user evaluates the impact of the puppet with the child.
D	**Debrief:** The user meets with the child without the puppet present and identifies how the child felt, what worked well, what could have been different, and what the child learned.
(KRS Simulation)	
KRS	***Knowledge***—of the user in guiding the interaction between puppet and child ***Realistic***—suspending the child's disbelief ***Spontaneous***—the interaction with the puppet is spontaneous

about their thoughts and feelings, or for procedural or educative play activities. However, the living puppets do not usually have medical equipment inserted or attached.

Reid-Searl et al. (2016), in a qualitative study of nurses using puppets in a children's ward in regional Australia, found that the living puppets in conjunction with the Pup-Ed framework were an effective way to optimize pediatric care. They reported that the nurses who used the puppets found them useful to connect with the child, to introduce play and distraction, to reduce the child's fears, and to break down barriers. The study also revealed that the use of puppets by nurses also had challenges including the confidence, or lack thereof, in using the living puppets and time constraints within the medical setting (Reid-Searl et al., 2016). The study stated that the integration of a guided framework, such as Pup-Ed (KRS simulation), was useful for nurses to enhance the provision of medical puppet play for children in the hospital (see Table 18.1).

The Pup-Ed (KRS simulation) framework provides the practical steps based on an educational structure to teach professionals ways to engage children using puppet play in their work. Within the training are some important aspects that may be explored and adapted to other settings, such as in conjunction with directive play therapy models (Parson, 2016), and therefore it is useful to explain in further depth.

The puppet preparation phase requires that the puppet be worn by the trained and informed professional, such as a nurse or play therapist on the ward. The informed professional is one who is able to connect with the child for the purpose of providing health care or procedural education. The informed person is knowledgeable about the issue at hand and will be able to respond and answer any questions the child may ask of the puppet. However, before this can take place, the professional needs to work with the puppet. Wearing the puppet—that is, either placing two hands in the gloves of the puppet or one hand in the mouth and the other in the puppet glove—enables the professional to use the puppet's hand(s) as his or her own. This is useful for manipulating medical equipment. However, getting to know and playing with the puppet begins the process to "bring the puppet to life." Moving the puppet in various ways, such as turning it away and toward the operator, talking to the puppet as if it were "alive," and developing specific characteristics and a scenario, all work together to establish and enhance the puppet's identity. If the professional is a sole user, he or she may choose to develop a distinct voice for the puppet, which requires practice. However, if multiple users are going to be using the puppet, such as on a pediatric ward, then it is advised that the puppet be silent, as not everyone will create the same voice for the puppet (Reid-Searl, 2012). In this scenario a whisper technique is used by the professional to and from the puppet to communicate with the child.

One aspect of puppet preparation includes creating a puppet character by giving the puppet a name, age, gender, address, diagnosis, past history, medical and surgical history, family and social situation, medication, and any unique attributes and idiosyncratic characteristics (Reid-Searl, 2012). So in essence, it involves creating baseline information that would normally be collected from a child being admitted to the ward.

Understanding the emotional, behavioral, psychosocial, and learning needs of the child requires entering the world of the child and assessing for any therapeutic or educational needs. Using a humanistic stance to create the conditions to enter the child's world—that is, unconditional positive regard, empathy, and being congruent (Rogers, 1957) together with a playful, curious approach—facilitates engagement and develops the therapeutic relationship. For example, Jenny, an 8-year-old girl, had just been given a diagnosis of insulin dependent diabetes mellitus (IDDM), also known as type 1 diabetes, which will require frequent blood tests and daily insulin injections or an insulin pump. How will Jenny cope with this news and long-term medical treatment? What is her understanding of IDDM? What information needs to be given now? In a scenario like this, a puppet with already existing diagnosis, prescribed medication, and family history may be able to connect with Jenny to demystify any concerns or fantasies. The puppet, through the skills of the professional, takes on the therapeutic play role in providing counseling and educational opportunities. This point is important in the KRS simulation concept, which is discussed below with reference to procedural puppetry.

Play in action refers to when the child can "suspend disbelief," which means that the child engages in the puppet play and may speak directly to the puppet rather than the health care professional using the puppet, and the puppet has "come to life" in the child's mind. The puppet whispers to the health care professional, who in turn rephrases, clarifies, summarizes, and probes using humanistic and solution-focused techniques to enhance engagement with the puppet (Reid-Searl, 2012). Reid-Searl (2012) also reminds professionals to consider both the timing and content of the puppet play in action. The child may or may not be receptive to the puppet in the first instance, and therefore assessing the engagement level is pivotal in the first few moments of puppet play.

Evaluation is essential to ascertain the effectiveness of the puppet play session, and this is incorporated by reflecting on the session and the interpersonal interactions to continually improve the professional's approach to teaching and learning through puppets. Evaluation of the child's knowledge acquisition occurs during this stage.

Debrief, the last letter of the Pup-Ed acronym, refers to coming out of the puppeteer role, where the professional critically appraises the puppet play session by asking the child or family member specific questions about what happened in the puppet play, how it happened, and what the interaction meant in the scheme of things (Reid-Searl, 2012).

For first-time users, it is recommended that they practice sessions of puppet play in front of a mirror or by video recording interactions to review and reflect on puppet play practice in order to develop the art of puppet play. Practicing with the puppet enhances the "Knowledgeable, Realistic, and Spontaneous" (KRS) aspects of the Pup-Ed training, which are based on humanistic simulation techniques. For this strategy to work, the educator must be: **knowledgeable** about the discipline and the use of the puppet in the context of the child's diagnosis and life-world while being developmentally aware; **realistic** in responses by incorporating the puppet characteristics and movements in response to the context and the medical environment; and finally, **spontaneous** in the interactions between the puppet and child through the whisper technique, and as such the interactions cannot be rehearsed or scripted but must demonstrate a more natural discourse, responsive to the learning needs of the child (Reid-Searl, O'Niell, Dwyer, & Crowley, 2017). These are professional attributes that are also used when applying procedural puppet play techniques in the medical setting.

Procedural Puppets

Procedural play, including the use of puppets, has been used in medical settings to inform children about medical and nursing interventions through puppet play and simulation. Tilbrook, Dwyer, Reid-Searl, and Parson (2017) recently reviewed the literature on the use of puppet simulation in children's health care and found health care professionals and play therapists use a variety of ways to integrate puppets into their practice, including puppet modeling and storytelling, and having children create their own puppets. Of particular interest was the considerable evidence that indicated puppet play was beneficial to children to prepare them for hospitalization and/or for painful or distressing procedures (Athanassiadou, Tsiantis, Christogiorgos, & Kolaitis, 2009). Puppet play was helpful in modeling medical procedures, which increased the child's comprehension of the procedure and enhanced the child's coping during the procedure (Athanassiadou et al., 2009). Puppet play also improved the child's reactions post-operatively and reduced behavioral responses such as aggressive behavior. Tilbrook et al. (2017) stated that puppet play has an important role in providing psychological care as complementary to standard medical care.

Typical preparation is used for a range of pediatric medical or procedural interventions such as insertion of a nasogastric tube (NGT), intravenous catheter (IVC) insertion, Port-A-Cath insertion, blood drawing, and other minor surgical procedures and radiological tests. In most cases the health care professional or therapist will demonstrate hospital or medical setting-specific procedures and provide sensory information while demonstrating the procedure on the puppet (Parson, 2009). The child is given an opportunity to play with the medical equipment, exploring the texture, smell, and flexibility of the equipment, with the aim to enhance familiarity prior to the procedure. With guided puppet play, the therapist will simulate responses in the procedural play as if it were a child reacting to, for example, a nasogastric tube insertion, and by exaggerated procedural educational opportunities, such as swallowing while the tube is being inserted, and by instructing the puppet on specific roles it has like staying really, really still so the procedure will be over as quickly as possible.

Children may have anticipatory concerns about having an NGT or IVC inserted or blood test completed. However, if provided with a playful, educative, and hands-on experiential simulation, the child is more likely to experience a less traumatic procedure and ultimately a more positive health care experience (Athanassiadou et al., 2009). The professional may simulate the procedure on the puppet for the child, and the puppet may respond according to the child's reactions, fears, questions, and wonderings. The health care professional is in a situation to impart knowledge and/or clarify any misconceptions in a realistic and spontaneous manner and in real time based on the moment-to-moment needs of the child.

Another innovative toy, while not technically a puppet but useful all the same for the medical setting, is Rabbit Ray. This is a robust therapeutic medical toy, made of hard plastic and easily cleaned, that is designed to support children's preparation and procedural knowledge regarding, for example, blood glucose monitoring, vaccination injections, taking blood (phlebotomy) with a butterfly (scalp vein) needle, IV cannulation, and setting up a drip or giving medication intravenously. For more details, see https://rabbit-ray.joytingle.com/. The nurse or therapist demonstrates on the rabbit how the specific procedure will unfold. The child then has an opportunity to play with the medical equipment, such as the syringe and tubing and so forth. The child may ask any questions and have them answered by the therapist. Similarly, and on a much more sophisticated level, there is the use of a silicon puppet to demonstrate medical procedures (see Reid-Searl et al., 2017).

Calico Puppets

Children relate particularly well to puppets when they are actively involved in their development (Fisher, 2009; Hartwig, 2014; Pélicand et al., 2006), and the medical setting is no exception. Calico dolls have been used in children's wards and emergency departments for decades to explain procedures to children. The child is offered a calico hand puppet to decorate and color, give voice, and to elicit information that he or she may not normally be able to ask.

Pre-made calico puppets can be purchased ahead of time, and one is offered to the child to decorate and personalize using permanent marker pens, a variety of felt and fabrics, wool and string, buttons, feathers, and glue. A hot glue gun is really useful for a quick result, although with supervised care and caution for young children and children who may have limited movement in their hands due to an intravenous cannula.

Summary

This chapter has provided an overview of three different ways to use puppets in the medical setting: to enhance communication between children and health care professionals, to promote procedural education and medical equipment exploration, and to project thoughts and feelings onto the puppet. The research supports the psychological education and reduction of emotional and behavioral reactions if children are informed of any upcoming procedures. Children have a right to be informed of anything that will happen to them in a developmentally sensitive and age-appropriate manner. Puppet play in medical settings is strongly recommended to complement and enhance communication to and from children when they are requiring medical care.

References

Athanassiadou, E., Tsiantis, J., Christogiorgos, S., & Kolaitis, G. (2009). An evaluation of the effectiveness of psychological preparation of children for minor surgery by puppet play and brief mother counselling. *Psychotherapy Psychosomatics*, *78*(1), 62–63.

Bernier, M., & O'Hare, J. (2005). *Puppetry in education and theatre: Unlocking doors to the mind and heart.* Terre Haute, Indiana: Authorhouse.

Blumenthal, E. (2005). *Puppetry: A world history.* New York: Harry N. Abrams Publisher.

Ekra, E. M. R., Korsvold, T., & Gjengedal, E. (2015). Characteristics of being hospitalized as a child with a new diagnosis of type 1 diabetes: A phenomenological study of children's past and present experiences. *BMC Nursing*, *14*, 4. doi:10.1186/s12912-014-0051-9

Fisher, J. (2009). *Puppets, language and learning.* London: A & C Black Publishers Limited.

Haiat, H., Bar-Mor, G., & Shochat, M. (2003). The world of the child: A world of play even in the hospital. *Journal of Paediatric Nursing*, *18*(3), 209–214.

Hartwig, E. K. (2014). Puppets in the playroom: Utilizing puppets and child-centered facilitative skills as a metaphor for healing. *International Journal of Play Therapy*, *23*(4), 204–216.

Irwin, E. C., & Shapiro, M. (1975). Puppetry as a diagnostic and therapeutic tool. In I. Jakab (Ed.), *Transcultural aspects of art: Art and psychiatry* (Vol. 4, pp. 86–94). Basel: Karger Press.

Landreth, G. (2012). *Play therapy: The art of the relationship* (3rd ed.). New York: Routledge.

Parson, J. (2009). Play in the hospital environment. In K. Stagnitti & R. Cooper (Ed.), *Play as therapy: Assessment and therapeutic interventions* (pp. 132–144). London: Jessica Kingsley Publishers.

Parson, J. (2016, June 25). *Bringing puppets to life in play therapy*. Presented at the Putting Theory into Practice in Creative Arts, British Association of Play Therapy BAPT Conference, Birmingham.

Pélicand, J., Gagnayre, R., Sandrin-Berthon, B., & Aujoulat, I. (2006). A therapeutic education programme for diabetic children: Recreational, creative methods, and use of puppets. *Patient Education and Counseling, 60*(2), 152–163. http://doi.org/10.1016/j.pec.2004.12.007

Reid-Searl, K. (2012). *Pup-Ed™ KRS simulation*. Rockhampton, Australia: CQ University.

Reid-Searl, K., O'Neill, B., Dwyer, T., & Crowley, K. (2017). Using a procedural puppet to teach paediatric nursing procedures. *Clinical Simulation in Nursing, 13*, 15–23. http://dx.doi.org/10.1016/j.ecns.2016.09.013

Reid-Searl, K., Quinney, L., Dwyer, T., Vieth, L., Nancarrow, L., & Walker, B. (2016). Puppets in an acute paediatric unit: Nurse's experiences. *Collegian*. http://doi.org/10.1016/j.colegn.2016.09.005

Rogers, C. (1957). The necessary and sufficient conditions of therapeutic personality change. *Journal of Consulting Psychology, 21*, 95–103.

Schaefer, C. E., & Drewes, A. A. (2014). *The therapeutic powers of play: 20 core agents of change*. Hoboken, NJ: John Wiley & Sons.

Tilbrook, A., Dwyer, T., Reid-Searl, K., & Parson, J. (2017). A review of the literature: The use of interactive puppet simulation in nursing education and children's healthcare. *Nurse Education in Practice, 22*, 73–79.

UN General Assembly. (1989). *Convention on the rights of the child: Adopted and opened for signature, ratification and accession by general assembly resolution 44/25 of 20 November 1989*. Retrieved from the office of the United Nations High Commissioner for Human Rights website www.ohchr.org/EN/ProfessionalInterest/Pages/CRC.aspx

19 The Application of Therapeutic Puppet Play in the Schools

Siobhán Prendiville

Chatter fills the room of a class full of 5- and 6-year-old children as they happily make welcome cards for the new student due to join their class today. Some draw pictures illustrating the school activities their new friend will be able to join in with, others write simple messages about themselves to share with their new classmate, while more decorate their card using their favorite colors and designs. They talk in their groups about how they will help the new boy feel welcome in school, the games they might play with him, jokes they will tell, and stories they will share. Silence filters through the room at the familiar sound of a knock on the door. "He's here!" "He has arrived," "Quick, open the door!" exclaim some of the children excitedly. Ms. P. smiles and moves knowingly to the door, opening it with a bright smile on her face. The principal stands at the other side, with Billy in tow. Billy moves closer to Mr. Barry, cowering in and hiding his eyes from the children. "It's okay, Billy," Ms. P. says to him, "I know you're feeling scared right now, this is all new for you. The children are very excited to meet you and can't wait to show you all of the things in your new classroom." Ms. P. helps Billy find his way into the room and he gazes around, taking in the children. Their eyes follow Billy as he moves with Ms. P. They look at him with interest, some grinning from ear to ear, others taking a moment to ponder the new arrival, to check their peers to see their reactions. Some reach out to touch Billy, others giggle hello, all are actively engaging with this new friend. And so the puppet journey begins . . .

Puppets are naturally engaging, attractive, fun, and versatile; they have long been used in therapeutic work with children and are utilized within a variety of theoretical models (Reynolds & Stanley, 2001). Puppets provide opportunities for children to express thoughts and feelings, gain understanding and insights, release fears and overcome worries and aggressive impulses, develop feelings of mastery and competence, foster and develop verbal and nonverbal communication skills, address psycho-educational issues, and address affective and behavioral dysregulation and cognitive distortions (Prendiville, 2014).

With appropriate resourcing, and adult intervention, children across a wide age span can also benefit from therapeutic puppet play outside the therapy room, including within educational settings. Most of the approaches presented in this chapter can be successfully used with the whole class in the mainstream or special needs class setting; they can also be used with individuals or small groups in education or therapy settings. Parents may also adapt techniques for family use.

Choosing Puppets for the School Setting

There is a wide range of commercial puppets available, including small finger puppets, glove and hand puppets, sleeve puppets, and full-bodied puppets; many have moving mouths, tongues, hands, and even legs. In order to stimulate interest and offer choice, a good range and variety should be provided for children's use (DeLucia-Waack, 2006; Prendiville, 2014; Crenshaw & Foreacre, 2001). However, it is not necessary to have a complete set to begin with; the collection can grow over time to include more variety in terms of size, type, and range of characters. In the school setting puppets can easily be shared between class groups and levels, and, of course, the children can also make puppets themselves.

Suggested Range of Puppets

People Puppets—various age, gender, and ethnic groups
Animal Puppets—tame and wild, e.g., rabbit, mouse, tiger, crocodile
Mystical Creature Puppets—dragon, wizard, fairy, mermaid, etc.
Special Character Puppets—police officer, doctor, judge, etc.
Royalty Puppets—king, queen, jester, etc.

Children's Spontaneous Puppet Play

A group of 7- and 8-year-old children are exploring a box of puppets. They are laughing as they remove them from the box and try them out. The lion roars and then laughs, the crocodile snaps, the kitten gives a soft miaow and rubs against a girl's cheek, the tortoise hides in his shell, peeking out every now and then. After a while, the king announces that it is time to start the show! The children share ideas: "Let's do doctors." "No, a jungle show." "We could do superheroes," chimes another. They thrash their ideas out together and decide on the jungle theme. "One of the animals can be a doctor, or even a superhero," suggests Tom, aka the king. Mary throws a sheet over the nearby table and this becomes their stage. The children choose one or two puppets each and the play expands. The giraffe and elephants are playing together when the tiger arrives and starts to tease them, calling them "long neck" and "big ears." The king moves in and out of role to direct the play. The classroom assistant watches closely, providing commentary and reflections on what she observes. The superhero parrot flies in and offers words of advice and encouragement to the elephant and giraffe. "Use your strong voice," he says. As the story evolves, the children try out different roles, some being more vocal than others, some clearly taking the lead and others following, but all engaging in a way that fits for them.

Children's spontaneous puppet play offers a myriad of developmental and therapeutic benefits. Puppets are projective play materials that provide a nonthreatening means through which children express thoughts, feelings, preoccupations, problems, fears, worries, inner conflicts, fantasies, and joys (Jennings, 2005). Puppet play facilitates the child's development of feelings of mastery and competence; the child can take the lead, can take charge of the puppet and the play. He or she can act out real-life experiences and situations, try out different roles, and verbally and kinesthetically explore and express emotions. Such play enables children to feel empowered, communicate strong emotions, gain understanding, resolve inner conflicts, find solutions to problems, learn to identify feelings in themselves and others, and control their anxieties, all while having fun and simply playing (Prendiville, 2014). In addition, spontaneous puppet play allows for the development of language and imagination, and promotes positive social interaction between children (Seach, 2007). Fostering a playful atmosphere that promotes and values puppet play within the school setting facilitates the pupils accessing these benefits. Children can be given the freedom to play with and explore the puppets. The adult must provide the resources, space, and time for play and, critically, must spend time with the children as they engage in this play. Initially, children will engage in exploratory play with the puppets, put them on and off, begin to make sounds and utterances with them, and gradually move toward attributing characteristics and personalities, making the puppets speak, and communicate with other puppets. The more opportunities the children have for such activity, the more developed their puppet play skills will become. As these skills develop, in addition to the increased opportunities to experience affective expression, children will be enabled to further develop their executive functioning skills of planning, organizing, monitoring, paying attention, and self-control.

Technique: Children's Spontaneous Puppet Play
Age Range: Preschool to Upper Primary
Group Size: 4–6 children (can be within the whole class setting)
Materials Required: Puppets, space to play, materials to create a puppet theater
Adult's Role: Spend time observing the play, give nondirective feedback and commentary, joining in as deemed appropriate (either as narrator or as a puppet character).

Structured Puppet Play

There is a flurry of activity at the puppet corner in the second-grade classroom. It is the children's "planning for play" time; the class teacher has just proposed the idea that the children explore the theme "A Big Adventure" through their puppet play. The children sit in a circle and excitedly talk to each other, debating what the big adventure could be—"a trip to the circus," "a space adventure," and "the adventures of Superman" are all offered as suggestions by the children themselves. Adam, today's executive planner, jots down the suggestions on the group clipboard. The teacher supports the children as they tease these ideas out. They settle on "a space adventure," and so the planning continues. "What other things might you need?" asks the teacher. "Playdough to make planets and asteroids," replies Tom. "Empty shoe boxes for the space rockets," suggests Avril. Next, the teacher asks the children to think about where their story might begin, and how it might develop and finish. Adam takes out the prompt cards—who, what, where, when, and why—and the children use these question prompts to help them tease out their plan for play. Who will be in the puppet play? Where are they and where will they go? What will happen? Their plan soon starts taking shape, puppets are selected, roles are divided, props are made, and a possible story line emerges. Captain Adventure has been called upon to fly to the moon to rescue two astronauts who have been kidnapped by Martians. He must be brave and face his fear of flying alone! When he arrives he will need to search for the astronauts and bargain with their captors for their release. The children are excited by their story line and keen to start playing. The timer sounds, signaling that it is time to move from planning to playing. The puppets go on and the big adventure begins!

School-based practitioners can also plan a more sequential approach to puppet play. In this approach, the practitioner presents a theme and guides the children's puppet play in such a way to enable the children to gain a deeper understanding and knowledge of a particular topic. Such themes may include "The Doctor," "Fire, Fire!" "Bullying," "The Best Day of My Life," "A Trip to the Dentist," and so forth. Additional props can be added to extend and elaborate the play and learning. Language and self-expression flourish as the children delve into the topic, free of the fear of failure often present in more formal lessons (Woodard & Milch, 2012).

Technique: Structured Puppet Play
Age Range: Lower to Middle Primary
Group Size: 4–6 children
Materials Required for Sample Topic, "The Doctor": Planning prompt cards, clipboard, planning page, people puppets, doctor play props, e.g., doctor's kit, bandages, telephone, money, cash register, receipt book, etc.
Adult Support: One adult practitioner in the classroom will suffice, extra personnel a bonus!

Planning for Play (10–15 minutes)

1. The teacher explains that today's play is going to be about the doctor. Five subgroups are set up to explore the theme; puppet play, small world play, sociodramatic play, creative arts play, and sand and water play. Each subgroup will contain 4–6 children.

2. An executive planner is selected for each group. The executive planner will record the group plan using the planning sheet and clipboard. This can be done using symbols, words, or sentences (depending on the ability level of the executive planner).
3. The children are encouraged to sit in their small group for the planning stage. The teacher, classroom assistant, and any other practitioners available in the room will move from group to group.
4. The executive planner takes out the question prompt cards to help shape the planning process: Who? What? Where? When? Why? The level of adult support needed here will depend on the developmental level of the children and their experience level of planning for play. Prompt suggestions may include:

Who will be in the play and what puppets are needed? (doctor, patient, receptionist, etc.)
Where does the play happen?
When is it happening?
Why is the doctor needed?
What might each puppet say/do?

Playing (20–40 minutes)

1. Invite the children to create a puppet play based on the topic.
2. Observe the play, provide reflective commentary, reflect actions, emotions, etc.

Reviewing the Play (10–15 minutes)

1. The children gather in their small group again, this time to review their play.
2. The executive planner leads this discussion, using the prompt cards and group plan as a guide. Adult support can be given to suit the needs of the group.

Prompt Suggestions

Who did you play with?
What did you play with?
What did you do?
What happened in the puppet show?

3. Each play group has the opportunity to tell the other groups what they did.

Extension Ideas

- The children complete a written review of their play experiences; this can take the form of symbols, words, or sentences. For younger children, or children experiencing literacy difficulties, the adult can act as a scribe.
- Photograph the children playing. Use these in follow-up lessons to sequence the play events or create a photo story about "The Doctor."
- Extend the doctor theme into more formal lessons.
- Invite parents and carers to view the puppet play area and see the photographs of the children's play.

In a similar way, puppet play can be used by children in the school setting to respond to and explore stories, poems, songs, and rhymes. As part of a creative arts lesson, children can design and create a series of puppets themselves. Paper plates, envelopes, wooden spoons, paper bags, and socks can easily be made into puppets (Woodard & Milch, 2012; Jennings, 2008; Kennedy, 2004). The children can then use their own puppet creations to reenact or extend a story, or respond to a song or rhyme. One child can narrate a story as the others play it out with their handcrafted puppets. Or the children can play at re-editing or elaborating the story by responding to "What if" questions through the puppet play. For example: What if the three bears arrived home while Goldilocks was eating the porridge? Older children can create more elaborate puppets and dramatize situations and experiences relevant to them, for example the latest series of *The X Factor* or interviews with sports stars or television personalities. Simple finger puppets can be made by younger children to accompany songs and rhymes such as "Five Little Monkeys" or "Old MacDonald Had a Farm." A strip of paper, decorated with crayons and taped around a finger, can easily become a frog, a pig, a boy, or a queen. The creation and use of puppets will add fun and excitement to the lesson, and inspire the children to take a more active, participatory role.

Technique: Responding to Story or Song Through Puppet Play
Age Range: Preschool to Upper Primary
Group Size: Small group or whole class
Materials: Storybook or music, puppet-making materials
Adult's Role: Read a story/play a song to the class. Invite the children to create puppet characters to represent the characters from the story/song.
Activity: The children create puppets (paper plate puppets, finger puppets, wooden spoon puppets, etc.). The children are then invited to dramatize the story/song using their puppet characters.

Class Puppet

> *It is lunchtime in Ms. P.'s classroom. Most of the children chat easily to each other as they eat their lunch. Others sing along to the nursery rhymes that are being played, and some flick through the library books on their table. Max, a quiet and shy 6-year-old boy, sits cautiously in his seat, eating his lunch without speaking to anyone. Ms. P. moves to Max's side and says, "Max, Billy is feeling a bit lonely today, can he come and sit next to you for lunchtime?" "Yes!" replies Max, as a sheepish grin emerges on his face. Ms. P. places Billy on the seat next to Max and moves away. She can see Max whispering in Billy's ear and rubbing his arm gently. He continues to offer Billy some of his juice and even places one of his crackers on the table in front of Billy. When Max has finished eating, he pulls out his book, places it between himself and Billy, and starts reading aloud.*

The practitioner's use of one specific puppet, over an extended period of time, is one of the most useful tools in the application of therapeutic puppet play in the school setting. In this approach, I recommend the use of a full-bodied child puppet, which is going to join the class, or indeed be used in individual or group therapy sessions.

The practitioner selects and tailors the life story, living arrangements, personality, behavior pattern, and temperament of the puppet to suit the needs of a particular child or group of children. The practitioner, not the child, will be the puppeteer and will manipulate and talk for the puppet. It is critical that the practitioner is comfortable with the puppet, has practiced using it, and is confident to present the puppet in a realistic manner to the children. The more confident, comfortable, and playful the practitioner is with the puppet, the more successful the intervention will be. Before introducing this puppet, take time to build a profile for him or her. Assign and get to know the puppet's personalized characteristics. What would the puppet say and do in different circumstances, how does the puppet look when he or she is happy, sad, worried, and so forth, what does the puppet like to play with and eat, what does he or she hate doing, has he or she any specific fears, worries, or problems? Practice manipulating your puppet while looking in the mirror, so you get the chance to experience what the children will see when you are presenting him or her. As you engage with the puppet, so too will the children. The aim is that the children will have fun and connect with and form a bond with this character, who will become a member of the group, a friend, someone whom they can share things with, talk to, play with, learn from, and teach.

Tips for Manipulating Your Puppet

Eye contact, puppet posture, and consistent character voice help to bring your puppet to life and enable the children to better relate and respond to the puppet.

- Eye Contact: When working with your puppet, look at your puppet; you do not need to disguise the fact that you are talking by covering your mouth. When your puppet is talking, you can look at the back of the puppet's head; when you are talking as yourself, you look at the children. This helps the children to keep eye contact with the puppet as he or she talks and you as you talk as yourself. If you want the group/child to look at you, have your puppet look at you, as this will draw their attention from the puppet to you.

- Puppet Posture: This is critical. Nonverbal movements breathe life into puppets. As the puppeteer moves a hand gently up and down, the puppet appears to be breathing. Small shaking head movements up and down suggest laughter, while side-to-side head movements can demonstrate the puppet's fear. Tilting the puppet's head toward the ceiling while bunching his or her fists together shows the puppet's anger. Moving the puppet's head slowly down toward his or her chest coupled with the puppet's hand covering his or her eyes can illustrate embarrassment or dismay. It is important to play around with your puppet and become familiar with how the puppet looks when you move him or her in different ways. It is possible to demonstrate a wide array of feelings through puppet posture alone.
- Consistent Character Voice: Some puppets may never speak directly to the child/children, instead whispering in your ear and allowing you to retell his or her words to the children. However, the joy that comes when a puppet looks at and speaks directly to a child is quite amazing. Play around with voices before settling on one for your puppet. You do not have to speak in a manufactured voice; you can simply vary your voice tone according to the age, gender, and mood of your puppet; a quiet voice, a deeper voice, a slower or quicker pace all work well. The important thing is not that you muster up the most elaborate puppet voice in the world; rather, it is that you manage to keep the puppet voice consistent.

You will refer to the puppet as your friend. This really helps the character come to life for the children, helps them see the puppet as part of the group, and illustrates the practitioner's full engagement in the make-believe world of puppetry (Prendiville, 2014). The ability to be playful and build up a good story is critically important in facilitating the development of a positive relationship between puppet and children and thus ensuring the success of this approach. Tips for bringing your puppet to life and facilitating the development of this positive relationship are outlined below.

- Treat your puppet as if he or she were real.
- Information and photographs of the "new friend" can be shared before the puppet even arrives. Letters, postcards, or emails can be sent from the puppet, sharing information and expressing a desire to meet.
- The puppet should appear alive at all times—do not stuff him or her in a cupboard!
- The puppet will need a place to sit, a chair, a coat hook, and a bag, just like the other children.
- Take photographs of your puppet engaged in various activities and in a variety of settings. Share these with the children.
- Have your puppet talk to and share personal information with your class.
- Talk to your puppet regularly, include the puppet regularly in class lessons, and acknowledge him or her at various stages throughout the day.
- Provide sanctioned opportunities for the children to touch and talk to your puppet, e.g., allow them all to shake the puppet's hand, give him or her a high five, and share their news with the puppet.
- Puppet Bag: Have your puppet arrive with a bag filled with some of his or her favorite things—favorite story, food, toy, etc. The puppet can also bring along resources for specific lessons the teacher is planning on presenting.

By bringing the puppet to life through puppet skills, photographs, and sharing of personal history, the children begin to develop a deep and fulfilling relationship with the puppet. For some the puppet will become a friend and a confidante, someone they talk to, share their lunch with, cuddle, and play with. Through the relationship that emerges, the children can develop a multitude of prosocial behaviors and skills such as sharing, turn taking, positive listening skills, use of gentle touch, altruism, empathy, and self-esteem. In addition to facilitating positive interactions, the use of a puppet friend in this way can also enhance the development of language, imagination, and play skills. For some who may struggle with peer relationships, the skills that are learned and practiced through this relationship will become transferable to real-world relationships.

Technique: A New Friend
Age Group: 4- to 8-year-olds
Materials: One large, preferably full-bodied, puppet

Preparatory Work

1. Prepare a profile: detailed information about your new puppet.
2. Get to know your puppet.
3. Practice manipulating your puppet.
4. Take some puppet photographs.
5. Send an email to the class from the puppet character.
6. Class emails puppet back—share info.
7. Prepare space for the new "child"—desk, coat hook, etc.
8. The arrival! Have fun with the arrival: Use your imagination and playfulness to engage the children. The puppet can introduce himself or herself, either by talking directly to the child/children or whispering in your ear for you to retell. The puppet can share photographs of himself or herself and his or her family, a favorite story, or an activity sheet. Whatever suits your particular group or child.
9. Continue to foster the relationship between children and puppet. Refer to the puppet throughout the day; have the puppet bring storybooks, play and art materials, and resources for lessons.
10. The puppet can be used in various lessons and activities throughout the year. He or she can also be used as a means to model cognitive, behavioral, and emotional regulation strategies.

The Puppet as a Model

Billy is talking to the class about his big angry feelings inside. "Sometimes it feels like there's a volcano in my tummy. I get angry when someone bumps into me or pushes me. When I get angry I hit and kick, and then I get into trouble and this makes me even more mad and sad." "Wow," says Ms. P., "that sounds really tough. We need to find a way to sort out that volcano in your tummy and help you to stop kicking and hitting." Ms. P. explains that she has a friend "Tommy Tucker" who has learned a wonderful way to manage angry feelings. She takes out her turtle puppet and demonstrates how he learned to tuck inside, take deep breaths, relax, and think of a solution before reacting to the big angry feelings! Billy is amazed when he sees this new trick and agrees to give it a try himself.

Social learning theory conceptualizes the influence of modeling on promoting learning, change, and growth (Bandura, 1977). One can never underestimate just how much children can learn from watching others act and react to situations. Practitioners in the education setting can use a puppet to model prosocial behaviors, learning strategies, coping skills, and positive ways to handle big emotions. The school-based practitioner would purposefully have a puppet, act, react and talk in a particular way in order to help the children strengthen or develop a new behavior or cognitive thought pattern, or indeed to weaken preexisting ones.

Billy is telling the children how he is getting on trying to think like Tommy Tucker when he notices the angry feelings building in his tummy. He explains that he has found squeezing his special squidgy ball a great help when he tries to relax instead of exploding! He shows the children how he squeezes his ball between his fingers. Next he shows them another trick he has learned. He bends down, pretends to pick up a flower, smells it, and then blows the petals away. "It helps me practice my breathing," he says. Next he encourages all the children to join in his new breathing game with him!

The practitioner can have the puppet friend model positive and desired behaviors, such as gentle touch, good sitting and listening, raising a hand to ask a question, and so forth. Reinforce the behaviors by giving the puppet specific praise for the targeted behavior. In this way the puppet can be used as a tool in proximity praising.

Tony is 6 years old and is easily distracted. He finds it very difficult to adhere to basic classroom rules such as sitting, waiting his turn, and looking at the teacher as she teaches specific concepts. Ms. P. has decided to sit Billy, the class puppet, at the same table as Tony. Billy is placed so he is looking directly at Ms. P. During a formal teaching time, Ms. P. notices that Tony is distracted; he is swinging on his chair and looking out the window. Instead of commenting on this, she praises Billy's positive behavior. "Wow, Billy, I love how you are sitting on your seat, I can see your two eyes looking straight at me, well done!" Tony notices this praise and adjusts his sitting and looks up at the teacher also. Ms. P. immediately reflects on this behavior: "Oh, Tony, you are sitting perfectly on your seat, your two feet are on the ground and your eyes are looking at me. Well done, Tony."

Alternatively, the puppet friend can be used as a coping model (Knell, 2011), whereby he initially displays less than ideal behaviors and gradually becomes more adept at following class rules and routines. In this approach the children are enlisted to help the puppet learn new behaviors, for example, how to tidy up, use gentle touch, or use an indoor voice.

Ms. P. gathers her class of 5- and 6-year-olds together to tell them about a new friend of hers who needs some help. "Alfie is his name," she says. "He has been to a few different schools already, but he has had a lot of trouble in each of them." The children's eyes widen as she explains how Alfie found it very hard to follow the school rules. "He didn't know how to use kind words and gentle touch, and instead he hit, kicked, spat, shouted, and said hurtful things to his classmates and teachers. He had moved around a lot; he had lived in different houses with different people, first his mom, then his mom and his stepdad, and now he was going to be living with his nana instead. It's tough for children when they move around so many times. It can cause them to have lots of mixed-up feelings,"

Ms. P. explains. The children nod in agreement. Ms. P. continues to explain how Alfie's nana had heard all about Ms. P.'s class. She had heard that these children were known for using gentle touch and kind words, and that they were really good at helping people. She wondered if they might be able to help Alfie learn new ways to manage his mixed-up feelings and troublesome behaviors. She really wants to find a new forever school for Alfie, a place where he can be happy and make real friends.

The children are delighted at the prospect of helping Alfie; they eagerly plan ways in which they will help him change his behaviors. They brainstorm their ideas and start setting up the classroom for his imminent arrival.

This strategy is particularly useful in the classroom setting, as it draws attention away from a child's problem behaviors and puts the child into the teaching position instead. In this way the child who is engaging in disruptive behaviors similar to Alfie's can be enlisted to help Alfie use gentle touch and kind words by showing him how to do it. This approach really empowers children who are displaying challenging behaviors, as they now have a reason to improve their behavior, and the focus is on their ability to carry out the target behavior rather than their inability to do so. It is particularly successful when the child has already built up a relationship with the puppet, as the child will want to help his or her friend out. Practitioner use of specific praise and positive affirmation for all attempts to teach the puppet will work to further reinforce the positive behaviors displayed by the child, for example, "Tommy, well done for showing Alfie just how to stay seated on his seat during story time. You are a great help to him, and to me!" If the target child or children deviate from the desired behavior, you can draw their attention back by reminding them of the important job they have to help Alfie learn to sit, eat his lunch, tidy his toys, and so forth.

Technique: Puppet as a Model
Age Range: 3–10 years
Group Size: Individual, small group, or whole class
Materials: Puppet and any other resourcing tools necessary, for example, a fidget toy
Adult's Role: Have your puppet tell the children about specific problem behavior, thought patterns, or feelings he or she is experiencing. The puppet will explain, in age-appropriate language, how this problem is impacting on his or her life. The teacher, or indeed the children, is then enlisted to offer advice and support to the puppet on how he or she can overcome the difficulty. The puppet tries out the advice, demonstrates the technique to the children, for example, playing with a fidget toy instead of banging the table, and subsequently returns at a later stage to let the group know how he or she is managing now.

Puppets to Explore Feelings

Puppets are also a wonderful resource for enabling children to learn to identify emotions in themselves and others and to manage and express big feelings in healthy ways.

> *It is the first day of the new school year, the very first day of primary school for Ms. P.'s class. Some children ran in the door, happily waving good-bye to their parents; others were much more hesitant, clinging on for reassurance, looking worried and anxious at the prospect of spending the day apart. A large box, decorated with wrapping paper, sits under Ms. P.'s desk. Inside there is a gentle rabbit puppet tucked inside a head of lettuce. Ms. P. holds the colorful box in the air and encourages the children to sit in a circle to see what is inside. The children stare in interest as she slowly reveals a head of lettuce with a tiny ear poking out. "It's my friend Rita Rabbit," Ms. P. says in a quiet voice. "It's okay, Rita, the children are very kind," she whispers to the puppet. "She is very shy. It is her first day meeting you all. She is feeling a little scared," Ms. P. announces to the children. "Will you help me get her to come out and say hello?" "Yes," call the children. "Okay, we need to use our quiet voices because she is very frightened. So please, on the count of three, say 'Hello, Rita' with me. 1 . . . . . . 2 . . . . . . 3!" "Hello Rita," whisper the children, eyes wide in anticipation. Rita slowly begins to emerge. With two more counts she is fully out of the lettuce, and the children are happily telling her their names.*

Technique: The Shy Puppet
Age Range: 3–8 years
Group Size: Individual, small group, or large group
Materials: Puppet that can hide in itself, such as a rabbit in lettuce or a turtle
Adult's Role: The practitioner introduces the puppet while it is still tucked inside itself. The adult recognizes the puppet's feelings and encourages the child/children to help coax the shy puppet out.

School-based practitioners can also use puppet friends to address more specific, emotionally sensitive life events, issues, and problems, for example, bottling up feelings, explosive temper tantrums, anxiety, parental separation, bereavement, and so forth. The use of a puppet provides dramatic distance, which is often necessary to enable children to feel more comfortable and safe enough to explore more sensitive issues (Nash & Schaefer, 2010). In this technique, the school-based practitioner facilitates the projection of the children's experiences and/or feelings onto the puppet. The adult can comment on the puppet's experiences and emotions and reassures the puppet of his or her safety. The puppet, as a model, can provide children with practical, emotionally healthy alternative ways to handle these issues. The puppet can model aspects of modulation of emotions, affect expression, and regulation skills, and coach children in ways of handling feelings. Often when the puppet introduces a new idea or demonstrates a skill, the child is more receptive to it than if the adult introduced it. In addition, the adult and the puppet can talk to each other, within earshot of the child, in a meaningful way designed to be helpful to the child. The puppet can speak about something that is worrying the child, for example, a disturbing event or negative and disruptive behaviors and feelings. Either the adult or the puppet can present possible solutions within the course of these conversations. Alternatively, the practitioner can engage the children in caring for and supporting the puppet. The child or group of children can be enlisted to give advice to the puppet and help the puppet overcome particular difficulties (Prendiville, 2014).

Michelle, the school-based play therapist, is working with a group of 7- and 8-year-old children dealing with anxiety. In session one Michelle introduces her friend "Molly" to the group. She explains that Molly spends most of her time feeling very frightened. Michelle invites Molly to open up and talk about her many worries. Molly speaks directly to the children. She has a very quiet voice and cuddles close to Michelle as she speaks. "I am scared of so many different things," she says, "like monsters, the dark, loud noises, and even going to my dance class. . . . Sometimes I feel like just staying at home and not going outside at all."

In session two Molly brings along a story to share with the group—"Teenie Weenie in a Too Big World"(Sunderland, 2003). She shares how she met a special friend who gave it to her and told her it would help her beat her worries. The children are eager to hear the story Molly has brought for them. Michelle sits Molly in the circle with the other children and reads the story to them. The children listen with interest as they hear about Teenie Weenie being lost and alone in a very scary place. They smile when he meets Hoggie and the Wip Wop bird; some cheer as he realizes that being together with others helps his worries go away. After the story Molly announces that she is going to try some of this together thing. The following week she returns and proudly tells the children that she went to her dance class last week and even managed to stay without her mom, because she had her toy bunny with her. "That was my bit of together," she announces gleefully. "Well done," the children chorus, before sharing some of their own success stories from the week.

Later, Molly tells the group how she has found another way to help her worries go away: "I share my worries with my mom now," she chimes. "We have a special together time each evening and I give my worries to her, that way I don't need to worry about them at night. After our together time I find it much easier to fall asleep." As the weeks go by, Molly gains confidence and shares her ups and downs with the children. From breathing techniques to meditations, positive self-talk to fidget toys, Molly has a lot of new strategies to share!

Conclusion

This chapter has described therapeutic puppet play approaches for the school setting. It has included innovative puppet play ideas that can be used by teachers, play therapists, classroom assistants, parents, and caregivers to support the development of children's social, emotional, cognitive, and behavioral competencies. There are many other ways to make use of puppets in school settings, including preparing children for upcoming events, engaging children's full interest in learning tasks and activities, as a classroom and behavioral management tool, and having a puppet that children take turns to bring home for weekends and school breaks. The possibilities for therapeutic puppet play are endless. I urge you to bring your own playfulness and creativity to your work with puppets. Have fun and allow the magical world of puppets to capture your imagination and take center stage in your school setting.

References

Bandura, A. (1977). *Social learning theory*. Oxford: Prentice-Hall.

Crenshaw, D., & Foreacre, C. (2001). Play therapy in a residential treatment centre. In A. A. Drewes, L. J. Carey, & C. E. Schaefer (Eds.), *School-based play therapy* (1st ed., pp. 139–163). Hoboken, NJ: John Wiley & Sons, Inc.

DeLucia-Waack, J. L. (2006). *Leading psychoeducational groups for children and adolescents*. Thousand Oaks, CA: Sage Publications.

Jennings, S. (2005). *Creative play with children at risk*. Oxon, UK: Speechmark.

Jennings, S. (2008). *Creative puppetry with children and adults*. Oxon, London, UK: Speechmark.

Kennedy, J. (2004). *Puppet mania: The world's most incredible puppet making book ever!* Cincinnati, OH: North Light Books.

Knell, S. (2011). Cognitive-behavioral play therapy. In C. E. Schaefer (Ed.), *Foundations of play therapy* (2nd ed., pp. 313–328). Hoboken, NJ. Wiley.

Nash, J., & Schaefer, C. (2010). Clinical and developmental issues in psychotherapy with preschool children: Laying the groundwork for play therapy. In C. E. Schaefer (Ed.), *Play therapy for preschool children* (pp. 15–29). Washington, DC: American Psychological Association.

Prendiville, S. (2014). The use of puppets in therapeutic and educational settings. In E. Prendiville & J. Howard (Eds.), *Play therapy today: Contemporary practice for individuals, groups, and parents* (pp. 97–112). London, England: Routledge.

Reynolds, C., & Stanley, C. (2001). Innovative applications of play therapy in school settings. In A. A. Drewes, L. J. Carey, & C. E. Schaefer (Eds.), *School-based play therapy* (1st ed., pp. 350–367). Hoboken, NJ: John Wiley & Sons, Inc.

Seach, D. (2007). *Interactive play for children with Autism*. Oxon, UK: Routledge.

Sunderland, M. (2003). *Teenie Weenie in a too big world*. Oxon, UK: Speechmark.

Woodard, C., & Milch, C. (2012). *Make-believe play and story-based drama in early childhood: Let's pretend!* London: Jessica Kingsley Publishers.

Index

Page numbers in italic indicate a figure, and page numbers in bold indicate a table on the corresponding page.